Enterprise Software
Delivery

D1556571

Enterprise Software Delivery

Bringing Agility and Efficiency to the
Global Software Supply Chain

Alan W. Brown

✦✦ Addison-Wesley

Upper Saddle River, NJ • Boston • Indianapolis • San Francisco
New York • Toronto • Montreal • London • Munich • Paris • Madrid
Capetown • Sydney • Tokyo • Singapore • Mexico City

Many of the designations used by manufacturers and sellers to distinguish their products are claimed as trademarks. Where those designations appear in this book, and the publisher was aware of a trademark claim, the designations have been printed with initial capital letters or in all capitals.

The author and publisher have taken care in the preparation of this book, but make no expressed or implied warranty of any kind and assume no responsibility for errors or omissions. No liability is assumed for incidental or consequential damages in connection with or arising out of the use of the information or programs contained herein.

The publisher offers excellent discounts on this book when ordered in quantity for bulk purchases or special sales, which may include electronic versions and/or custom covers and content particular to your business, training goals, marketing focus, and branding interests. For more information, please contact:

U.S. Corporate and Government Sales
(800) 382-3419
corpsales@pearsontechgroup.com

For sales outside the United States, please contact:

International Sales
international@pearson.com

Visit us on the Web: informit.com/aw

Library of Congress Cataloging-in-Publication Data
Brown, Alan W., 1962–
  Enterprise software delivery : bringing agility and efficiency to the global software supply chain / Alan W. Brown.
     p. cm.
  Includes bibliographical references and index.
  ISBN 978-0-321-80301-6 (pbk. : alk. paper)
   1. Software engineering—Management. 2. Agile software development. 3. Enterprise application integration (Computer systems) 4. Management information systems. 5. Business logistics. 6. International business enterprises. I. Title.
  QA76.758.B7625 2013
  005.1068—dc23   2012012882

ISBN-13: 978-0-321-80301-6
ISBN-10:   0-321-80301-9

Text printed in the United States on recycled paper at Courier in Westford, Massachusetts.
First printing, June 2012

Contents

Figures

Foreword

If your business future depends on software—and there are very few organizations left that don't—you should find this book invaluable. Most organizations are facing at least the following challenges:

- Their core competence and competitive differentiation increasingly depend on a mastery of software delivery.

- Their track record is weak, with more than half of their software projects failing to deliver satisfactorily within acceptable scope, budget, and schedule constraints.

- There is a greater premium on development time and delivery quality.

- There are not enough good software people to go around. Great architects and project managers are particularly scarce.

Facing these challenges is a daunting task. To be competitive, businesses feel pressure to move faster in delivering new capability to business users. Without appropriate levels of governance, management, and measurement, the advantages of speedy innovation can be short lived or marginalized by uncontrolled complexity in software development and delivery.

Modern enterprises need access to the best technical know-how to solve these challenges. They also need a strong understanding of the economics of software delivery so they can exploit economic governance and measurably improve their software delivery capability. Traditional engineering governance has its place, but software delivery organizations must steer through far greater levels of uncertainty to deliver better economic outcomes. Managers that have transitioned to a more agile "steering" leadership style, based on effective measurement, can optimize their projects' scope, design, and plans, reducing unnecessary scrap and rework. Steering implies frequent course corrections based on testing, measurement, and trends in defects and cost-of-change. Effective steering eliminates uncertainties earlier and significantly improves the probability of win-win outcomes for all stakeholders.

In this book, Alan Brown provides you with a pragmatic foundation for good economic governance of enterprise software delivery. The early chapters build strong foundations for enterprise context, project context, software supply chains, and software factories. The meat of this book discusses pragmatic approaches for improved collaboration, agility, quality, and measurement. Finally, this book delivers some industrial-strength case studies to illustrate these techniques being applied under game conditions. Our industry needs more good case studies like these.

I have worked with Alan for about ten years at Rational and IBM. We have collaborated in assessing and collateralizing good industry practices, in training technical field professionals, and in the direct selling and deploying of tools, methods, and skills to improve the software delivery capabilities of many large Fortune 500 clients. Alan has earned his stripes in the field by listening, observing, synthesizing, and doing it side by side with many successes and some failures. He knows what practices will improve economic outcomes in software delivery, especially at large scale. This book is loaded with from-the-trenches know-how and it provides practical guidance in the disciplined use of agile practices for software delivery organizations. Alan has packaged a tough topic into an enjoyable read, with a well-balanced mix of text, graphics, data, and experience.

—Walker Royce
Chief Software Economist, IBM Rational

Preface

A dramatic revolution in the planning, design, development, and production of software-based solutions is turning the world of software delivery on its head. We are changing what we build, how we build it, who takes part in constructing it, where we develop it, how we manage its quality, what users expect from it, how frequently we update it, and much more. I have seen examples of enterprise software delivery organizations whose methods are unrecognizable from how they worked only five years earlier. They are now more closely aligned with their business colleagues when prioritizing needs, they rapidly innovate to deliver new features to the market, they are taking advantage of a diverse worldwide workforce to increase flexibility in delivery, and they are consequently viewed by executives as a vital component of business differentiation.

Yet some sectors of the software engineering industry remain in denial or trapped in a world of poorly functioning practices and techniques. Unfortunately, we often bring false assumptions, outdated data and delivery models, and lack of real-world experience to our approaches to strategy, innovation, education, and research. This polarization is perhaps more evident in enterprise software delivery today than it has ever been.

More than twenty years ago, a similar situation occurred in the US car-manufacturing sector. In a short time Asian car manufacturers had substantially changed their approach to the design, production, and delivery of vehicles. Not only were the new cars cheaper; they were more reliable and better suited to modern driving conditions, contained more of the features customers wanted, and could be customized and realigned to different market needs.

In response, US car manufacturers accelerated vehicle design approaches to bring new, more flexible solutions to customers, whose demands for greater customization and adaptation were not being met. With what came to be called *lean manufacturing*, vehicle production adopted a supply chain approach. Specialist parts providers were organized into an optimized product-line assembly model that featured increasing levels of automation, standardized interchangeable components, and flexibility through worldwide multisourced supply of critical components and subassemblies. New business models that more closely aligned customers with suppliers contributed to innovations in design, production, and distribution.

This book examines the analogous revolution now taking place in enterprise software delivery and focuses on the key drivers for change, the impact of those changes on the work of software engineers, and the reforms under way in enterprise software delivery organizations to meet the changing needs.

In particular, this book showcases a global software supply chain view of enterprise software delivery. Within the concept of the "global software supply chain," the book positions some of the latest technology shifts in areas such as global outsourcing, collaborative application life cycle management, and cloud computing. The book aims to be informative and practical and uses real-world experiences to stimulate thinking about how to take best advantage of this revolution in enterprise software delivery.

The Key Proposition of This Book

In enterprise organizations, software delivery is essential for the efficient and stable delivery of core capabilities to the business, and it is the driving force for the innovation and differentiation of new services and products to the market. Businesses are enhancing their own enterprise software delivery organizations with system integrators and technology partners to create centers of excellence and capability centers that specialize in delivering value to the business. This is an industrialized view of software delivery. At its extremes, we see examples of software factories where large, dedicated teams create standardized solutions or maintain large software codebases governed by explicit efficiency criteria.

At the same time, enterprise organizations are demanding the rapid innovation and evolution of existing enterprise software solutions to support deployment to new platforms, address new market needs, and overcome competitive threats. While standardization using software factories helps reduce cost and improve predictability of enterprise software delivery, agile ways to approach innovation are essential for solution differentiation and for enhancing the value delivered to the enterprise's clients. Significant invention, adaptation, and flexibility is essential in research and development activities to drive forward the solutions brought to market and to improve the services made available. Yet we often find these aspects to be in conflict with the needs for efficiency and control.

This book proposes that success in enterprise software delivery highly depends on an organization's ability to balance agility and efficiency. In particular, enterprise software delivery organizations must strive to create the process and technology backbone for today's software factories through the following:

- A standards-based infrastructure to encourage and support a supply chain with multisourced component assembly and reuse of key technology components

- Adaptive factory setup and reconfiguration in support of changing market needs and demands

- Real-time feedback to optimize the factory's delivery quality and efficiency

- A virtualized collaborative infrastructure connecting worldwide teams for creating software services and assembling and delivering solutions

These strategies must be supported by team-based practices that encourage and enhance scalable approaches to agility that allow the organization to do the following:

- Collaborate among and across global teams, transcending barriers due to diversity of geography, organization, skills, and culture.

- Deliver solutions with agility and flexibility in light of dynamic market needs and frequent feedback from close interactions with all stakeholders.

- Focus on quality to ensure delivery of high-value capabilities that meet stakeholder needs and expectations.

- Continuously monitor and measure enterprise software delivery to offer honest, accurate assessments of progress and value.

In this context, this book discusses global enterprise software delivery, explores approaches to enterprise software delivery in use today, and provides a set of examples and recommendations for effectively balancing agility and efficiency across the global software supply chain.

Audience and Goals for This Book

The primary audience for this book is the practitioners responsible for delivery for all kinds of enterprise software and solutions. For practitioners in strategy and management roles, it presents a realistic portrait of an industry in flux and offers a context for making sense of the challenges and tensions currently being experienced in many enterprise software delivery organizations. For practitioners in delivery roles, the book gives guidance to improve your ability to make strategic decisions, revise your methods of adopting agility practices in view of an essential focus on cost management and efficiency, and make sense of current trends and future directions in enterprise software delivery.

A secondary audience for this book is the academic community of educators and advanced students seeking a contemporary companion to more formal software engineering textbooks. Reflecting current industry practice, this book brings to that community a realistic underpinning for teaching and research activities, supported by numerous examples and illustrations from real enterprise software delivery situations.

The goals of this book are as follows:

- Highlight the significant changes in enterprise software delivery over the past few years.

- Illustrate the changing face of enterprise software delivery today.

- Describe the key challenges facing enterprise software delivery and the common approaches to address those challenges based on a software supply chain view.

- Suggest practical ways organizations can address challenges in improving their enterprise software delivery approaches to balance the need for innovation with the pressures to cut costs and standardize delivery activities.

- Provide examples from real-life situations to inform and inspire practitioners, educators, and researchers.

The book is organized into three major parts:

- The first three chapters provide an introduction to enterprise software and enterprise software delivery. They discuss the challenges being addressed, explore the nature of enterprise solutions today, and highlight the ways in which enterprise software organizations are structured to achieve their task.

- The middle chapters examine the key themes in enterprise software delivery: collaboration, agility, quality, and governance. A series of examples and cases studies illustrate these topics, emphasizing the practical lessons readers can apply.

- The final two chapters offer practical observations on the current state and future directions of enterprise software delivery.

Relationship to Previous Work

Much has already been written on the challenges of enterprise software delivery. This rich history of work falls broadly into four categories.

The first category focuses on understanding software engineering techniques and approaches. This category includes a large number of seminal works, such as the books on software engineering principles by Fred Brooks [1], Capers Jones [2,3], and Tom DeMarco [4,5], and key software engineering texts such as Ian Somerville's book [6], now in its ninth edition. Offering insights into enterprise software practice, such works introduce a plethora of perspectives on the challenges of software engineering, survey specific techniques to address challenges across the software delivery life cycle, and often aim to highlight one or more particular approaches to software development for more detailed analysis and review.

The second category promotes a specific approach to software delivery that offers distinct benefits for practitioners in certain situations. The classic examples are manuals on specific software development techniques (such as the unified modeling language [UML] books from Grady Booch and many others [7,8,9]), texts describing common solution patterns for software in specific domains (led by the work of "the gang of four" [10] that inspired many subsequent works), and a vast array of "how-to" materials of diverse forms (including the majority of the IBM Redbooks and the Microsoft Practitioner series).

The third category describes specific software development environments, tools, and processes. This work varies widely but includes descriptions of specific software delivery processes (such as the recent wave of books on agile [11,12] and lean practices [13]) and works on software delivery models (such as Philip Kruchten's books on the rational unified process [14]). This third category also includes detailed process-and-tool combinations that may be based on specific functional domains (e.g., the many books focused on requirements management, configuration management, or testing) or based on specific solution domains (such as a less available but growing body of work on delivering web-based enterprise software and large-scale safety-critical systems).

The fourth category addresses the broader business and societal implications that result from the critical impact of many aspects of software delivery and offers a broad perspective on the changing nature and role of software in delivering solutions in which software plays an increasingly vital role. This work offers a range of views, from the polemic (such as Nicholas Carr's *Does IT Matter?* [15] and *The Big Switch* [16] and Thomas Friedman's *The World is Flat* [17]), to the social (such as works by Ravi Kalakota [18], Douglas Brown [19], and many others that address the global aspects of software outsourcing and offshoring), to the financial (including Barry Boehm's work on software economics [20] and

Walker Royce's work on software management [21]), to a wide variety of software process improvement materials from various organizations (such as the Software Engineering Institute [SEI], the Association for Computing Machinery [ACM], and the Institute for Electronic and Electrical Engineers [IEEE]).

Each of these, of course, plays an important role in helping us understand and deliver better enterprise software. However, the most obvious and straightforward questions often remain unaddressed or buried in the vast amount of details and overlays of ideas explored in such works. In particular, this book seeks to address three fundamental questions:

- What is the nature of today's enterprise software delivery?

- What is driving the approaches being taken to improve enterprise software delivery?

- How can these observations provide an informed view of the current trends as the basis for a strategic approach to balancing agility and efficiency in enterprise software delivery?

Addressing these questions will provide an important chance to reflect on, understand, and validate contemporary thinking on the nature of enterprise software delivery. Furthermore, it will allow both practitioners and academics to refocus their current efforts. The material will consolidate, expand, and challenge current activities in enterprise software delivery, to help practitioners view the decisions being made in a more appropriate context, with a broader view of the evolving nature of software delivery challenges. For academics, this book provides an excellent source of information, case studies, and examples to guide the formation of research activities and stimulate more informed and realistic discussions with students on enterprise software delivery.

Finally, you can join the conversation and obtain additional information and insight into the themes explored in this book at the following website: www.enterprisesoftwaredelivery.info.

Acknowledgments

The primary intent of this book is to provide a realistic view of current practices in enterprise software delivery. Consequently, I've used many examples and illustrations drawn from a wide variety of sources, primarily directly from real-world situations. By necessity, I removed confidential or extraneous information, and in a few cases I've simplified the material for presentation. In all cases, my goal has been to keep the examples as realistic as possible.

In assembling these ideas and examples, I have enjoyed the advice, help, and support of many people. It is my great pleasure to acknowledge their contribution and highlight their importance to this book. In particular, I have had incredible support in three main areas:

- The concepts and principles explored in the book have benefited from many discussions and interactions with a wide range of people. My particular thanks go out to Scott Ambler, David Bishop, Grady Booch, Peter Eeles, Tony Grout, Tommy Lennhamn, Dave Lubanko, Martin Nally, Walker Royce, and Jack Verstappen.

- The examples in this book draw on excellent work by several people. I would like to thank David Bishop, Christian Bornfeld, Erich Gamma, Niek de Grief, Arthur Jurgens, Ana Lopez, Antonio Lopez, Luis Reyes, Scott Rich, and the many people I have encountered during my work in numerous client projects over the past few years.

- Numerous detailed reviews of earlier drafts of this book have greatly improved its content and form. Particular thanks are due to Christian Bornfeld, Tommy Lennhamn, Jean-Yves Rigolet, Ian Sommerville, Scott Tilley, Walker Royce, and Rob Witty.

Finally, a very big "thank you" to my family, who have had to put up with my absences and late nights throughout the process of creating and delivering this book. This book would not have been possible without their endless patience, love, and support.

About the Author

Alan W. Brown is a distinguished engineer at IBM Rational software. Alan is currently IBM Rational's chief technology officer (CTO) for Europe, where he works with customers across Europe, consulting on software engineering strategy as it pertains to enterprise solutions, process improvement, and the transition to agile practices. In this role, Alan engages in strategic discussions in areas such as enterprise solution delivery, software delivery economics, and distributed software and systems delivery.

Alan has worked in many strategic roles in the software industry in Europe and the United States, including vice president of research and development at Sterling Software, research manager at Texas Instruments Software, and senior technical staff member at the Software Engineering Institute (SEI) at Carnegie Mellon University.

Alan has published over fifty papers, authored four books, and edited an additional three books. Alan holds a PhD in Computing Science from the University of Newcastle-upon-Tyne, UK.

You can contact Alan at alan@alanbrown.net.

Chapter 1

Why Is Enterprise Software Delivery So Difficult?

Chapter Summary

This chapter introduces the book's main themes: globalization of the enterprise, cost efficiency in delivery, and agility in meeting new market needs and expectations. To establish these themes, I discuss today's enterprise systems delivery challenges, review the current focus for enterprise software delivery organizations, and outline the evolving expectations and demands on enterprise software delivery. I draw the following conclusions:

- Economic pressures have focused attention in enterprise software delivery organizations on cost-cutting activities, severely stretching existing delivery practices.

- New organizational models are required to support enterprise software delivery organizations with greater geographic diversity and where integrated software supply chains are being created.

- Greater demands and diversity of needs from clients are driving significant demand for new services and improved access to existing capabilities.

- A primary focus for the coming years will be on balancing the need for governance and control with increased flexibility and agility in enterprise software delivery.

1.1 Introduction

Working in a large multinational software services company some years ago, I knew what to expect on the very first day of each new quarter—a speech from the head of the enterprise software delivery organization that started with the comment, "Today we begin the most challenging quarter in the most challenging year in the history of this company!"

Of course, the speech, intended as a motivational "call-to-action" for everyone in the company to redouble their efforts, was received with a collective sigh. But what if he was right? What if with each new quarter the challenges *are* more difficult, the stakes *are* higher, and the pressures on enterprise software delivery *are* increased?

Almost every day we hear that more and more people are connected to the Internet (already about 2 billion people, or about 28 percent of the world population),[1] substantially more transistors are being packed on the newest generation chip (already in excess of 2 billion),[2] greater numbers of people now carry around mobile Internet-connected devices in their pockets (with the number of mobile phone subscribers in early 2012 estimated at almost 6 billion, with 1.2 billion mobile broadband users),[3] and a majority of businesses rely on online purchases to meet their objectives (with US online retail sales reaching almost $250 billion a year).[4] Today's world is significantly more technologically advanced than it has ever been. The drive to take advantage of these advances to make our world more interconnected and intelligent is changing our everyday lives and our businesses—giving us smarter cities, more innovative health care, more intelligent industrial systems, and improved consumer experiences.

Yet these technological advances are possible only with significant innovation in software systems. Software is the "invisible thread" enabling smarter products and services and more intelligent enterprise software and solutions. The latest automobiles, for example, contain dozens of microprocessors running tens of millions of lines of code to manage the engine and braking system, monitor the pressure in the tires, navigate safely on the roads with real-time traffic updates, and provide an extensive entertainment system connected to personal devices such as phones and MP3 players. A constant stream of new customer demands means this software will continue to get more complex: for example, software will connect your vehicle to multiple external systems, such

---

1. www.internetworldstats.com/stats.htm.
2. www.physorg.com/news121350597.html.
3. http://mobithinking.com/mobile-marketing-tools/latest-mobile-stats.
4. www.reuters.com/article/idUSN0825407420100308.

as dealer networks, monitoring centers that respond to in-car emergencies, GPS navigation systems, and more.[5]

This software-driven world does not come without challenges. We've seen high-profile failures in much of the deployed enterprise software, which is inherently complex. We're all aware of horror stories from the popular press describing vehicle recalls due to software failures in engine management and braking systems, inaccurate bank statements showing funds inexplicably removed from accounts, misdiagnoses in patient monitoring systems, or erroneous calculations that send multimillion-dollar missiles off into space rather than toward their designated targets. In fact, a recent analysis[6] examined 288 deployed enterprise applications from 75 organizations (with more than 108 million lines of code) and found structural errors that on average would require an investment of more than $1 million per application to fix.

The bottom line is that there is a challenge to control the large amount of software currently in production, and the many billions of lines of code that must be deployed over the coming years need to be developed, delivered, managed into production, and maintained. Enterprise organizations whose businesses rely on software must learn how to balance the relationship between necessary investments in enterprise software delivery and the business value these investments bring to the organization.

So while software engineers are busy "inventing the future" they must also take care of current and past investments. And while enterprises must invest in future needs and innovation, they also must understand and control the "technical debt" inherent in their currently deployed systems.[7] Companies have already created millions of applications to drive existing devices and manage their businesses. For example, an estimated 200 billion lines of COBOL code execute every day to control the enterprise software running many of these businesses.[8] Each of these systems requires effort to manage, maintain, upgrade, and evolve.

A software delivery manager for a large European financial services company and I recently examined challenges in four areas affecting software delivery in his organization, as shown in Figure 1.1.

---

5. http://gizmodo.com/5467388/software-bug-causes-toyota-recall-of-almost-half-a-million-new -hybrid-cars.

6. www.itq.ch/pdf/cast-report-on-application-software-health.pdf.

7. The idea of "technical debt" was described by Ward Cunningham in 1992 (http://c2.com/doc/ oopsla92.html) as the increasing price of fixing development inaccuracies and shortcuts over the lifetime of a deployed system.

8. www.ibm.com/software/jp/zseries/seminar/pdf/cobol_news.pdf.

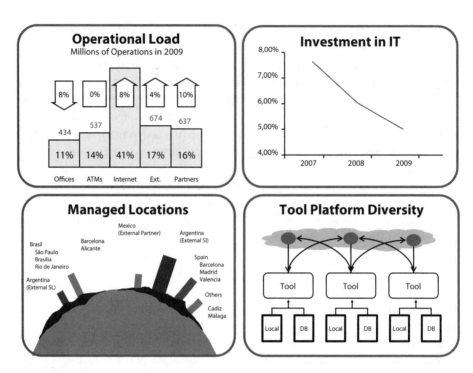

Figure 1.1 *A summary of four key challenges for a large financial services organization*

In the first area, *operational load* (top left of the diagram), the challenge is the significant increase in the volume of operations on this organization's currently deployed systems, particularly through Internet and partner channels. In the second area, *managed locations* (bottom left), the challenge is an increasing geographic diversity across many locations as the business expands into new areas (in this case dominated by Spanish-speaking populations) and the use of multiple providers as primary delivery agents in these locations (especially system integrators). In the third area, *investment in IT* (top right), the challenge is a decreasing investment trend in enterprise software delivery support, with a three-year reduction from more than 7 percent to less than 5 percent of the organization's revenue devoted to IT. In the fourth area of Tool Platform Diversity (bottom right), the challenge is the need to address the increasingly complex tooling environment for the development and delivery of the enterprise software being managed, with many tools, multiple data sources, and complex interdependent delivery processes.

When faced with these pressures, we need to ask some important questions about how best to deliver new capabilities in the context of our existing obligations to manage what we have in place. Reflecting on the current state of enterprise software delivery, we must determine how to focus our efforts on areas that will help improve and accelerate our ability to deliver increased functionality more quickly and to maintain what is in place more efficiently.

In this chapter, I address some of the fundamental questions about enterprise software delivery. Additional historical details, analysis, and commentary on the role and structure of enterprise software delivery organizations are provided in Appendix A, where I take a more detailed look at the role and function of a typical enterprise software delivery organization.

1.2 What Is an Enterprise System?

Throughout this book I use the terms *enterprise software* and *enterprise software delivery*, yet I purposefully avoid defining these terms. This may seem rather perverse. But any attempt at defining them undoubtedly results in a futile effort to explain what is meant by *enterprise* and *system*. These words are so heavily overloaded historically and so open to multiple interpretations contextually that any attempted definition produces unsatisfactory results. Instead, I characterize *enterprise software* more simply as software-based solutions used or created by an organization to benefit one or more of its stakeholders. This simple view of the term puts the focus on situations where executing that software is critical to the mission or business function of the organization and where it is essential to invest in continued operation of that software over some period of time.

Of course, I recognize that the context in which enterprise software is conceived, developed, deployed, and maintained affects many of those activities, perhaps in profound ways. Specific development and delivery techniques and approaches may be important (or mandatory) in one domain, while unnecessary or inefficient in others. Certain artifacts and documents are highly valued for control and governance in some classes of projects but may prove redundant and distracting for others. Therefore I want to point out that some of the guidance and observations in this book will have more applicability in some domains than in others. I illustrate key points with real-world examples drawn from a variety of domains, but the majority are from financial services industries, such as banking, insurance, and credit-card management, and from the perspective of software teams within large suppliers of software-based systems and services.[9] However, I believe this situational variance does not detract from

---

9. I focus on the financial industry primarily because of my firsthand experience in that field. However, this also brings to mind the story of Willy Sutton, a depression-era bank robber wanted for robberies in Miami, New Orleans, and New York. After his capture in 1950, a reporter asked him why he robbed banks. His reply was "Because that's where the money is."

the importance of the wider perspective and commentary I provide. So while I describe concepts that have broad value and use in enterprise software delivery, I'm careful to offer contextual descriptions for use in applying the ideas in practice.

In addition to a diversity of contexts, there is a wide variety in the role, function, and structure of an "enterprise software delivery organization." Typically, such an organization is responsible for many different activities, covering the development, deployment, maintenance, and operation of the enterprise software. The exact scope is determined by the specific context of the business being supported. For example, in Figure 1.2, I illustrate how the enterprise software

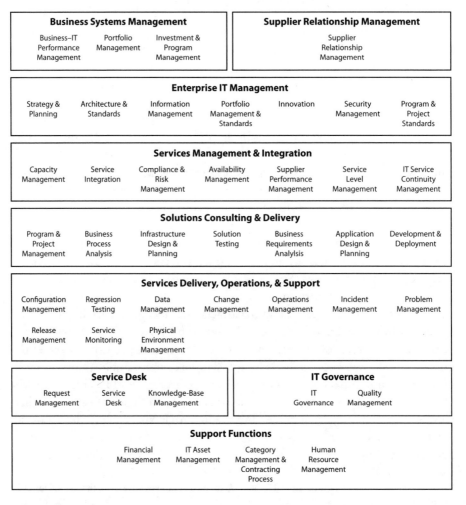

Figure 1.2 *An example of the scope of activities supported by an enterprise software delivery organization*

delivery organization for a large multinational utility company views the range of capabilities it supplies to the business. Here we see that the broad perspective of the role includes not only development and delivery of enterprise software but also a number of supporting activities, such as service-desk management and supplier-relationship management. This set of functions may be directly offered by the enterprise software delivery organization or shared with other third party groups. Consequently, the enterprise software delivery organization sits at the heart of a web of relationships that cuts across the business and reaches outside to a potentially large ecosystem of suppliers and stakeholders.

To restate, a core tenet of this book is that many important ideas and approaches to enterprise software delivery are widely applicable. This is true whether the early discovery aspects of a project are referred to as "business analysis" or "mission planning" or whether maintenance activities are described as "fixes and upgrades" or "through life-cycle capability management."

1.3 What Is Different Today?

From the earliest days of computers, "software crises" of various kinds have arisen: the lack of scientific programmers in the 1950s, an inability to access expensive shared computers in the 1960s, the growing software backlogs in the 1970s, and so on. Thus it is important to establish some context for the current challenges facing the software industry.

Although many factors contribute to the current enterprise software delivery challenges, the financial crisis experienced by most major world economies from 2005 onward has had a powerful polarizing effect on enterprise software delivery, accelerating trends that were perhaps already in motion. On the one hand, the drive for efficiencies in all aspects of business operations has raised the visibility and importance of enterprise software delivery. Many organizations are discovering just how dominant and influential a role their enterprise software plays in delivering value and differentiation to their clients. As a result, many organizations seek to accelerate their enterprise software delivery to increase automation of key business processes, work more closely with their business partners, and drive out unnecessary costs throughout their business supply chain.

However, on the other hand, organizations are much more closely examining the costs involved in delivering and maintaining existing enterprise software. Unfortunately, many organizations have found that they have too little insight into and control of their enterprise software delivery costs, and they're hard-pressed to clearly align their spending in this area with the value delivered to the business. Furthermore, when pressed to make yet another round of cuts in expenses, it is often far from clear where and how to make them without a severe impact on the business. Frequently, there is no clear visibility into the trade-offs across various strategies to achieve necessary economies and their effect on the enterprise delivery organization's ability to perform its function.

As a result of these trends, enterprise software delivery organizations are under increasing pressure to manage costs, be productive, reduce time to market, and enable maintenance and evolution of those systems over extended periods of time. In addition, they must achieve all this with greater transparency and accountability to the business.

The increasing heterogeneity, complexity, and distributed nature of deployment architectures compound the problems faced by enterprise software solutions providers. A driving force for these changes over the past decade has been the massive adoption of the Internet as a deployment target for many systems. From its origins as a means to share documents and perform collaborative research in academia, the Internet (and its related technologies of intranets and extranets)[10] has become the primary platform for highly interactive systems of all kinds, supporting commercial transactions, information gathering and dissemination, and many forms of education and entertainment.

Clearly the Internet continues to have a major impact on the way business is conducted and the way enterprise software delivery organizations organize and operate. In 2010, the US Department of Commerce stated that e-commerce worldwide is estimated at $10 trillion annually.[11] Additionally, existing businesses are being transformed. Economic efficiencies of e-commerce are contributing to lower cost distribution, tighter inventory control, increased productivity, and improved customer service.

Similarly, enterprise software delivery organizations are themselves transforming. Internet-based technologies have revolutionized the typical way in which software is created, delivered, and maintained. Today it is rarely the case that the enterprise software delivery organization is based in a single location, has ownership for all the software it manages, maintains fixed lines of communications with its stakeholders, or is governed by a single company. The very nature of enterprise software delivery has changed, including the scope, shape, and situation in which enterprise software delivery takes place. This creates challenges of many kinds, even in such fundamental areas such as tracking releases, aligning updates, identifying system patches, and so on. In such activities, many groups are involved with scheduling, planning, and executing software deliveries.

More recently, Internet solutions have extended the domain of desktops and PCs to mobile and embedded devices. By 2015 there will be an estimated

---

10. For ease of discussion, we shall refer to these technologies simply as *the Internet* or *the web*.

11. As reported in December 2010 at www.commerce.gov.

1 trillion interconnected devices around the world,[12] producing a very complex mesh of interconnected capabilities, services, and applications. Participating in Internet-based commerce is no longer simply a matter of making back-office core business functions accessible to a handful of browser technologies. Many enterprise software delivery organizations must understand and support a vast array of delivery platforms and technologies and offer a high quality of service when participating in complex, unpredictable networks of systems.

A wide collection of Internet, device, and web-based technologies support these changes, spawning a revolution in the way in which systems are designed, deployed, and evolved. Many organizations see the need to take advantage of these technologies. But few organizations have the knowledge, technology, or skills necessary to do so. Arguably, this mismatch between the needs of organizations and their ability to execute based on these needs represents the greatest challenge since the first software programs were being deployed more than forty years ago. Those that have succeeded have been rewarded with more efficient services meeting the needs of a growing customer base, the flexibility to support the move into new markets, and inflated stock evaluations based on their future potential to dominate their chosen domains. Those that have not embraced this technology have at best been sidelined as niche players or at worst failed to survive at all.[13]

The challenges faced by organizations assembling software-intensive solutions also provide the greatest opportunity for enterprise software delivery organizations. Recognizing the strategic importance of these new technologies to their businesses, many organizations have raised the importance and stature of their enterprise software delivery to levels not seen in the past twenty years. Successful organizations understand that their ability to compete is substantially increased by strengthening their ability to deliver enterprise software with and for web-based and mobile-accessible technologies and by using the infrastructure of the Internet to rethink the nature of a global enterprise software delivery approach.

1.4 What Is the Focus of an Enterprise Software Delivery Organization?

In general, enterprise software delivery organizations conduct three basic kinds of activities:

---

12. For example, see www.readwriteweb.com/enterprise/2010/06/ibm-a-world-with-1-trillion-co.php.
13. There have also been some very notable e-business failures. For example, see the discussion of why boo.com failed at www.learnebusiness.com/ebusiness_articles/Most_Famous_Dotcom_Failure.pdf.

- *Remediating and repairing existing systems.* Currently, many existing resources are dedicated to fixing and upgrading existing systems to extend their useful life. These are tactical efforts aimed at addressing compelling short-term needs, reducing ongoing investment, or preparing these systems to be outsourced to third parties.

- *Leveraging existing assets to improve productivity and performance.* To supply new services in a cost-effective way, organizations are putting a great deal of effort into extracting value from existing systems, wrapping those pieces for access to new technologies, and assembling new applications. Building solutions from existing pieces will always be a key part of building cost-effective systems. However, opening up existing applications to new devices and Internet-based access requires the significant rework of many systems to ease access, optimize performance, implement additional security checks, and consolidate information from multiple sources.

- *Supporting new business opportunities.* Software delivery organizations are rewriting strategic plans to comprehend the need to support new markets, new customers, or new usage models. Often these strategies involve new technology adoption to make use of web-based technologies and Internet-connected devices. These tasks represent the most important strategic development efforts now under way in most organizations.

Very few people could have predicted the massive changes that have occurred over the past decade in the business environment and technical landscape. In particular, the use of the Internet and its related technologies has been accelerated due to the economic crises and turmoil experienced in many business domains and in many regions of the world. As a result, end users of enterprise-scale systems have significantly higher expectations about the flexibility, availability, and usability of these systems. These translate into a whole new set of demands on enterprise software delivery organizations and their supporting technologies.

There is a strong mutual relationship between an enterprise system delivery organization's strategic approach to these tasks and the structure and evolution of the systems themselves. The large diversity in the scope, size, technology, and context of enterprise systems is also reflected in the enterprise software delivery organizations. This book is not intended to be a primer on enterprise software; rather, I refer the reader to some of the many excellent existing materials that provide an overview of software engineering techniques [6,22], describe approaches to enterprise software development [23], review architectural patterns for enterprise software design [10,24], and discuss evolution of enterprise software [25].

However, it is worth noting that the evolving nature of enterprise software systems influences (and is influenced by) the organizational structure creating it. In short, I note that the backbone for enterprise systems today is characterized by at least three important trends:

- Application servers constitute the middle tiers of an n-tier architecture for large-scale distributed systems. Many changes are being made to data centers to enhance their effectiveness in providing such capabilities. In addition, more frequently virtualized, externally hosted, or cloud-based approaches are being introduced to improve efficiency and flexibility in delivering enterprise infrastructure services.

- An enterprise-integration approach combines existing packages and systems as part of a comprehensive integrated solution, connected via an enterprise service bus.

- Component approaches and technologies form the underlying design metaphor, supported by a robust set of methods and tools conforming to an emerging set of industry standards.

These critical elements of enterprise software delivery today shape the focus for enterprise software delivery organizations.[14]

1.5 How Are the Needs for Enterprise Software Delivery Evolving?

A very significant shift in the delivery of enterprise software systems is being driven by several convergent factors, including the following:

- *End-user expectations.* End users require more timely, synchronized information to be available everywhere, on demand, with no downtime. This increased access and transparency is significantly changing reporting, governance, management, and deployment practices across the organization. The variety of roles, particularly for nonspecialist software users, has continued to grow. The range of needs of those users can be very wide. With software playing an increasingly important role in all our lives, the solutions being developed must be easier to use by a broader community of people on numerous devices and provide more accurate and reliable

---

14. If further background is needed, Appendix A contains a detailed review of the structure and role of enterprise software delivery organizations.

information with greater availability. Briefly stated, enterprise organizations must attempt to bring themselves much closer to the users (in terms of the user's context, providing convenience of access to services and support for their intent).

- *Cost to create solutions.* Expanding business and technical demands are increasing the pressure to augment business expertise to meet nonfunctional requirements on a diverse set of new platforms. To be competitive in meeting these needs, enterprise software delivery organizations must take advantage of lower labor rates around the world, integrate components from a variety of suppliers, and reuse solutions across product lines and solution families. The emergence of a global "software supply chain" places the organization at the center of a series of business and technical relationships that may not be entirely under its control yet may largely determine its delivery success. This rethinking of the software supply chain and emphasis on cost control exposes inefficiencies in current development practices. It also requires an improved visibility and transparency of ongoing activities and overextends existing team-collaboration approaches.

- *Auditing and compliance.* Increased accountability is forcing greater transparency about how software is developed to ensure it meets the business needs. Increased regulations and oversight are placing additional requirements on adoption of well-documented best practices with mandated control points to aid auditing. In many domains, it is not sufficient to simply deliver an enterprise solution that functions correctly; it is now also essential to prove that it does function and to demonstrate that appropriate practices were used in its creation, evolution, and management.

- *Speed of change.* The fast pace of business change has required the delivery of more software more often to more stakeholders, resulting in a greater number of enterprises having to adopt accelerated delivery styles aimed at quickly producing solutions that are "good enough" rather than face missing key business deadlines. This pressure to meet demands quickly has led to a fundamental shift toward greater flexibility in delivery through a more incremental phased approach. This often results in smaller but more frequent deliverables of software. For many enterprise software delivery organizations, such approaches are in direct conflict with their governance structures, and they may be hampered by inflexible enterprise software and overly constrained development practices.

- *Adaptable business platforms.* Increased architectural control and insight into where solutions are deployed help to ensure support for current business needs and allow greater flexibility to adjust deployment according to those needs. Enterprises are increasingly global in nature, form alliances with partners more frequently, offer far more products in a variety of markets, and are constantly redefining their core business competencies. Today's distributed solution platforms must allow optimization around current business needs and support reconfiguration as those needs change. A rich collection of distributed infrastructure technologies has emerged to allow greater flexibility in the deployment, optimization, and redeployment of core application capabilities as business needs change. Enterprise software delivery organizations must devote a great deal of their resources to introducing, adapting, and optimizing these business-driven platforms.

As a result of these factors, enterprise software delivery organizations are looking ever more carefully at how to evolve the portfolio of systems they are managing, the technology base in which they operate, and the skills they have available in their teams. The goal, naïvely stated, is to "do more with less." A primary focus for their strategic planning is the balance they must strike between two competing pressures: On the one hand, they seek greater agility and flexibility in how they work with business stakeholders, adopt new technologies, and meet customers' needs. On the other hand, they seek to standardize, reuse, and economize to maximize efficiency and value to the business. The pressure to control costs and deliver software in compressed timeframes continues to require creative management of development and test teams.

How an enterprise software delivery organization faces this paradox is one of the most interesting and compelling challenges that will largely determine an enterprise's success. This book examines the global nature of this problem, the approaches that are being taken, and the range of measures that can be taken to focus efforts more effectively in areas of greatest value to the business.

1.6 Conclusions

The pressures on enterprise software delivery are growing. At the same time that they are being required to cut costs and provide greater accountability to the business, enterprise software delivery organizations are being asked to accelerate innovation in the systems they deliver and maintain. Success in enterprise software delivery highly depends on an organization's ability to balance the demand for agility and efficiency and align global resources to deliver based on those needs. In particular, enterprise software delivery organizations must strive to build the process and technological backbone for today's software factories while creating the team-based practices that encourage and enhance scalable approaches to agility that optimize the global software supply chain.

The rest of this book discusses the characteristics of enterprise software being delivered today and the approaches enterprise software delivery organizations are adopting to improve the balance they must achieve between innovation, efficiency, performance, and value.

Chapter 2

Anatomy of an Enterprise
Software Delivery Project

Chapter Summary

I present an example of a typical enterprise software delivery project. I examine its key characteristics and analyze specific areas for improvement. I explore both the enterprise-level and project-level issues within this specific example, and conclude the following:

- A systematic approach to enterprise-level improvement is essential to achieve the benefits over short-, medium-, and long-term periods.

- Substantial project-level improvements can be made by focusing on several critical application life-cycle management areas.

- Optimizing the global work force requires a balance of resources and a focus on collaboration across people, assets, and processes.

2.1 Introduction

To provide the context for this book, it is important to have a clear view of the current challenges faced in enterprise software delivery. To enable this view, I take a specific enterprise software delivery organization and describe how it executed a particular enterprise software delivery project. After discussing the project's critical elements, I analyze where and how improvements to that project are possible.

While many facets of this real-world enterprise software delivery project are of interest, I choose to highlight four areas that amplify key themes I will address in detail throughout the book:

- Collaboration across distributed teams, particularly when those teams span geographic, organizational, and company boundaries. In such projects, we frequently find that inefficiencies and misunderstandings are a major source of errors, frustration, and waste. Clear approaches to communication and coordination greatly improve the team's performance.

- Agility in the enterprise delivery team's means of organization and operation, which enables effective delivery, and in its interaction with the business. A project's progress and delivery rhythm is based on how it reacts to changes in its goals, context, and delivery environment.

- Continuous quality assurance, which provides superior solutions using efficient, predictable techniques. Late software breakages are often a result of misunderstood requirements, unstable architectures, and poor communication across the team. They prove very costly and highly disruptive to the project's success. Early and continuous attention to quality is essential.

- Governance and metrics to provide insight into a project's status and ensure the project stays on track. Lack of governance can lead to chaotic behaviors. Furthermore, good governance approaches based on poorly defined metrics schemes can result in suboptimal decision making. Visibility and traceability across the project are essential to manage the project complexity.

In this chapter, I establish the context for this enterprise software delivery project, and I then explore these key themes within this real-world example. I conclude with a number of observations about what we can learn from this study.

2.2 MyCo and the MyProj Enterprise Software Delivery Project

Drawn from a real-world project, this case study is illustrative of a wide variety of situations. A multinational utility company is supported by an enterprise software delivery organization under significant cost and efficiency pressures to deliver IT services to the business. For ease of reference, I'll call this company

MyCo, and I'll name the project we'll examine *MyProj*.[1] Faced with many challenges over the years, MyCo has invested in several different facets of its enterprise software delivery, making the following changes:

- From very siloed, geographically dispersed solutions and technologies to centrally driven technology platforms

- From wholly onshore to a mix of onshore, offshore, and outsourced application development and support

- From globally dispersed in-house-managed to outsourced IT infrastructure services

- From ad hoc vendor engagements to use of preselected vendors for defined domains

- From undefined core software delivery processes to the implementation of common, centralized IT processes

- From company-specific governance of enterprise software delivery to governance and improvement supported by standardized activities, particularly in enterprise architecture with the open group architecture framework (TOGAF) [26] and the control objectives for information and related technology (COBIT) framework for IT governance and control [27]

- From a collection of uncoordinated enterprise software delivery improvement schemes to significant investment in measured improvement against the capability maturity model (CMM), currently assessed at level 2 and on a path to level 3 compliance

Within this broad context, I'll analyze the structure, staffing profile, and delivery approach of MyProj. I'll then examine where improvements to enterprise software delivery are possible, and I'll assess their potential impact on this project.

2.3 Business and Organizational Context

MyCo is a large multinational organization with a presence in more than a dozen different countries around the world and a work force of over 100,000 employees. As with all utility companies, its business includes very high levels

---

1. Although this example is based on a real-world situation, I have simplified the example for presentation purposes, and I use fictitious names for reasons of privacy.

of innovation, research, and development in areas such as energy production and distribution. However, it also has a large historical investment in infrastructure, systems, and processes that have been in place for decades. Pressures are placed on costs and levels of efficiency to both drive innovation to be more effective and optimize operational costs to be more efficient.

The MyCo enterprise software delivery organization has a key role in addressing these challenges. Its strategy involves four areas:

- *Collaboration across global delivery teams.* The common mode of operation involves multiple suppliers, multiple geographies, and multiple business units.

- *Waste reduction and optimization of resources and assets.* Aligned practices provide a consistent and integrated development approach with standardized tooling across the organization.

- *Optimized reuse of core assets and practices.* An ongoing effort to catalogue, categorize, and assess the value of the current asset inventory aims to make it more accessible across the organization. These asset categories are aligned across all aspects of software development, delivery, and deployment.

- *Business cost management.* Increased cost transparency is enforced in all activities through continual monitoring of project health across the portfolio of projects and across a wide variety of tools and practices. A specific move toward virtualized and cloud-based infrastructures is foreseen, with several pilot efforts already in progress.

2.4 Project Context

Within this strategic context, the MyProj project is particularly critical to MyCo. In this project, a core back-office system for customer management is being redesigned to improve customer-handling activities and provide greater analytical capabilities across several disparate customer data sources. MyProj has the following important characteristics:

- *Worldwide delivery and deployment.* MyProj involves not only the collaboration of development and delivery resources from many locations but also the global deployment and management of the resultant solution.

- *Significant criticality, size, and investment.* MyProj is a 2-million-euro investment and involves almost 2,800 staff days of effort within a broader

10-million-euro system improvement program. The planned elapsed time of the project is 1 year, with some significant business impact if that date is not met.

- *Outsourced delivery model.* The majority of the effort on MyProj is contracted with an external system integrator in a "time and materials" contract.

- *Focus on reusable assets.* MyProj both uses and contributes assets that have been used and can be reused in other projects. These assets include software code, component specifications, and documentation.

To manage costs, MyProj's system integrator uses delivery centers across the world. Using up to 80 percent of resources in offshore locations, MyProj's offshore delivery model features the following:

- Offshore teams that are handpicked based on required skill sets

- Offshore project managers and technical leads who spend an initial period colocated with the onshore management team (a so-called landed phase) before returning to their offshore locations

- Regular *high-touch* visits by a core team and the customer to manage progress and create more informal relationships among the extended team

- Explicit expectation management of surface risks as early as possible

- The enactment of a collaborative solution-oriented management approach to analyze and resolve any blocking problems that arise

- High levels of collaboration across the teams to ensure synchronization at all stages of development and delivery

2.5 Project Execution Results

Figure 2.1 illustrates the staffing profile for the execution of MyProj. Here we see the loading of resources over the lifetime of the project and the levels of effort for each development phase. MyProj was completed within a few weeks of schedule (1 year elapsed time) with a peak effort of almost 300 staff days per month and a total investment of almost 2,800 staff days from inception to delivery of the enterprise software.

The profile depicted in Figure 2.1 is typical of many projects (both within MyCo and elsewhere), with a characteristic peak loading of effort late in the

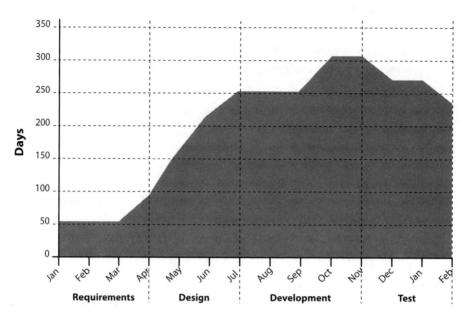

Figure 2.1 *The resource profile for the MyProj project*

development phase as unit test efforts give way to integration and system test-ing. Often in this phase of the project, the majority of the more complex bugs are found, usually as a consequence of misunderstandings in requirements, architectural weaknesses, and failures in communication across the team. Throughout the testing phase, this high level of staffing is maintained to address these concerns, correct errors, and bring the resulting system to a deliverable state. In this regard, MyProj displays many aspects typical of such projects. For this analysis I do not explicitly address some of the issues concerning postde-ployment costs; instead, I simply note that this high level of staffing continues through the first weeks of deployment due to the large number of late fixes and changes in the system.

2.6 Post Hoc Analysis

As a consequence of the MyProj resource profile, MyCo undertook a detailed post hoc analysis of effort across the project phases. This analysis aimed to identify key areas where a more effective delivery approach would provide measured improvements while maintaining or improving the predictability and quality of the delivered results.

Two levels of analysis were undertaken: one at the level of the enterprise software delivery organization and the other based on the specific details of the MyProj project.

2.6.1 Enterprise Software Delivery Organization Analysis

The first level of analysis considered the areas for improvement across the enterprise software delivery organization. Specifically, there are improvement areas in which efficiencies are possible as a result of addressing systemic issues in the enterprise software delivery approaches currently in use. These would have broad applicability and show value to the organization in the short, medium, and long term.

This analysis was multifaceted. Working with management personnel, we looked at results from several similar enterprise software delivery projects that had taken place over the past two years. We then compared that information with benchmark materials from several industry studies (such as [2,20,28]), examined data from our internal project delivery analyses, and engaged a third-party enterprise software industry analyst organization to offer a critical review of our findings, comparing them with data from their current clients and with their own analytical approaches.

Figure 2.2 shows a summary of the results of this analysis. For simplification purposes, the graph shows major areas for enterprise-level improvement across two dimensions: the long-term impact and the timing of potential benefits. Here, there was focus in seven areas, each represented as circle on the graph identifying how that area was considered to contribute to impact and the likely timing of that impact. In each area, we performed quite detailed analysis of savings and improvements by examining representative project data, typical labor rates, and project organization sizes and structures. Using that information, we then were able to show the potential improvements in terms of productivity savings (labor reduction) and quality improvements (defect rate reduction). For example, in the areas of Requirements Management Linked to Quality Management, we used company-specific project information and industry-wide benchmark data to identify that improved life-cycle management techniques could result in a reduction as large as 10 percent in defect density for delivered software in the first year. With added attention to test case management and test planning, this would also provide up to a 7 percent saving in labor costs in the first year. Similar analyses were performed in all seven areas identified in Figure 2.2.

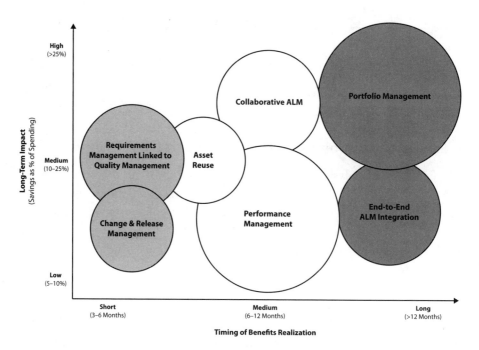

Figure 2.2 *A summary of efficiencies across the enterprise software delivery organization*

A full description of the analysis approach is not necessary here. Rather, I'll provide a short summary of the key features of the techniques used to highlight its key characteristics.

While a number of analysis approaches are possible, in this case we selected a practice-based approach. Each practice and its associated tools have an underlying benefit for each practitioner. For example, the adoption of an improved change management practice and associated tools will save a developer 1 percent on average. Considering the loaded costs of each resource, we can calculate a benefit, per year, and by multiplying this figure by the number of practitioners, we can calculate an annual saving. While each individual practice improvement is actually quite small (perhaps a saving of one to four hours a week), the accumulation as more practices are adopted results in a significant overall benefit.

As shown in Figure 2.2, our analysis approach, then, assesses a series of selected practices in terms of potential improvement. Each practice is a collection of tools and services aimed at enhancing the development capability of a team or project. It was concluded, for example, that near-term improvements in areas such as change and release management and requirements management could have delivered labor savings of 5 percent and 7 percent, respectively, with additional reductions in defect density of up to 10 percent in the first year.[2]

2.6.2 Project-Level Analysis

While the first level of analysis considered the areas for improvement across the enterprise software delivery organization, the second level directly examined the MyProj project. Focused on several areas, the analysis involved detailed discussions with the delivery team,[3] analysis of processes executed, inspection of actual defect rates and error-fixing practices, document reviews, and experimentation with real data.

We concluded that improvements could be made in the following areas:

- *Quality management.* Difficulties in project status reporting were commonly experienced. To increase the effectiveness and productivity of the onshore management team, in particular, better decisions could have been made with enhanced real-time quality assessments supported by automated quality data collection tooling.

- *Data management.* Errors in data analysis and models were detected late in the development cycles. Improved integrated tooling would help improve data analysis and modeling, increasing quality of data used to test and reducing development and test timelines.

- *Requirements traceability.* Poor connections between requirements, development, and test activities resulted in several misunderstandings across the team. Greater integration and tracking could have the effect of removing design gaps and misunderstandings. A consequent decrease in the continual need to query requirements to ensure their currency and to understand unclear design implications could result in a significant time savings in development. Similarly, a decrease in the need for such queries results in better estimation for change analysis and reduced critical and major defects in test activities, as build activities are more aligned with the requirements and design status.

---

2. In practice, many additional factors were also taken into consideration, such as the interactions among the practices, capacity for change across the teams, phasing of changes, and so on. Such factors are part of an internal IBM "business value analysis" tool that was used.

3. The approach was to use a structured risk analysis technique similar in many respects to the approach used by the SEI and based on previous experiences with its application to large software projects and programs [29].

- *End-to-end environment management.* Several administrative activities caused time delays in creating and maintaining appropriate working environments. These delays can be eliminated with faster environment procurement and easier access to predefined developer profiles, thus making necessary resources, such as tools, data, and test equipment, more accessible.

- *Onboarding to access the development and test tooling.* Situations arose where new project members, or existing members switching to new roles, had difficulty getting information or access to the tools for software development and delivery. This time loss can be greatly reduced with faster onboarding, improved documentation, and access to communities for peer-level advice.

The result of this project-level analysis is shown in Figure 2.3. Here we show how MyProj could have been executed as a result of these software factory delivery improvements in the areas stated. In particular, we produced data that shows a one-month reduction in cycle time, with reduced peak effort through

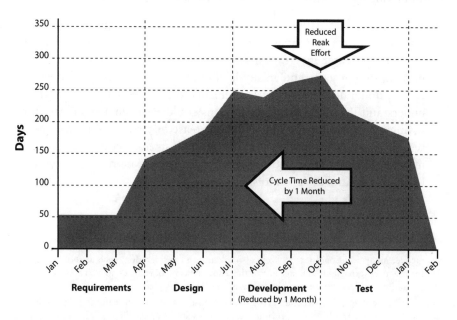

Figure 2.3 *Adjusted project profile for the MyProj project*

the elimination of certain blockages, reduction in costly misunderstandings, and improved communication channels.

A more detailed view of the efficiencies and cost savings is shown in Figure 2.4. Here we view the change in resource and cost profile over time as a result of these enterprise software delivery improvements.

2.7 Commentary

This review of the MyProj project has enabled us to look in some detail at a typical enterprise software delivery project with respect to the project's delivery context, resource profile, and execution history. In the subsequent analysis, we considered areas that could improve from adopting additional software factory delivery techniques and automations. We can now make a number of important observations.

First, it's useful to summarize the sources of potential improvements we identified from our analysis of both the enterprise and project levels. We can express these as recommendations for improvements in four areas. Each recommendation represents a challenge and an opportunity:

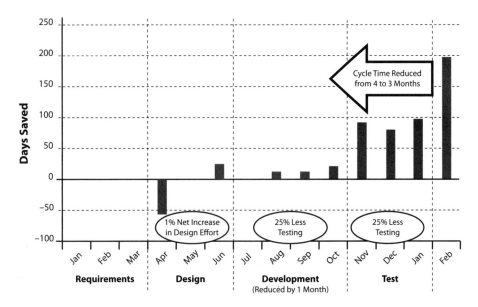

Figure 2.4 *A more detailed efficiency analysis of the MyProj project*

- *Collaborate globally.* The global approach to delivery deserves particular attention. Many challenges to enterprise software delivery are a result of intercommunication issues. In a globally distributed development team, we must ensure that the value gained by using people in other regions (whether to make use of scarce resources or to optimize costs) is not lost. When cross-organization issues are added to the challenge, investment in processes and technology to ensure smooth collaboration becomes essential and proves to be a determinant factor in the project's success.

- *Deliver with agility.* A great deal of flexibility is needed to manage the continual change inherent in these kinds of projects. Agility is necessary in not only the style of development but also the management of interactions with the business stakeholders; the manner in which project objectives are assessed, understood, and evolved; and the way in which the solution is provided to the operational teams to be moved into production. This broader view of agility in enterprise software delivery is essential. Our analysis takes into account the increased confidence that results from early attention to testing available software and the benefits of guidance from continuous stakeholder feedback.

- *Focus on quality.* We've always known that the peak effort and cost of enterprise software delivery is during testing and delivery phases. During these phases, the real quality issues become more concrete, and many of the more complex problems surface. This project analysis again confirms that a "total quality" view of enterprise software delivery reduces that peak effort substantially and provides the major source of early savings to an organization. The reduction of high-impact late changes is of the utmost importance in any project.

- *Monitor and measure continuously.* Poor decision making was primarily a result of incomplete information and lack of clear insight into the project's real status. The challenge was increased due to the distributed, multiorganizational aspects of the project. Far too much time was spent chasing information, finding relevant data, and making sense of the data gathered from multiple sources. The project would have benefited from an increased focus on automated information gathering, together with a more clearly defined view of the project's most relevant business and technical measures.

Second, we note several additional areas where improvements could be made. For example, we did not spend time in areas of reuse. Many industry studies provide data that supports substantial improvements in productivity and quality through mature, systematic reuse practices. In the case of MyProj, while reuse maturity was low, attention to this area would undoubtedly bring additional rewards.

Another area of importance to MyCo is the move toward cloud-based delivery models. Through deployment of cloud technologies, the company is looking to reduce investments in underused technology infrastructure and increase standard services for areas such as testing. Again, these areas were considered important, but their impact could not yet be sufficiently understood and qualified to include in this study. Further work is ongoing to get more detailed and reliable data in this area, with significant savings expected.

Third, I express a note of caution about broader interpretation and extrapolation from these results. While this analysis has produced very valuable data and provided many interesting insights, we must be careful in understanding the broader applicability of these results to both MyCo and other organizations. An important area of caution concerns the scalability of these approaches to broader enterprise software delivery contexts. It's clear that many of these process and tool optimizations are equally valid for other teams in other situations. However, additional review is needed to understand how broadly and how quickly these results could be applied, say, to the whole of the MyCo enterprise software delivery organization. I believe that many of the same results could be achieved by more broadly adopting such practices in other projects, but further investigation would help validate this assertion.

2.8 Conclusions

This chapter focuses on a concrete example of an enterprise software delivery project exhibiting many properties that characterize today's software delivery challenges: globally distributed delivery of core business capability in a mixed onshore–offshore team. The example has shown us in very real terms how and where efficiencies are possible with the focus on global enterprise software delivery.

As a result of this study, the key factors in enterprise software delivery improvements have been seen in four areas:

- Collaborate globally.

- Deliver with agility.

- Focus on quality.

- Monitor and measure continuously.

I examine each of these areas in more detail in the remaining chapters of this book, focusing specifically on case studies that highlight the results obtained by applying many of the improvement suggestions provided in this study.

Chapter 3

The Software Supply Chain and Software Factories

Chapter Summary

I discuss the software supply chain and its role in delivering the vision of an industrialized model for global enterprise software delivery, exemplified in a software factory. I highlight a software factory's core characteristics, illustrating them with several examples. The main lessons drawn from this review include the following:

- A supply chain perspective is a relevant and useful way to look at today's global enterprises, and it provides insights into several challenges in enterprise software delivery.

- Adoption of an industrialized approach places the focus on cost efficiency, reuse, and standardization in enterprise software delivery.

- Global enterprises organized as a collection of software factories require an infrastructure of processes and technology that highlights collaboration, automation, and visibility across the global supply chain.

- Real-world examples of a software factory model illustrate the viability of this approach and provide practical organizational models for enterprise software delivery.

3.1 Introduction

More than forty years ago, the original NATO reports [30,31] focused attention on some of the core elements of an industrialized approach to enterprise software delivery: increasing productivity and quality of software delivery in the face of severe skills shortages, the importance of standardized processes to improve predictability, and the role of measurement and metrics in gaining insight into project progress and for optimizing development and delivery activities.[1] In the succeeding years, a great deal of attention was turned toward these themes, particularly in understanding how different forms of software process improvement could raise the quality and consistency of software delivery [32,33]. This research resulted in "spiral" and "iterative" models of software development [34,14] and measured improvement schemes such as the capability maturity model (CMM) [35].

More recent work on the industrialization of software has focused attention toward automation and verification aspects of software production [36]. From one perspective, component-based design techniques and reuse libraries were seen as key elements to create catalogues of parts for assembly of systems from predeveloped pieces [37]. While from another perspective, the key to automation was the role of more formal modeling languages amenable to improved analysis techniques from which working systems could be generated [38].

Indeed, many existing texts have discussed the scope of enterprise software, the many challenges faced in their delivery into production, and their ongoing maintenance. Broadly speaking, we see that delivering quality enterprise software is challenging as a result of many factors. But it's useful to highlight three of these:

- *Increasing complexity.* The scope and capability of software and systems has increased significantly in recent years. In addition, many products containing software must now be integrated with other software or subsystems, including multiple subassemblies, in-house-developed code, supplier-created code, and packaged application elements.

- *Geographically distributed teams.* The advent of distributed delivery teams and a global supply chain of enterprise software and engineering teams have made managing an enterprise software delivery organization

---

1. It is remarkable how, forty years later, the reports from those workshops remain a touchstone for the move from software delivery as a "craft" to an "engineering" approach. Their coining of the term *software engineering* was explicitly aimed as a provocation and as a vision for the future—and so it remains.

more challenging. Geographic dispersion introduces communication challenges, and effective stakeholder collaboration is often overlooked.

- *Lack of standardization.* Many teams operate with little standardization or without a common foundation, resulting in a lack of shared processes and little automation.

Ultimately, the proliferation of interconnected devices and the globalization of software delivery have highlighted how software is increasingly seen as a strategic business asset, key to unique customer value and sustained business differentiation. Best-in-class product and services companies are those that have built a strong competency in enterprise software delivery—approaching this as a core business process. Their attention is placed on enabling innovation, lowering costs, and managing change. Critical to this global view of effective enterprise software delivery, all these tasks must be industrialized to deliver the services necessary with the speed, quality, and flexibility essential to meet the new demands.

These significant factors draw attention to an aspect of enterprise software delivery that is becoming increasingly dominant in today's interconnected world. Specifically, we see many organizations that have begun to rethink the delivery model of enterprise software, moving away from perceiving it as a series of discrete islands of activity that are visible and under the control of a single organization and instead considering it a "distributed integrated supply chain" where parts of that software supply chain may be delivered by partners and third-party suppliers.

In this chapter, I examine this view of enterprise software delivery in detail. I first explore the idea of the "software supply chain" and introduce the concept of the software factory. I then detail the characteristics of the software factory approach and illustrate those concepts using real-world examples. I conclude with some observations and recommendations.

3.2 Toward a Software Supply Chain

Many business domains have experienced a great deal of change over the past few years due to the evolution of the business environment, financial upheavals, societal changes, and technical advancement. To understand and evolve their businesses to meet the new context, enterprise organizations have analyzed their core business processes to see how they can be refined and optimized, and subsequently restructured. This business process reengineering has helped organizations refocus on the most compelling and valuable aspects of the business, and it is often part of an organization's process of readjusting investment priorities toward those business activities that are considered essential while looking to divest those considered secondary [39].

The resulting business supply chain is composed of a collection of directly owned and governed business activities, integrated with those that may be acquired and customized from other sources. Business areas considered secondary for many organizations include customer relationship management (CRM), human resource management (HRM), and some aspects of sales management. Many organizations now use standard package applications to implement these functions, or they entirely outsource delivery of these business processes to third-party organizations.

We can apply this same business process reengineering approach to enterprise software delivery activities. With this view, we can reconsider enterprise software delivery in terms of separating functions that are core to a business's value from those that are ancillary. For example, analogous to business processes such as HRM and CRM, many enterprise software delivery organizations see no differentiating value in having specialized approaches to core elements such as technical infrastructure management, operations management, and even some aspects of asset management or test management. This mindset produces several results:

- Recognition that enterprise software delivery is itself a business process that can be modeled, analyzed, and reengineered. This means that enterprise software delivery is amenable to many existing business process optimization techniques and a number of well-understood improvement practices can be readily introduced.

- Measurement and management of enterprise software delivery through standard value analyses is more easily applied. The investments in enterprise software delivery can be understood in terms of how much value they bring to the business, and those investments can be directly compared to the return from moving them to other areas of the business.

- A focus on a multivendor software supply chain is a realistic way to deliver enterprise software. Parts of the enterprise software delivery process that may be considered secondary to the function of the organization become candidates for consolidation, outsourcing, or fulfillment by other partners. Multisourcing can be used to create competition, drive down cost, and improve the quality of delivered systems.

- Enterprise software delivery can be considered as an integrated value chain. While individual activities in the supply chain are important, an end-to-end view highlights the essential nature of the whole process and treats integration of the supply chain as a determining factor in managing and optimizing the value delivered. Techniques can be applied from areas such as lean manufacturing (to eliminate waste) and agile production practices (to increase flexibility in delivery).

- Mature supply chain measurement and optimization techniques can be applied. For more than a decade, there has been a great deal of work in operations research and various engineering management disciplines to improve measurement and analytical approaches to production systems and supply chain optimization [40,41]. These approaches lend a set of mature practices to the domain of enterprise software delivery.

This "software supply chain" viewpoint is in many ways an interesting maturation in the role and contribution of enterprise software delivery. We've already seen it adopted in other industries as a natural step in their industrialization.

3.3 Industrializing Enterprise Software Delivery: An Analogy

Enterprise software delivery is not the only industry that has dealt with the challenges of massive increases in demand, where handcrafted techniques are no longer sufficient to meet consumer needs. We can learn from the progression of the industrial sector:

- *Prior to the twentieth century,* most manufactured products were made individually using labor-intensive, manual processes. A single craftsman or team of craftsmen would use their skills and basic tools to create each part. Then they'd assemble them into the final, one-off product, making incremental changes in the parts until they fit and worked together. Ultimately, these practices were expensive and led to unpredictable time to market, cost, and quality. Standardized parts and processes made manual labor more effective. As a result, the assembly line was created, transforming industrial development by enabling manufacturers to produce less expensive and better quality products. However, a manually driven assembly line approach relied on large numbers of people organized across a variety of skills and areas of expertise. This couldn't be adapted to meet changing market needs, and it provided limited oversight and control, leading to quality issues.

- *In the mid-to-late twentieth century*, increased levels of automation were introduced into the industrial process. Automation was optimized with

the right blend of skilled work force and specialized robotics, and products were built from a multitude of standardized components sourced
from a global supply chain to exploit the economies of scale, cost, and
quality. This greatly improved the volume of production. However, despite higher product quality and predictability, assembly lines remained
inflexible to change.

- *Today*, the industrial sector is driven by the need for cost optimization,
flexibility, and reduction in waste. Just-in-time production processes create a highly efficient globally sourced supply chain, while lean processes
driven through real-time, team-based collaboration in "centers of excellence" drive down costs and enhance flexibility. Consequently, today we
have efficient and flexible manufacturing processes and ever-improving
product quality, delivered at the lowest cost.

We can use the progression of the manufacturing industry as an analogy for
the development of software today. Many organizations centered on software
delivery are taking an approach similar to the industrial sector, and addressing
the challenges faced by enterprise software delivery via a modern-day, software-
factory approach to enterprise software delivery. This approach focuses heavily on real-world collaboration, maximum automation, and intuitive real-time
metrics and reporting.

3.4 A Software Factory Approach to Enterprise Software Delivery

As we've discussed earlier, organizations today face an unparalleled rate of
change in their business environments, while at the same time, they're managing and lowering operating costs across the organization. The direct implication
is that they must not only minimize waste and inefficiency but also increase
productivity. The software and systems industry is evolving from using a craft-
based process focused on individuals to a mature, repeatable process that produces consistent high-quality output but with the flexibility to be adjusted to
variances in individual consumer needs.

In defining a software factory approach to enterprise software design, development, and delivery, we can apply key characteristics from the industrial
sector to reduce time to market, increase flexibility and agility, and reduce costs,
while increasing quality and end-user satisfaction. An integrated approach can
help software delivery organizations achieve business agility, collaborate more
effectively, and deliver higher quality products and services.

3.4.1 Aligning Business and Engineering

A software factory approach to enterprise software delivery requires a well-established, multiplatform process with tooling that aligns business strategy with engineering and system deployment. Such multiplatform processes prove critical in building applications that meet the needs of the customer. Helping to identify business needs and stakeholder requirements, they then drive those business goals into enterprise software delivery projects and solutions, ensuring that the final product meets the business objectives with the lowest possible cost and highest possible quality.

Executives and management teams need to focus their attention on making appropriate strategic decisions, selecting the "right" products to execute, and choosing the "right" assets to retain in their infrastructure. Key factors that enable organizations to be leaner, more agile, and more profitable include identifying and prioritizing potential areas of consolidation, reducing redundancy and recurring costs, and improving operational efficiency.

Fine-tuning the organization requires better enterprise decision making and an understanding of business/technological dependencies. Management teams must have access to an easily searchable, corporate-wide repository of related business and technical information that can support enterprise analysis, planning, and execution.

3.4.2 Automating Processes and Tasks

Automating the enterprise software delivery life cycle can help reduce errors and improve productivity, leading to higher quality products. An integrated portfolio of tools can help teams automate specific, labor-intensive tasks—similar to the way automation is used to perform repetitive manual tasks in manufacturing processes. Automation enables practitioners to focus on creating more innovative solutions with industry-leading design and development environments that support the delivery of high-quality, secure, and scalable products. Companies that invest in automation and a more efficient means of production and delivery can experience a sizeable jump in productivity, quality, time to market, and scalability.

3.4.3 Leveraging Assets across the Enterprise

Modern architectural and product development frameworks can introduce complexity, as they often include third-party, custom, off-the-shelf, or outsourced components in the overall enterprise software solution. There are several ways to cope with this:

- Service-oriented architecture (SOA) frameworks can promote reuse across the enterprise. To achieve significant value from an SOA approach, applications are focused around shared interface descriptions and assembled from standardized software components [42].

- Product-line engineering (PLE) is an approach for achieving strategic reuse by developing portfolios of similar products that share a common domain understanding but are differentiated by variations in features and functions, as required by each solution in the family [36].

Each of these approaches is grounded in a searchable index of available shared assets. To truly achieve the benefit from reuse, organizations must be able to understand what assets they already have, and then leverage those assets to create reusable, flexible components that can be applied to extend architectural frameworks in meaningful, predictable ways.

3.4.4 Supporting Lean Processes and Integrated Infrastructures

Today's enterprise software delivery teams can be highly distributed geographically. Consequently, to reap the benefits of enterprise software delivery frameworks, they need flexible and agile processes with real-time collaboration and integration across disparate platforms, roles, and geographies. Globally distributed development can be facilitated through defined, customizable processes and best practices to support flexibility, mitigate risk with comprehensive quality management, and enhance developer productivity through task and process automation.

3.4.5 Automating Operational Measurement and Control

To help ensure predictable outcomes, the enterprise software delivery process must be governed so it can be continuously measured and improved. A fundamental aspect of this governance is the definition and codification of processes for developing products. These processes and best practices are corporate assets, and they must be captured in an actionable form so that teams can be guided to adhere to appropriate best practices through automated workflows.

Relevant metrics should be gathered automatically at each step, including after enterprise systems are delivered into production. By constantly and automatically measuring the specific key value aspects of processes, these metrics can provide insight into the efficacy of existing processes and identify areas for improvement. Automated measurement and control is particularly critical in tightly regulated industries, such as military, aerospace, and medical domains, and in many financial sectors.

Ultimately, it is return on investment that justifies introducing these concepts in a dynamic factory approach to enterprise software delivery. The productivity achieved through more efficient methods, and the quality improvements in the resulting software and systems, have quantifiable monetary value.

3.5 Key Elements of the Software Factory

Creating a software factory requires a blueprint to organize and structure the methods and tools that deliver the necessary capabilities. From a simplified perspective, enterprise software delivery focuses on a number of virtual centers of excellence [43]. Figure 3.1 illustrates a software factory blueprint as a collection of capabilities that support the management and delivery of enterprise software, covering five key areas [44]. I'll briefly review each of these in turn.

3.5.1 Business Management

Effective business and IT planning and portfolio management help streamline the business and reduce costs by empowering faster, better-informed decisions, and prioritizing enterprise software investments to support business goals. Ultimately, proficiency in this area allows strategic intent to be converted into executable processes with measurable business results. Achieving this proficiency typically requires several elements:

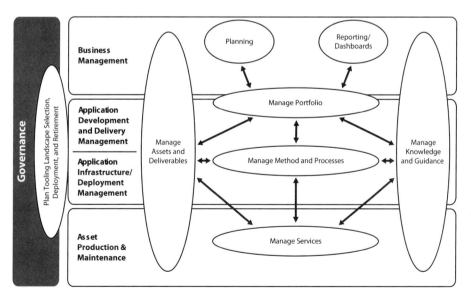

Figure 3.1 *Key elements of the software factory*

- *Enterprise architecture management* helps managers make faster, better-informed strategic and tactical decisions; prioritize enterprise software investments to support business goals; and analyze, plan, and execute change with reduced risk.

- *Business process management* helps optimize business performance by discovering, documenting, automating, and continuously improving business processes to increase efficiency and reduce costs.

- *Requirements definition and management* minimizes the number of inaccurate, incomplete, and omitted requirements. This helps teams collaborate effectively with stakeholders, reduce rework, accelerate time to market, and respond better to change.

3.5.2 Asset Production and Maintenance

Knowledge management and reuse best practices allow organizations to discover and leverage existing data and assets. With an understanding of the key assets, it's possible to enforce policy and best practices, manage model dependencies, and even trace assets to versioned artifacts.

It's important for organizations to determine what assets exist by providing the ability to search and select across multiple asset repositories and data warehouses, relate assets to one another, and leverage existing assets for reuse. Such solutions can also help administrators enforce policies and best practices, manage model dependencies, and trace assets to versioned artifacts, creating a link between systems, subsystems, code, requirements, test cases, and delivered solutions. Finally, teams create new assets, transforming code into standardized artifacts, such as web or business process execution language (BPEL) services that can be used as components for building value-added applications.

3.5.3 Application Development and Delivery Management

Smart product design and delivery optimization requires collaboration across teams to deliver quality enterprise systems. In addition, applying lean processes with disciplined teams in centers of excellence ensures flexibility and facilitates globally distributed enterprise software delivery. Collaborative services, automation, and measurement feedback throughout the software development life cycle are essential to achieve levels of productivity and consistency beyond those accomplished using traditional, craft-oriented software development tools.

To provide these capabilities, management solutions must focus on the following:

- *Change and release management* improves quality and productivity by effectively unifying distributed teams by managing change processes from requirements gathering to deployment.

- *Quality management* advances quality across the entire software delivery life cycle from requirements, design, development, quality assurance, security, and compliance to deployment. Teams collaborate to mitigate business risk and reduce costs, automate and boost productivity to speed time to market, and analyze for ongoing quality improvements and greater project predictability.

- *Architecture management* introduces software development tools for design, development, and delivery that support modeling and coding activities in appropriate high-level languages, supported with a range of analysis capabilities for maintaining the architectural quality of the delivered solution.

3.5.4 Application Infrastructure and Deployment Management

Today's application infrastructures allow organizations to cost-effectively build, deploy, and manage applications and products for varying business needs. Integrating service delivery across organizational boundaries and all stages of the life cycle helps to improve time to market and reduce cost and risk while providing the visibility, control, and automation needed to deliver a dynamic infrastructure that adapts to changing business requirements. These solutions provide the following capabilities to help organizations develop a robust application infrastructure:

- *Product deployment* capabilities that help automatically deploy, track, and manage applications across the life cycle

- *Application foundation* technologies that support tasks aimed at build and deployment across mainframe and distributed environments

- *Connectivity and application integration* that foster collaboration, insight, and cost effective reuse of data and knowledge across the organization

3.5.5 Governance

Automated capabilities to monitor operational environments and provide feedback to the enterprise software delivery processes are critical. Iterative improvement across the entire life cycle ensures timely problem resolution and ensures flexibility to adapt to changes in today's business environment. These solutions for operations provide capabilities to help organizations develop a robust set of practices for automating operational monitoring and measurement. These solutions can help in the following areas:

- *Application health monitoring*, to ensure the continued operation of key business capabilities at required levels of service

- *Performance management*, to gather statistics on the operational aspects of the current system and its environment

- *Security and compliance*, ensuring that the systems in production offer appropriate levels of confidence in operation and are resilient enough to handle various categories of errors or attacks

- *Service management,* for ensuring consistency of approaches to incident, change, and other management activities that enable quality service delivery and support

- *Performance optimization,* to continually monitor and improve system performance to end users

- *Monitoring and measurement*, focusing on key services levels and performance indicators to obtain a realistic status of current operations, trends, and directions

3.6 Examples and Illustrations

To make these concepts more concrete, I'll introduce three examples of software factory approaches from real-world situations. In the first example, I look at how IBM is applying an application assembly approach to global software delivery. In the second example, I focus on one key area of enterprise software delivery—software testing—and I examine how specialized software testing factories are being used to optimize the testing process. In the third example, I look at a large financial services organization that is delivering a major insurance solution platform for deployment in locations around the world, using a software factory approach to delivery and maintenance.

3.6.1 Example: IBM Application Assembly Optimization (AAO) Approach

Application assembly optimization (AAO) is a recently initiated delivery approach and a key component of IBM's globally integrated capabilities strategy [45].

The approach was launched to introduce an industrialized approach to enterprise software delivery by aligning responsibilities, strategies, and priorities across a number of worldwide "competency centers." With these centers, supported by a centralized governance model, IBM can quickly assemble critical expertise for substantial opportunities across key industries to bring the right skills to each situation, as needed without unnecessary duplication or delays. This more integrated, repeatable approach is aimed at increasing operational efficiencies through global deployment of application assembly techniques across IBM global business services teams.

In terms of a software factory approach to enterprise software delivery, AAO enables the following process transformations:

- *Delivery*. From a skills- and time-based model to a reusable assets- and automation-based model

- *Cost*. From an hourly rate-based model to an outcome-based model

- *Metrics*. From utilization measures to performance-based value measures

- *Control*. From direct line of management to a more centralized pool of shared resources

- *Workflow*. From location-based global delivery centers to a virtual workflow distributed among centers and geographic locations

Fundamental to the AAO approach is a collaborative environment with strong global management disciplines, automation techniques, and innovative approaches to measurements and incentives. To realize this, the AAO solution has four basic components:

- *Centers of competency*. These are concentrations of skills around specific industry or domain needs that form a network of expertise and asset libraries to be rapidly aligned and used as needed in specific client situations.

- *Technology assembly centers (TACs)*. TACs apply factory-floor concepts and automated processes to enterprise solution delivery at IBM global delivery centers. The TACs are specialized service areas (e.g., testing, web-based architectures) that form a virtual global team of highly skilled practitioners to deliver work products in their areas of expertise.

- *Collaboration and measurements*. Using real-time, in-context team collaboration, distributed teams can think and work in unison. AAO uses tools with deep collaboration functions and supports them with social networking sites, wikis, blogs, and mobile offerings specifically targeted at business interests of the practitioners. The measurement framework for AAO is a dynamic system with automation, extensibility, and flexibility. The framework supports multiple dimensions of measurements that include customer value, strategy, operations, risk, quality, and governance.

- *Lean processes.* Each AAO process is developed using a lean approach and is regularly reviewed to provide continuous operational improvement by addressing any bottlenecks and waste proactively.

The operating model of the AAO approach uses "work packets" as the key mechanism to deliver enterprise software. A work packet is a prescriptive, self-contained unit of work that can include instructions, assets to be reused, schedules, exit criteria, and any input work products needed. The receiver of the packet designs, plans, and executes the work requested. Application optimization is the umbrella term for the processes, procedures, tools, metrics, and governance management, and multisite locations where work is performed.

As illustrated in Figure 3.2, to deliver on these work packets, virtual teams are created and organized into "cells." These cells allow flexible configurations of people and resources to come together with a collection of deep expertise

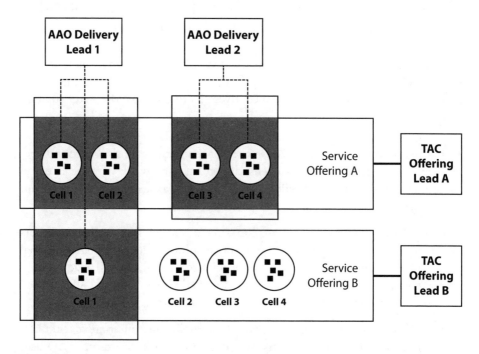

Figure 3.2 *An illustrative AAO governance structure*

in the service or solution being delivered, armed with appropriate tools and reusable assets and frameworks to accelerate delivery and maintain high quality in delivery. Governance, measurement, and control of software delivery are optimized around this flexible organizational model to allow each delivery to be composed of the appropriate cells, as required to complete a specific work packet.

In summary, we see that the AAO approach can be viewed as the software and services equivalent of a traditional manufacturing approach, applied to enterprise software delivery in an organization consisting of thousands of people delivering software-based solutions to its clients. Work packets form the heart of an assembly-line approach with real-time measurement across work-packet progress and delivery. The underlying supporting tool platform provides information on in-progress and completed work, gives the status of resource utilization, and helps identify bottlenecks in software delivery. In this way, real-time optimization of key delivery processes is possible.

3.6.2 Example: IBM Test Factory Approach

A key objective for many organizations is to maintain high levels of quality while reducing costs in enterprise software delivery. Most testing solutions available today have focused on the test execution and test management functions in areas such as functional and performance testing, automatic regression testing, and test defect management. Currently, market pressures are driving significant improvements in enterprise software quality and cost reduction by forcing a consolidation of many expensive testing capabilities into specialist centers of excellence, where skills, tools, and practices can be centralized as common services across an organization. In several organizations, these testing-focused centers are referred to as *software testing factories*.

A software testing factory is particularly suited to organizations that need to set up a test project quickly or execute software testing on a recurring but non-continuous basis. It can also be used to supplement an existing large program, support multiple lines of business with a common service, or provide specialist testing capabilities in short demand in operational test teams. By pooling the resources and optimizing the costs, such capabilities help to alleviate the costs and effort needed to maintain test assets and test knowledge for existing applications across a variety of projects.

The approach is particularly effective in organizations that are more complex, with numerous departments, vendors, and locations. From a testing perspective, this complexity must be managed and coordinated into one smoothly operating, reliable test management system with automation of key practices and a clear measurement framework to govern its activities. A software testing factory provides a basis for effective standardization and communication across the testing organizations and business units to, ultimately, the end users and clients.

System integrators (SI) such as IBM Global Business Services, Sogeti, Atos Origin, and Accenture have all created specific practices based on the software testing factory model. They are coordinated around a common governance structure, methodology, and set of tools and processes, and they use a factory approach toward execution and delivery of results to maintain efficiency in the face of highly fluctuating consumer demand for their services. As a result, the SI acts as the focal point for all change management into the test cycle and takes responsibility for best practices in test management and test execution areas such as test planning, cost estimation, and various forms of code analysis.

In summary, a software testing factory approach is considered useful in many organizations for the following reasons:

- It provides cost-efficient and effective testing on-demand for different kinds of software.

- It introduces standardized business-driven test processes and can enforce consistent approaches across key test practices.

- It centralizes test equipment provisioning across multiple projects and lines of business.

- It focuses a common approach to metrics and measures on developed and delivered quality for all enterprise software.

- It introduces a simple, direct handling approach to test service requests that can be centrally governed and managed.

Figure 3.3 illustrates a software testing factory approach used by IBM in one of its European regions. IBM's testing solution provides managed testing services via a software testing factory in a two-tier model using teams in Europe and Asia. It provides an accelerated and phased method for transforming current methods, processes, and tools into an industrialized approach. The solution aims to achieve the following kinds of target results with clients:

- On-demand resource model (typically up to 40 percent core team, 60 percent flexible resources)

- Optimized onshore–offshore resource profile, with often 90 percent of work performed off-shore

Corporate Test Factory

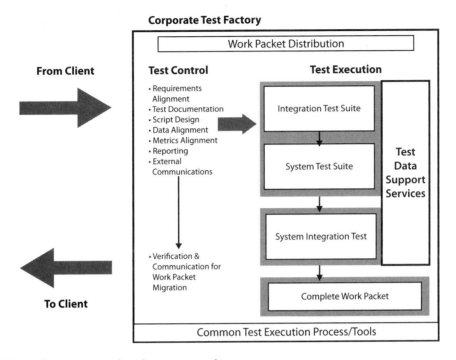

Figure 3.3 *An example software testing factory*

- Productivity improvements resulting from high levels of test automation (50 percent to 70 percent)

- Unit-based pricing using a test-case-based approach or focused on testing as a service for its clients

- Transparency of factory performance metrics through shared dashboards containing as many as twenty service level measures that are continuously assessed by the test provider and the client

3.6.3 Example: A Large Financial Organization's Core Insurance Platform

As financial services organizations seek to reduce costs in delivering new core capabilities, many are also turning to new delivery models such as software factory approaches. One such large multinational organization has focused on improving its general insurance (GI) business platform as an integral part of its approach to creating a centralized business model through a single supporting enterprise software delivery group. This center of excellence is responsible for delivery of the GI platform. This platform must address many requirements, including the following:

- A wide variety of multicountry, multicurrency, multilanguage, and multi-company requirements

- A great deal of variation in country-specific regulatory requirements

- Many local cultural issues and country-specific market practices

In addition, this GI platform must integrate with numerous other systems and data sources, including HRM, CRM, document management, and several other third-party data sources and data feeds.

To achieve this goal, executive management at the company decided that the new platform would be based on an existing enterprise system that was already successfully in use in one region of the world. The existing system underwent an extensive reworking based on the new, broader needs to be fielded world-wide. The center of excellence is responsible for the entire enterprise software delivery life cycle for the GI platform:

- Analyzing and addressing the business-specific requirements

- Designing the underlying application architecture

- Baselining architecture and implementing solutions

- Testing of functional and nonfunctional requirements

- Testing user acceptance testing

- Promoting and deploying the application into production

- Performing ongoing application maintenance

With the very high priority of this complex project, the center of excellence has adopted a software factory approach to the delivery and ongoing support of the GI platform. In particular, they decided to work with multiple vendors and SIs to create a software supply chain in which those vendors contribute to the success of the solution through the following:

- Specializations in key areas (e.g., one SI dedicated to test functions providing a level of external governance across three other SIs responsible for project delivery)

- Use of offshore delivery centers to reduce labor costs and manage fluctuations in staffing needs (including specialist providers in India and Latin America)

- Reuse of a standardized application framework that supplies the key capabilities of the GI platform to all delivered instances through well-managed customizations for each regional variation

- A common hosted set of enterprise software delivery services that are used by all suppliers regardless of organization, role, and location (in areas such as source code management, configuration management, build management, etc.)

- Centralized collection, analysis, management, and execution of change management from many different stakeholders across the world with customized instances of the GI platform

The heart of the software supply chain approach adopted by this organization was a focus on the broader change management process that crossed all aspects of this complex set of organizational and technical relationships. In particular, a clear, well-specified change process was defined, around which each of the suppliers in the supply chain is able to integrate their specific activities and assets. This set of change processes defines the areas of integration between the suppliers and the major control points for the overall software supply chain governance.

To reiterate, the main software factory processes in the center of excellence aim to support change management across the supply chain. As illustrated in Figure 3.4, the center of excellence focuses on four core activities: incident management, problem management, change management, and release management. Each of these activities produces a series of specific artifacts that are controlled and governed as the basis for ensuring a consistent approach across the supply chain.

3.7 Observations and Commentary

Industrialization of the software supply chain is seen as fundamental to cost control and efficiency in enterprise software delivery. Software factory situations such as those described here provide important insights for an industrialized view of enterprise software delivery, from which several observations can be made:

- A different set of ideas is needed for monitoring progress and effective status management in software factory approaches. Most traditional metrics highlight two kinds of measures: productivity in terms of function points or source lines of code delivered and quality in terms of defects per delivered module. Such measures are useful but insufficient for a supply chain view of enterprise software delivery. Instead, measures must focus on a broader set of service level agreements (SLAs) across providers, which may include measures of cost, predictability, variance to schedule, volatility in requirements, responsiveness to new requests, and so on. Similarly, the transparency of the supply chain delivery process becomes critical. This transparency may vary in degrees between a "black-box" view, where suppliers have complete control over how they deliver (what processes, tools, and practices they use), and a "white-box" view where all activities are open to discussion, inspection, and review. Deciding on an approach (and coordinating and managing across these activities) becomes critical to the supply chain's operation.

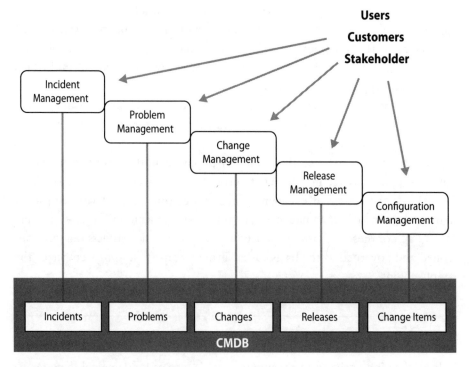

Figure 3.4 *The key change processes in the center of excellence's software factory approach (based on the ITIL service model)*[2]

---

2. See www.itil-officialsite.com.

- In many cases, organizations will choose a variety of different partners in the enterprise software delivery process. Organizations will not only choose different suppliers for different specialist tasks, they'll also implement multisourcing in some areas to reduce risk, increase flexibility, and enhance competition. While such schemes can provide value, they also significantly increase the management costs across such complex supply chains.

  An extreme version of multisourcing is the use of crowd sourcing for component delivery. Some organizations are already experimenting with delivery approaches in which new demands are essentially "put up for auction," with the goal of finding the cheapest supplier that can meet the stated needs. This is an extension of the typical request for proposals (RFP) approach in which a more open marketplace is used to increase the flexibility of component suppliers to a much wider constituency. Of course, organizations must address many challenges with such an approach, particularly those around security, intellectual property, and quality.

- A more standardized approach to the software factory infrastructure is beginning to emerge. Expanding on the traditional source code management and change management tools, collaborative application lifecycle management (CALM) is becoming important to organizations adopting a software factory approach [46]. CALM centers on the recognition that many different distributed teams must be coordinated in enterprise software delivery. These teams may be from different companies and geographically dispersed. Hence the CALM technology reinforces a set of software factory practices with tooling that comfortably adapts to widely distributed teams in various levels of cooperative delivery scenarios. At one extreme, these teams may consist of outsourced suppliers with very clear roles, handover of responsibilities, and artifact ownership. However, many other more blended situations are also common, and the software factory infrastructure must be adaptable to those arrangements.[3]

- A healthy ecosystem of suppliers of components in a supply chain proves critical. Supplier organizations in a software factory must be able to optimize the delivery of components, often for many potential consumers. One of the most interesting approaches we see today involves model-driven architectures (MDA) and PLE techniques [47].

---

3. The topic of CALM is addressed in much greater detail in subsequent chapters.

In these approaches, abstract models of system characteristics are used to generate components and subassemblies. Organizations can analyze and customize these models for different usage contexts more easily than they can with system-specific delivered code. With these approaches, specialist suppliers of components and component tooling have emerged. For example, some financial services organizations choose to start with a third-party core-banking framework and adapt it to their operating context by modifying its data and process models, rather than develop it from scratch themselves.

- Virtualized technology platforms are particularly attractive for organizations adopting a software factory approach. Analogous to other industries, a widely distributed, flexible supply chain requires an automation framework well matched to those characteristics. A natural extension of CALM technology is to look to supply those automation capabilities "on-demand" using cloud technologies [48]. Cloud-hosted services have advantages for the organization delivering the enterprise software (in terms of flexibility of infrastructure across the peaks and troughs of the life cycle, opening up the supply chain as widely as possible) and for the suppliers (in terms of permitting easy access to their services without expensive infrastructure investment).

  The move to cloud-hosted services has encouraged a growing number of software-as-a-service offerings as a way to deliver software factory capabilities [49]. For example, in software testing, many SIs and third-party companies have announced "testing on the cloud" approaches that enable enterprise software delivery organizations to obtain testing activities such as performance testing as a service. Rather than invest in significant infrastructure, organizations can provision load testing of an enterprise software system using cloud infrastructure as needed, and a variety of load tests can be configured and run on demand.[4]

3.8 Conclusions

Enterprise software delivery organizations face the challenges of developing more software more quickly with higher quality. Reflecting on the engineering and manufacturing approaches in other industrial domains, we can apply key concepts to the software supply chain.

---

4. The topic of cloud computing is addressed in much greater detail in subsequent chapters.

The software factory vision focuses on approaches specifically aimed to improve software delivery capability, helping teams understand how to scale lean practices, deliver more for less, correlate business outcomes with investments in processes and tools, and deliver higher quality products in less time.

A structured approach to helping enterprise software delivery teams drive business innovation through measured and continuous process improvement is an important foundation for delivering a dynamic factory approach to software and systems delivery.

Chapter 4

Collaborative Software Delivery

Chapter Summary

I examine collaboration aspects of global enterprise software delivery, introducing the elements driving globally distributed organizations, and discuss how distributed teams interact to deliver quality software and systems. I review characteristics of the technology that enables collaborative working and provide several practical examples. I draw the following conclusions:

- Successful global delivery requires a strong analysis of where and how shared responsibilities are managed across the global team.

- An integrated tooling platform is essential to support collaborative interactions and coordinate interteam activities.

- By identifying several models, or patterns, of interactions among the global organization, we can optimize processes and tools toward the interaction styles that typify collaborative behaviors.

4.1 Introduction

Recently I asked the chief architect for a large aerospace and defense company to explain the key elements of the architecture for an enterprise system his team was developing. I expected he would go over to the whiteboard and start to describe service interfaces, draw deployment diagrams, or elaborate on networking infrastructure details. Instead, he launched into a monologue describing the organizational structure of his teams, the key points in the outsourcing approach they were pursuing with several specialist providers, the levels of progress he was monitoring in service level agreements with third-party suppliers, and the coordination approach he was using to manage his software delivery centers around the world. After a while I interrupted, reminding him I was interested in the system's architecture. "This *is* the architecture!" he replied.

A dominant theme is emerging in the delivery of enterprise software: *collaboration is king*. Many more organizations view their enterprise software delivery as a web of interrelationships within their deployed system, across the teams, and throughout the software delivery supply chain. In many cases, the architecture and component-based structure of their systems is a direct reflection of this organizational approach. Also, these organizations realize that delivery success depends on the way these collaboration aspects are conceived, supported, governed, and managed.

Currently, many of the biggest challenges in enterprise software delivery are posed by misunderstandings among the different stakeholders, due to lack of a common view into projects, incompatibilities and errors in artifacts shared by distributed teams, and inefficiency in managing the complex relationships (both human and technical) that define the supply chain of enterprise software development and delivery. Progress in these areas requires enterprise software delivery organizations to adopt new communication and coordination approaches. Many of the informal aspects that keep teams connected and in-step have exceeded their capacity to support the kinds of complex supply chains that are emerging.

We are at the junction of several important trends that highlight the vital role collaboration plays in effective enterprise software delivery:

- *Flexible working practices.* Many organizations have introduced workplace flexibility that enables employees to work from a home office, use local shared office space and "mobility" stations, and adjust work hours to broader family and society needs. These practices have major effects on teamwork, interaction, and communication. It is not unusual that teams producing enterprise software are formed, execute, and disperse without ever meeting physically.

- *Globalization.* Driven by skill shortages, expanding markets, and labor cost pressures, organizations have set up software centers in geographic locations around the world. Such geographic distribution places pressure on communication across teams that must coordinate in the delivery of a single system and share a common view of status and progress.

- *Outsourcing.* From IT infrastructure to specialized software testing techniques, outsourced organizations now play a critical role in the success of enterprise software delivery. The variety of approaches to outsourcing is matched with very different ways to support collaboration with those external providers. Organizationally diverse supply chains require particular attention to areas such as privacy of data, security, and intellectual property management.

- *Faster time to market.* Driven by fast-paced market changes and increasing competition, business stakeholders demand more software more often, and enterprise software delivery organizations must react faster to these changing demands. To address this challenge, delivery organizations must develop better real-time awareness of the current status of projects, analyze change impact quickly, and understand how to reprioritize project resources as needed.

- *Agile development practices.* Hyperproductive teams demonstrate areas of agility that enable them to be more attuned to the changing project needs. Central to the approach of a range of popular agile development practices is the constant communication and coordination across the team that allows members to react and plan as needed and provide early intervention when problems arise.

- *End-user demands for transparency and self-service.* The past decade has seen the Internet have significant impact on consumer behavior. Due to the Internet, consumers are better informed, smarter, and more demanding of the enterprise systems that support the services they receive; generally, consumers desire to engage more in the customization, management, and optimization of those services.

In this chapter, I'll examine these underlying aspects of collaboration as it relates to enterprise software delivery. I begin by analyzing the impact of globalization. Next, I review how collaborative development techniques are changing the way enterprise systems are delivered. Finally, I provide some real-world examples of how improved collaboration practices are improving the industrialization of enterprise software delivery.

4.2 Globally Distributed Development

Global development has become the de facto approach to enterprise software delivery. The economic pressures facing all organizations require a global view of where to look for opportunities to reduce costs, efficiently obtain vital skills, and locate delivery centers in relation to the markets they serve [49]. Single, centralized enterprise delivery organizations are a thing of the past.[1] Enterprise software delivery organizations should expect to work with individuals and teams in many locations, operate in a variety of working relationships and structures, and involve different organizations during the development and delivery of a system.

Typically, today's enterprise software delivery organizations must support access to their software delivery platform from a variety of different locations. For example, Figure 4.1 shows a simplified view of the globally distributed development organization that supports a particular European retail company, "CompanyX," with outlets across several central European countries. Even in this simplified example, we see several distinct situations:

- A core location in Belgium functions as the coordinating central site for the enterprise software delivery organization. The majority of the product and project management team and the senior development architect reside at this location. It's also where system and software development resources, data repositories and administration, and remote service provision are concentrated. Projects use resources from the core site and often from other sites as well.

- Subsites in Belgium and the Netherlands contribute local resources to projects and coordinate directly with the core site. The subsites share metrics and reporting with the core site. However, depending on their location and usage model, they may or may not be trusted with respect to the core site regarding certain kinds of data access.

- Independent sites in India run by system integrators offer specialized support and staff augmentation. They share many of the characteristics of internal subsites. They independently extend or deliver to projects with local independent project management and development resources coordinated via explicit service level agreements (SLAs). These SLAs define the scope of their role and monitor their performance against defined objectives.

- A remote site in India provides assets for developers, who collaborate via remote services provided at the core and subsites. Mobile users or small teams in the remote location are supported by a minimal technology infrastructure. Again, they may or may not be trusted with respect to the

---

1. A few special exceptions remain (e.g., in sensitive government and military domains). Even there, however, we are seeing interesting collaborative approaches, such as the US Department of Defense's use of collaborative project delivery platforms such as forge.mil (http://forge.mil).

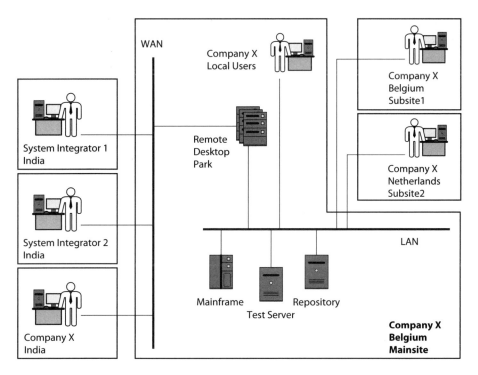

Figure 4.1 *A simplified example of globally distributed development for a European retail company*

core site. Often only some projects share resources across the core and remote site and require open access to all data, while other projects are isolated from the main set of delivery projects for reasons of privacy or data protection.

Such distribution in team organization and location is very common in today's enterprise software delivery approaches. I'll examine examples of three different dimensions of the challenges imposed by global software delivery approaches: distributed team working, organizationally distributed working, and globally distributed working.

4.2.1 Distributed Team Working

In today's world, every project is a distributed project. It's not just that we have teams in many locations around the world; it's that "local" teams are frequently working from different locations throughout the day—in their basement at home, in the local coffee shop, on the train traveling to work, on their "vacation" at the beach, and so on. This kind of flexibility in working practices makes heavy demands on the infrastructure, through which our teams connect with each other, share information, and coordinate around key artifacts and activities. Users who wish to work from locations that are remote from the core site (e.g., a satellite or home office) must often work with a model that reduces interconnectivity or introduces additional infrastructure to enable high levels of interaction.

Most organizations are now equipped with tools and technologies that work effectively over the Internet to support distributed working. Internet-based web clients provide remote users the ability to access the enterprise software delivery systems. However, situations that require trusted remote access pose additional challenges, further complicated by the need to scale support to multiple levels of trusted remote users at various locations.

Projects that contract work from untrusted, remote locations frequently use a different technology architecture. The core concepts of a remote usage model remain the same, but additional measures are taken to ensure data security. A separate set of repositories is typically established that allows access only to those software development artifacts that the untrusted remote users need.

4.2.2 Organizationally Distributed Working

In addition to the challenges posed by remote user access, organizational boundaries also pose challenges for enterprise software delivery. Here I highlight three organizational arrangements for collaboration:

- *Internal partnerships.* Perhaps a little surprisingly, an analysis of organizationally distributed working approaches must start with a view of what is happening within the organization. Many companies are not in fact a single legal or operational entity. It's not unusual to see companies with separate organizational groups as a result of mergers and acquisitions, as a consequence of distinct business domains (e.g., retail and personal banking as two separate units within a financial services company perhaps with roots in two separate companies that have been recently acquired and merged), or as a result of geographic needs and local laws. Such divisions between organizational units may have more or less direct impact on collaboration. Hence even within a single company, organizational barriers to collaboration exist. Taking one specific directional approach, a company might create a legally and organizationally separate enterprise software delivery organization that functions as a stand-alone unit in support of the company's core business. Such a move is driven by efficiency needs or attempts to broaden the market for the company's enterprise software delivery capabilities. Examples of such an approach can be found in many domains: for instance, the Spanish banking sector includes the enterprise software delivery organizations of the Santander Banking Group (ISBAN) and the La Caixa savings bank (SILK).

- *Supplier partnerships.* As part of their reengineering of recent years, many businesses have looked to use more commercial software packages in the delivery of their enterprise software systems. The most obvious example is the use of software packages from vendors such as SAP and Oracle, widely deployed as core elements of a company's enterprise software infrastructure. But this approach also now extends to use of online services from companies such as Amazon, Google, and Salesforce. com. Specific collaborative approaches to work with those suppliers are essential to the delivery success for the enterprise software systems that rely on them. Collaboration may include participation in vendor workshops, direct use of the vendor's service delivery services, and regular joint strategic reviews between the companies to align future plans. Recently these supply chains have become even more complex. More often today we see enterprise software systems largely constructed from several supplier-developed components and technologies, including in some industries major elements of the enterprise software infrastructure (e.g., core banking infrastructures that are supplied by large technology companies such as IBM and Microsoft and specialized banking platforms supplied by companies such as Temenos and Metavante). Collaboration tactics in these cases may include holding strategic workshops on mutually important topics for joint planning, sharing installation and customization details for debugging operational problems, and providing direct access to each other's development labs for immediate access to essential fixes and updates.

- *Outsourced partnerships.* A natural extension to technology partnerships for many companies is to outsource some or all aspects of their enterprise software delivery capabilities. A formal agreement, usually in the form of an SLA or a strategic outsourcing agreement, is typically defined as the context for the collaboration between the outsourcer and outsourcee organizations.

Due to its growing popularity and importance, here I give particular attention to the outsourced partnership approach [50]. Figure 4.2 illustrates many of the key elements of collaboration in outsourcing.

Following discussions and summaries of the outsourcer's needs and requirements, collaboration between outsourcer and outsourcee begins with a series of

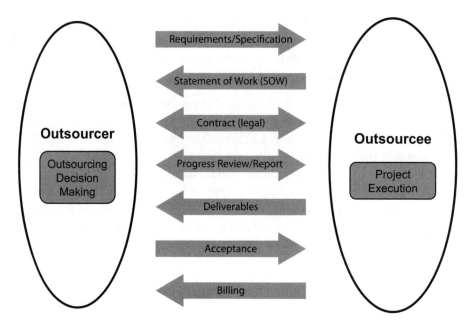

Figure 4.2 *Key elements of collaboration between outsourcer and outsourcee organizations*

requirements that are agreed upon between all parties in some form of a statement of work. As a consequence, a legal contract is defined that, in addition to costs and resources, may include elements of how the work will be performed and reported, escalation criteria in case of disagreements, and acceptance criteria for completed work.

While the elements of an outsourcing relationship as illustrated in Figure 4.2 may appear straightforward, in practice the required collaboration may necessitate a variety of agreed practices, coordination gates, shared documents, formal sign-offs on results, and so on. The variation in outsourcing relationships stems from decisions about which aspects of the enterprise software delivery process are to be outsourced, how to blend the responsibilities between outsourcer and outsourcee organizations, and which aspects of control are explicitly or implicitly ceded to the outsourcee organization.

As illustrated in Figure 4.3, many important discussions simply concern what should and shouldn't be outsourced and the how the collaboration and coordination will be addressed. One organization or another will have sole responsibility for some elements, while other elements will be shared among outsourcer and outsourcee organizations. In each of these areas, collaborative approaches must be agreed upon, best practices must be defined

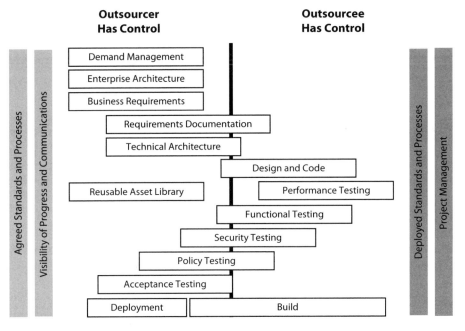

Figure 4.3 *Examples of the technical areas where collaborative agreements are important in outsourcing*

and automated using tools, and management systems must be installed and configured.

4.2.3 Globally Distributed Working

Much has been written about the globalization of enterprise software delivery (e.g., [18,51,52]). Market dynamics have driven all organizations to seek to supply various kinds of required resources from different areas of the world. A global approach addresses three primary aims:

- *Reduce labor costs in enterprise software delivery.* Labor costs represent the largest part of the budget for most enterprise software delivery organizations. To reduce these costs, organizations have located delivery capabilities in lower-cost areas, enabled by greater connectivity via improved transport links, high-speed Internet, and cheap, reliable telecommunications networks. Placing enterprise software delivery groups in locations such as India and China—where labor rates can be as low as 25 percent of those in most of Europe and North America—reduces direct labor costs and indirectly improves efficiency by supporting so-called follow-the-sun delivery approaches, where activities on a project can continue twenty-four hours a day, seven days a week.

- *Find skills in short demand.* In the last decade, we have seen a growing unmet need for many kinds of skills in enterprise software delivery. As a result of worldwide demographic trends and declining numbers of new business management and computer science students in colleges and universities in many parts of Europe and North America, organizations have had to look further afield to grow new capabilities and fill vacant positions. Across the world, a rich talent pool is available, but often in geographic locations far from the organization's current delivery centers.

- *Gain access to emerging markets.* A number of countries around the world have quickly growing economies, have invested significantly in many aspects of their infrastructures and services, and are requiring more consumer goods and services. They provide major market opportunities for businesses to expand and grow. Access to these markets can take place remotely, but local presence can help to understand local needs and culture, customize delivered goods to local specifications, and improve relationships between the company and the market being served. Expanding a company's operating and delivery capability on these growth markets are often seen as key criteria for success.

Consequently, the question for organizations is not *whether* they need to deliver their enterprise software globally, but *how* to accomplish this with the greatest efficiency. Success requires overcoming challenges in technology, organization, management, and culture.

Many enterprise software delivery organizations divide their delivery capabilities into three major segments, each with distinct collaboration issues to address. The first is onshore resources. These are the teams that geographically reside in the main delivery centers, typically in Western Europe and North America. They are the traditional business hubs for the company. The second is nearshore resources. These consist of expanded delivery centers typically located within the same country or region. Hence they have easy access to resources and share working culture with the main delivery center with minimal communication and coordination challenges. The third is offshore resources. These resources are generally in other time zones of the world, where they may not share a common language and working culture with the core sites. In such situations, additional challenges of collaboration must be addressed to overcome the difficulties of synchronizing all activities in the development and delivery chain.

Organizations use an overall distribution plan to understand and govern collaboration among these three segments. A simplified example of such a distribution plan is shown in Figure 4.4.

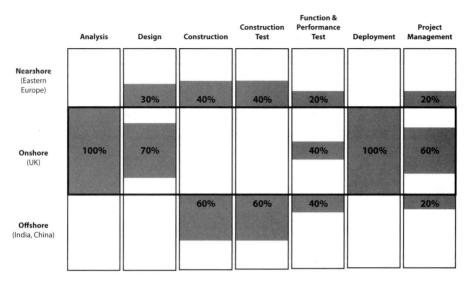

	Analysis	Design	Construction	Construction Test	Function & Performance Test	Deployment	Project Management
Nearshore (Eastern Europe)		30%	40%	40%	20%		20%
Onshore (UK)	100%	70%			40%	100%	60%
Offshore (India, China)			60%	60%	40%		20%

Figure 4.4 *An example global resource distribution plan for a large telecommunications organization*

In this simplified illustration of a global resource distribution plan for a large telecommunications organization, the main onshore resources are based in the United Kingdom, with nearshore facilities in Eastern Europe and offshore locations in India and China. The diagram depicts how the company has allocated each enterprise software delivery discipline with respect to the geographic location of the teams.

This telecommunications organization has a team at corporate headquarters in London that focuses on requirements analysis, enterprise architecture, and high-level design for all projects. As these elements are created, project specifications are communicated to St. Petersburg, Russia, and Bangalore, India, for development and component testing. Specialist performance and security testing is carried out in a test center located in Shanghai, China. As all testing is completed, work is delivered to the UK headquarters, where validation and final acceptance tests are executed. Project and portfolio management, as a core competency, is handled from the UK headquarters, where all components of application and resource portfolios are tracked and monitored. Additionally, local project management is performed at each site for the local activities taking place.

Although Figure 4.4 shows a greatly simplified view of the distribution of tasks, even this level of analysis provides important insights into the areas of the enterprise software delivery life cycle that require precise and clear communication between different teams.[2] In this situation, communicating changes in requirements was particularly challenging. Additional visibility and more frequent analysis of requirements volatility resulted in special training and major updates to the requirements management practices between the development teams in London, St. Petersburg, and Bangalore.

Many possible variations on this kind of global resource distribution scheme are possible. The key to success has been seen in the explicit recognition of the approach that is being used, aligned with approaches that define coordination and communication practices to match the implemented scheme supported by tools and automation to optimize the approach.

In practice, the role of automated support for collaboration among teams proves critical, particularly in complex resource schemes such as those described previously. Such automation provides a foundation for realizing a collaboration approach across the entire distributed organization. Also, it can enforce best practices in communication, automatically record critical interactions that occur, and act as the basis for future verification, validation, and auditing activities.

4.3 Collaborative Delivery Environments

The focus on collaboration has led to a great deal of attention on the scope and needs for collaborative technologies in enterprise software delivery. We can refer to this collection of collaborative technologies as a collaborative delivery environment (CDE) [53]. A CDE is a virtual space wherein all the stakeholders of an enterprise software delivery organization—even if distributed by time or distance—may negotiate, brainstorm, discuss, share knowledge, and generally work together to carry out some task (most often to create an executable deliverable and its supporting artifacts).

The purpose of a CDE is to create a frictionless approach for enterprise software delivery. A number of points of friction in the daily life of the developer individually and collectively impact the team's efficiency:

- The cost of start-up and ongoing workspace organization

- Inefficient work product collaboration

---

2. In fact, in summary it can be stated that every horizontal and vertical line in Figure 4.4 identifies a significant collaboration point between teams and between project activities that will require attention. Each such boundary exposes a need for synchronization of shared information, plans, resources, and activities.

- Ineffective group communication, involving knowledge and experience, project status, and project memory

- Time starvation across multiple tasks

- Stakeholder negotiation

- Stuff that doesn't work

I call these *points of friction* because energy is lost in their execution which could otherwise be directed to more creative activities that contribute directly to the completion of the project's mission. Addressing these six points of friction represents substantial return on investment for many organizations.

The *costs of start up* are related to Strubing's observations concerning organizing the working space [54]. As a team gets started or as new team members join a project, there is always an awkward, disorienting period of time until the new member gets settled into his or her space. Finding the right tools, knowing whom to talk to, knowing what documents to read first, and understanding the current state of the project are all activities that take time, and they're especially painful if the new team or member is not offered any initial guidance.

Work product collaboration involves the friction associated with multiple stakeholders creating a shared artifact. Often, one person is given the responsibility for owning a particular artifact and so serves as its primary author. Over time, however, critical documents involve many people in their evolution. Keeping track of changes, knowing who changed things and why, synchronizing simultaneous edits, and in general handling accountability for the life of the artifact are all activities that cost time and can create inefficiencies if not automated.

Communication is perhaps the largest point of friction. As Strubing noted [54], "negotiativeness" and the management of ambiguity are both critical nonprogramming tasks and both are at the core of sound communication. Typically, the memory of a project, its culture, and its design decisions are locked up in the heads of a few core individuals, and part of a team's activities involves a sort of tribal sharing. Insofar as such knowledge is inaccessible, the depth of information flow will suffer. And insofar as the communication paths among team members are noisy—such as it is within teams of teams—communication quality and hence team efficiency suffers.

Time starvation refers to the reality that there is typically never enough time to complete everything on an individual's to-do list. Developers are finite in their capacity to work. Although time cannot be expanded, projects on a death march will try to squeeze out every possible cycle by pushing those human limits, typically at great human expense (which is why death-march projects are not sustainable) [55].

Stakeholder negotiation involves the time necessary to steer different members of the team having different worldviews to some degree of closure so that the team can make progress. Within a project, time will always be spent on explaining to various stakeholders what's being built, the precise desired structure and behavior of the system, and the semantics of design alternatives and ultimately design decisions. In short, stakeholder negotiation is the process of ironing out ambiguity.

Surprisingly little has been written about the impact of *stuff (technology and tools) that doesn't work* upon the efficiency of the development team. Intermittent network outages, operating systems that behave in mysterious ways as if possessed, buggy-packaged software, and tools that don't work quite as advertised all eat up a team's time. Such interruptions are often small, but any loss will interrupt the concentration of the developer and, ultimately, losses will mount up, one minute at a time.

An explicit, targeted approach to deliver coordinated collaboration capabilities, a CDE, can address many of these points of friction. Making a virtual project environment just an URL away can minimize start up costs, and the ability to self-administer such sites means the team can manage its own artifacts rather than require the services of a dedicated support team. A CDE can minimize the friction associated with work-product collaboration by providing artifact storage with integrated change management and the storage of metaknowledge. Communication can be facilitated by the use of mechanisms for discussions, virtual meetings, and project dashboards. A CDE addresses time starvation not only by providing a hundred small creature comforts for the developer but also by making possible virtual agents that act as nonhuman members of the development team, responsible for carrying out scripted, tedious tasks. A CDE facilitates stakeholder negotiation by mechanisms that automate workflow. As for stuff that doesn't work, a CDE won't make much difference: the best I can suggest is that practitioners simply refuse to buy or use products of inferior quality. That notwithstanding, if stuff doesn't work, it is likely there are others in the world who have experienced the same problem and might have solved it or found a workaround. In the presence of an extended community of developers such as might interact with a CDE, mechanisms for sharing experiences can somewhat temper the problems of hard failure (and perhaps even offer a form of collective bargaining to put pressure on the vendor who has delivered up shoddy products).

Ultimately, technology is valuable to an organization insofar as it provides a meaningful return on investment. CDEs offer a potential for both tangible and intangible returns. Tangibly, CDEs can facilitate reduced costs in start-up, tool administration, and artifact administration. In difficult economic times, a company's travel budget is under pressure, yet collaborative work must continue.

The use of a CDE can actually reduce these company and human costs by eliminating the need for some travel. Intangibly, a CDE provides a sense of place and identity for the organization's nomadic developers who are geographically distributed and mobile; such a space helps jell the team. In addition, an examination of communication patterns within teams shows that healthy organizations create and collapse small tiger teams all the time for the purpose of wrestling specific problems to the ground. Facilitating the management of such teams with a CDE permits greater accountability and focus of mission.

4.4 Collaborative Application Life-Cycle Management

Perhaps the most tangible area of focus for a CDE is automation across the enterprise software delivery life cycle. In most aspects of delivery (especially in global delivery scenarios) the major collaboration challenges relate to synchronization and hand offs between the major delivery activities. Typically, many errors are found when tracking requirements to the tests that validate them, ensuring updates to code are reflected in their design documents, rewriting build scripts when component interfaces are realigned, and so on (as highlighted in studies by Capers Jones and others [3]).

Recognizing the importance of this cross-life-cycle view, many have come to refer to it as collaborative application life-cycle management (CALM). CALM focuses on the synchronization of the entire team and the hand offs that occur across domains.[3] These integration points facilitate a streamlined development process or, when they are missing, create friction and chaos among the team members.

Enterprise software systems are the product of many conversations, both within and among teams creating the solution and across a myriad of external relationships. Team members must be able to interact with each other in many ways. They must continually connect with other teams to synchronize activities, and they must communicate with external stakeholders to validate and refine their needs. Hence success in enterprise software delivery requires a collaborative approach. A CALM solution must support people regardless of who they are and where they are. It must also support their conversations and the assets they create as a result of these conversations.

Capabilities provided by CALM to help teams in their collaborative tasks should include the following:

- Team awareness to enable teams to know who is online so that they can engage in a discussion

---

3. This definition of CALM is adapted from Goethe et al. [46].

- Instant messaging to allow team members to communicate instantly regardless of their geographic location

- Event notification and subscription to allow users to know when an artifact is updated or a key event has taken place

- User-defined metadata to support augmentation of knowledge about artifacts based on experiences and perceptions

- Tagging to enable individuals to identify specific resources of interest and mark them using categories of significance to the user or shared among teams

The root of these capabilities lays with the configuration management systems that have been available for more than twenty years [56]. Those systems originated to help manage source code assets across teams and projects. However, as illustrated in Figure 4.5, such systems have evolved significantly. From their origins in basic version control using a common technology solution, configuration management systems have grown to support multiple locations, a wide variety of asset types, and different organizational structures [57].

As illustrated in Figure 4.5, the latest CALM solutions support distributed supply chain solutions using lightweight Internet-based integration mechanisms. They are capable of addressing the coordination and communication needs of complex multicompany collaboration scenarios typical of today's outsourcing arrangements.

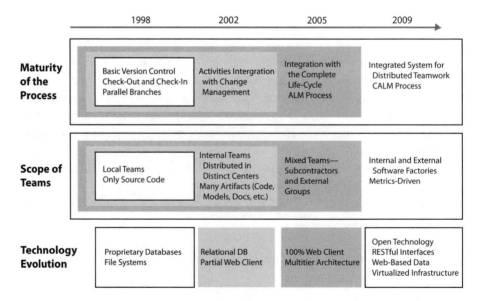

Figure 4.5 *The evolution from configuration management to CALM*

But furthermore, as these CALM capabilities have matured, three clear usage patterns for the adoption of CALM have emerged. These patterns map clearly to the changes in global delivery of enterprise software systems. I summarize these three patterns in Figure 4.6.

I call the first pattern of CALM adoption *vertically aligned*. Here, team members are closely aligned in their activities and working in a tight relationship where intercommunication is frequent, interactive, and often informal. This approach is typical of teams making use of agile delivery methods such as Scrum, XP, and DSDM [12]. The goal of any CALM approach for vertically aligned teams is to enrich and support that intense interaction style.

In the second CALM adoption pattern, *functionally divided*, delivery teams cluster more traditionally around functional areas of the life cycle, with specialist groups for requirements management, system design, code development, functional testing, and so on. Within each cluster there are frequent interactions around artifacts and processes. However, across these groups collaboration is much more controlled and based on milestones, shared artifacts, and process gates. Many of today's large-scale enterprise software delivery teams organize around a functionally divided model as a way to manage resources, people, and costs.

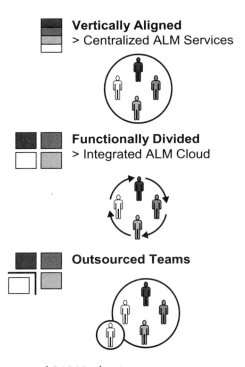

Vertically Aligned
> Centralized ALM Services

Functionally Divided
> Integrated ALM Cloud

Outsourced Teams

Figure 4.6 *Three patterns of CALM adoption*

The third CALM adoption pattern supports *outsourced* teams. In an increasing number of situations, individuals and teams work remotely from the main delivery resources (both in the physical and conceptual sense). The need for CALM is to allow interactions and communication as necessary, but in the context of additional organizational, technical, and legal barriers that may be in place.

Complicating this situation is a recognition that all three of these patterns (and a number of variations) may exist simultaneously in any realistic large-scale enterprise software delivery organization. Often, for example, an organization will have a large number of more traditional functionally divided maintenance projects, several vertically aligned situations where new innovation is taking place, and increasing outsourcing to third-party groups. Any CALM approach must understand and support these models as appropriate to the organization's needs. This categorization of CALM usage, however, enables us to understand when and how organizations apply distinct CALM approaches based on their differing needs and characteristics.

4.5 Examples

The following two examples illustrate the strategy and approach to collaborative software delivery in large enterprise software delivery organizations. In the first example, I look at the challenges of outsourced development in a financial services company, and I focus on the important relationship between outsourcer and outsourcee. In the second example, I examine the main improvement areas for enhanced collaboration and their impact in IBM Software Group, a large global software delivery organization.

4.5.1 An Outsource Application Delivery Solution for a Large Financial Services Organization

A large financial services organization (herein referred to with the fictitious name *ABC-Co*) was undergoing significant pressure to reduce enterprise software delivery costs and improve its innovation in new financial products delivered to its market. As a result, ABC-Co decided to outsource major aspects of the application delivery function to several partners. Its goal was to transform the way it delivered enterprise software solutions and to facilitate a company-wide transformation into a technology-led organization. ABC-Co assigned its outsourced partners to define and deliver a program that enabled a step-change in performance, quality, and effectiveness, with all the supporting processes and tools necessary for success. Enterprise software delivery through a partner-delivered approach was directly aimed at achieving the following:

- Enable faster speed to market for new financial product developments.

- Highlight and mitigate risks in project delivery early in the life cycle.

- Have short cycle times to allow business changes to be easily incorporated.

- Provide robust estimates allowing more effective decision making on budgets and dates.

- Communicate effectively and efficiently with all stakeholders.

- Enable professional delivery of quality solutions with verifiable levels of delivery and operational performance.

A key objective in selecting a partner-delivered approach was to use the partner's expertise as a spur to improve the overall approach to enterprise software delivery in local ABC-Co teams. In particular, ABC-Co wanted an enterprise software delivery methodology to do the following:

- Apply lean principles to deliver quickly, ensure quality of results, and eliminate waste.

- Be robust and easy to follow for all stakeholders and participants.

- Be flexible for different types of projects with widely varying characteristics.

- Provide a strong governance model (preferably well aligned with industry standards such as the COBIT framework [27]).

- Encourage and support technical excellence practices verified against benchmark metrics.

- Provide working software early to build confidence in the development teams and all project stakeholders.

- Encourage quick decision making based on accurate status information.

- Be deployed by ABC-Co's own teams, by offshore partners, and in a mixed sourcing environment.

The primary delivery partner addressed these needs by adopting a broad approach to collaboration with ABC-Co. This collaborative view concentrated in four areas:

- A robust organizational model with strong delivery governance to offer a blended model of ownership and control between ABC-Co and the partner

- Well-defined enterprise software delivery processes with automation by tools that best support this blended delivery life cycle

- A flexible delivery approach composed of onshore and outsourced services, with clearly understood trade offs between resource locations in the composition of delivery teams

- Shared key metrics that provide transparency across the organizations and a real-time view of progress and status

As illustrated in Figures 4.7, 4.8, and 4.9, the implemented approach focused on a shared collaborative model across three primary dimensions: *management*, *business functions*, and *value*. In each of these areas a series of roles and responsibilities were defined and agreed upon. The challenging nature of the collaboration across outsourced solutions is well illustrated in these figures. Here we see the complex series of interactions that must be understood and the variety of relationships between ABC-Co and its partner that require initial agreement and continued monitoring and analysis.

Figure 4.7 illustrates the management dimension and the blend of different management responsibilities required of ABC-Co and the partner organization. A joint team is required to share responsibilities across the areas of *strategic*, *program*, and *operations* management.

Figure 4.8 focuses on the business function dimension. Again, the partitioning of services indicates a combination of ownership relationships between ABC-Co and its partner. In this case, ABC-Co has the main responsibilities for strategic activities, while staffing functions and application management are the responsibility of the partner. Governance activities are a shared responsibility.

Figure 4.9 shows the value-cycle dimension of this relationship. While initial activities in the value cycle are owned by ABC-Co, their realization requires shared ownership between ABC-Co and its partner. In particular, it is a joint responsibility to evaluate the value implications of the delivered services and to optimize them based on the shared needs of ABC-Co and its partner.

To address these management needs and facilitate the collaboration between ABC-Co and the partner, a collaborative organizational structure was defined, as illustrated in Figure 4.10. This organizational structure is interesting from several dimensions. First, we can observe that attention is required in several perspectives that address strategic, program, and operational levels. Each of these requires collaborative processes, supported by appropriate tools. Second, we see that the partner must also be prepared to work with the other partners selected by ABC-Co. It's likely that multiple partners will be required to collaborate on the same set of projects. Third, we can note that the

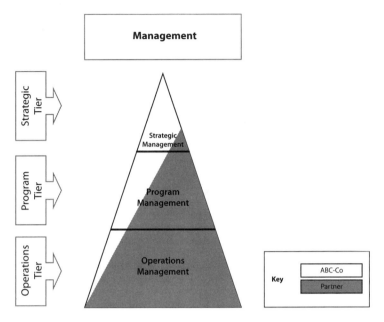

Figure 4.7 *The key management dimensions between ABC-Co and its partner—Management view*

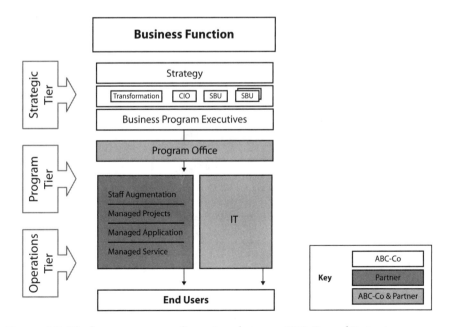

Figure 4.8 *The key management dimensions between ABC-Co and its partner—Business function view*

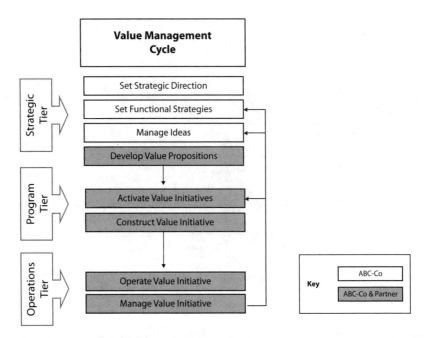

Figure 4.9 *The key management dimensions between ABC-Co and its partner—Value management cycle view*

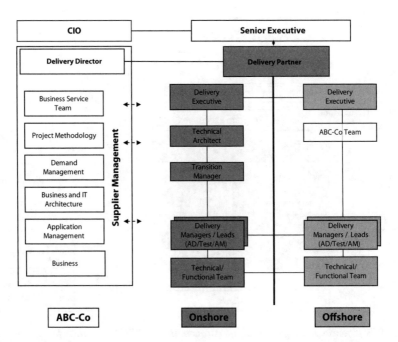

Figure 4.10 *The collaborative organization structure for ABC-Co and its partner*

obligations for clear collaboration across the teams fall not only on the shoulders of the partner. There are significant investments in collaborative processes for ABC-Co.

The way in which progress and status are reported proves critical to collaboration in outsourced projects. In this situation, ABC-Co provided a clear set of measurement objectives documented in an SLA with the partner.

Figures 4.11 and 4.12 illustrate the measures and metrics in use to assess the progress and status of the partner's effectiveness in enterprise software delivery with ABC-Co. Figure 4.11 shows the set of measures required by ABC-Co for application delivery and maintenance that must be reported on a periodic basis. These are augmented by additional metrics that the partner collects as part of its ongoing outsourced delivery function. Additionally, a key measure of success for ABC-Co is to have the new delivery practices, skills, and methodologies embedded within local ABC-Co teams that deliver enterprise software and thus become sustainable without continual intervention by the partner. As illustrated in Figure 4.12, together, the combined measures from ABC-Co and its partner can be combined to offer a "balanced scorecard" that provides an overall view of the collaborative relationship that exists between them.

4.5.2 IBM Software Group Product Delivery

For more than a decade, IBM has made increasing investments in software products and solutions. IBM Software Group, responsible for the development and delivery of these products, has quickly grown organically and by a myriad of acquisitions, so that by 2010 it included more than 26,000 people in software delivery activities around the world. These people are organized into nearly five hundred different product teams across five divisions. This organization is summarized in Figure 4.13.

This growth in IBM has not been without challenges. In fact, in surveys and analysis early in 2000, IBM became concerned that the productivity and quality of delivered solutions was under significant pressure as a result of this growth. The perception was that continued rapid growth would negatively impact IBM's ability to innovate to meet its customers' needs for new products and services. As a result, IBM chose to invest in changes influenced by several key observations:

- A need to respond to fast-changing approaches to software delivery, demanding more agility in the time to market for new products

- The recognition that many projects operated under a large overhead of existing processes that were costly to understand, manage, and execute

Standard Metrics Measured by Partner

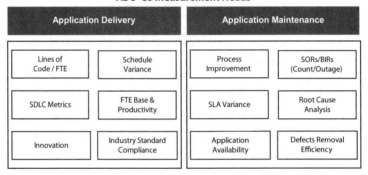

Human Resources	Client Satisfaction	Process Adherence	Quality (Development)		Quality (Support)
Skills Availability	Customer Satisfaction	CMMI Level Attainment	Schedule & Effort Variance	Delivered Defect Density	Bad fix %
Resource Utilization	Functional Quality	QA Process	Rework Effort	QA Process	SRs/Person per Month
Attrition/ Retention Variance	Transition Schedule/ Cost	Six Sigma	Review Effectiveness	FPs/Person per Month	Severity 1 & 2 Adherence

ABC- Co Measurement Needs

Application Delivery		Application Maintenance	
Lines of Code / FTE	Schedule Variance	Process Improvement	SORs/BIRs (Count/Outage)
SDLC Metrics	FTE Base & Productivity	SLA Variance	Root Cause Analysis
Innovation	Industry Standard Compliance	Application Availability	Defects Removal Efficiency

Figure 4.11 *Measures and metrics for ABC-Co and its partner*

Sample Balanced Scorecard

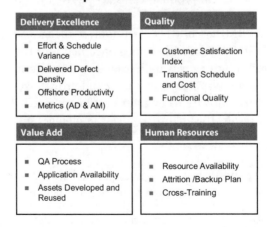

Delivery Excellence	Quality
▪ Effort & Schedule Variance ▪ Delivered Defect Density ▪ Offshore Productivity ▪ Metrics (AD & AM)	▪ Customer Satisfaction Index ▪ Transition Schedule and Cost ▪ Functional Quality

Value Add	Human Resources
▪ QA Process ▪ Application Availability ▪ Assets Developed and Reused	▪ Resource Availability ▪ Attrition /Backup Plan ▪ Cross-Training

Figure 4.12 *Example balanced scorecard for ABC-Co and its partner*

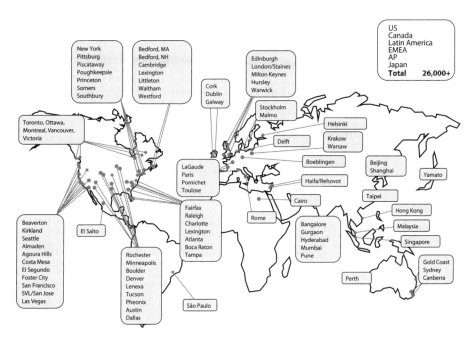

Figure 4.13 *An illustration of the global footprint of IBM software group resources*

- Growing awareness of pockets of experience in several teams where high productivity was witnessed, producing high-quality results in product innovation in reduced time frames

- Concerns with existing morale in some groups, where the daily grind of high-ceremony process controls induced a perceived "death march" feel to projects, which was reducing the organization's ability to motivate existing employees and hire new ones

- Market pressure from competitors where substantial innovations were taking place and IBM was often believed to be too slow to react

- Influence from external open-source projects and community activities where large, widely distributed teams had been able to produce innovative, high-quality products using many new collaborative techniques

IBM Software Group began a series of initiatives to address these concerns. One of the most influential of these initiatives proved to be in the area of collaborative software delivery. As shown in Figure 4.14, IBM Software Group focused attention in three areas of collaborative software delivery: *communities*, *coordination*, and *collateral*:

- Enhanced community support was provided to improve understanding and communication across groups with a common interest or need. The large scale and distribution of people required special attention to how teams improved knowledge of and interacted about areas of interest. IBM enacted a much improved technology infrastructure for setting up, sharing, and communicating in real time.

- In delivering IBM's enterprise software, it was critical to support more agile interaction styles with lighter-weight mechanisms for coordination and governance. This coordination within and across projects enabled team members to interact more dynamically on their daily tasks and allowed management to be more aware of project status.

- In terms of efficiency, greater reuse of artifacts across the software delivery life cycle allowed team members to reduce waste and improve quality. Communities and projects were connected to reuse repositories that cataloged and managed shared assets, making them more accessible and easier to adapt to new contexts.

These initiatives all had immediate and lasting impact in the IBM software delivery organizations. Over a three year period, IBM Software Group saw a 20 percent improvement in productivity, reduced head count per product by

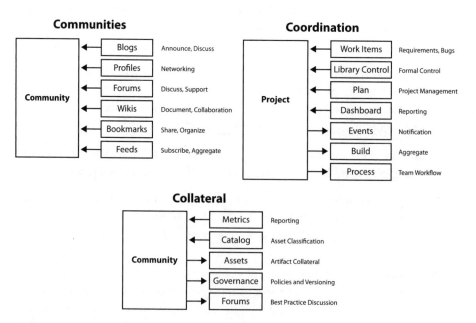

Figure 4.14 *The three key focus areas for collaborative software delivery improvements in IBM software group*

more than 10 percent, and experienced overall improvements in quality of released products through decreased levels of defects and improved customer satisfaction survey results.

However, with the accelerating demand for enhanced productivity, specific challenges persisted in areas where global software delivery team members were widely distributed across the world. In particular, more projects became a blend of onshore and offshore resources as IBM increased its software delivery presence in India, China, and Latin America.

To address these concerns, IBM Software Group focused on several areas, as illustrated in Figure 4.15. These areas spanned several levels, including organizational structure, roles and responsibilities, metrics and governance schemes, and shared collaboration technologies. Such investments have significantly smoothed the collaboration and effectiveness of distributed teams in IBM Software Group.

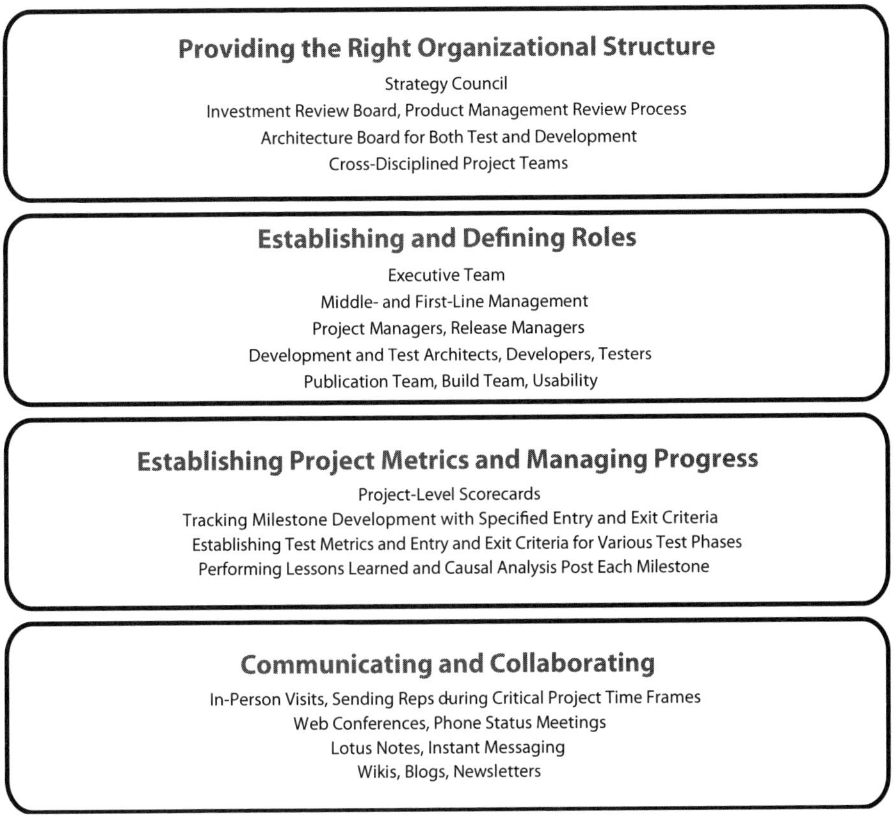

Providing the Right Organizational Structure
Strategy Council
Investment Review Board, Product Management Review Process
Architecture Board for Both Test and Development
Cross-Disciplined Project Teams

Establishing and Defining Roles
Executive Team
Middle- and First-Line Management
Project Managers, Release Managers
Development and Test Architects, Developers, Testers
Publication Team, Build Team, Usability

Establishing Project Metrics and Managing Progress
Project-Level Scorecards
Tracking Milestone Development with Specified Entry and Exit Criteria
Establishing Test Metrics and Entry and Exit Criteria for Various Test Phases
Performing Lessons Learned and Causal Analysis Post Each Milestone

Communicating and Collaborating
In-Person Visits, Sending Reps during Critical Project Time Frames
Web Conferences, Phone Status Meetings
Lotus Notes, Instant Messaging
Wikis, Blogs, Newsletters

Figure 4.15 *Areas of focus for IBM software group in improving globally distributed software delivery teams*

4.6 Conclusions

Enterprise software delivery organizations are under significant pressure to reduce costs while improving productivity and performance. A primary approach is to use global resources to reduce labor costs and locate specialized skills. However, a main impediment to delivering these improvements is the challenge of collaboration within teams and across the emerging software delivery supply chains. Unless organizations identify and address these collaboration issues, the benefits from global team working are lost.

In this chapter, I examine the main elements of collaborative software delivery from the perspective of team interaction, globalization, and multiorganizational supply chain management. We see that CALM plays a critical role in reducing the risk of failure. Automation through collaborative delivery environments helps to focus on CALM and can be customized to deliver a CALM model that is well matched to the global delivery approach in use.

Chapter 5

Agile Software Delivery

Chapter Summary

I define and explore agility in enterprise software delivery, focusing on the issues of agility at scale, as they apply to the global enterprise. I make a series of practical observations on the application of agile practices to global software delivery and come to the following conclusions:

- Scaling agile practices requires explicit attention to organizational transition aspects affecting many roles and activities across the delivery life cycle.

- Complexity occurs at many levels in the global enterprise; it is essential to use simplifying techniques to manage this complexity.

- Scaling the rollout of an agile approach must be based on a managed program with clear goals, objectives, and key performance indicators.

- A focus on the measurement, metrics, and visibility of project progress is a clear success factor in scaled agile approaches, and it is essential to flexibility in decision making.

5.1 Introduction

Organizations today feel mounting pressure to respond more quickly to their customer and broader stakeholder needs. Not only is the drive for increased business flexibility resulting in new products being brought to market; it's also accelerating evolution of existing solutions and services. Handling such change is a critical factor in enterprise software delivery, driven by market fluctuations, new technologies, announcements of competitive offerings, enactments of new laws, and so on. But *change* cannot mean *chaos*. In most of the organizations producing software, all activities, and change activities in particular, must be governed by a plethora of formal and informal procedures, practices, processes, and regulations. These governance mechanisms provide an essential method for managing and controlling how software is delivered into production.

However, over the years, we've also seen an overabundance of these controls—to the point that they can severely limit an organization's ability to be effective. Members of one large enterprise software delivery organization joked that they had recently completed an analysis that showed that even if they were to deliver a "null" project (i.e., a project where there actually was no new software produced), they would still require almost six months of elapsed time simply to write all the documents (presumably leaving them empty), go to all the meetings, and obtain the formal sign offs for the project to be considered in compliance with local procedures.

This example may seem rather harsh; however it's illustrative of the pressure on enterprise software delivery organizations to balance their delivery capabilities across four key dimensions, as summarized in Figure 5.1:

- Time to market for projects to complete and deliver a meaningful result to the business. This can be measured in average time for project completion.

- Productivity of individuals and teams. This is typically measured in terms of lines of code or function points delivered over unit time.

- Process maturity in the consistency, uniformity, and standardization of practices. Measurements can be made via waivers to common process norms or by maturity approaches such as the capability maturity model (CMM) levels.

- Quality in shipped code, errors handled, and turnaround of requests. Measures are typically combinations of defect density rates and errors fixed per unit time.

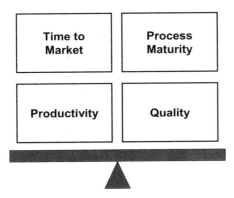

Figure 5.1 *Dimensions of a balanced approach to enterprise software delivery*

Finding an appropriate balance across these enterprise software delivery success factors is a constant struggle. One of the most interesting dimensions of this struggle is a change in perspective toward enterprise software delivery. Indeed, many organizations view the relationship between "operational risk" and "delivery risk" to be different today. Simply stated, there are many occasions in which the risk of delivering late or with capabilities that do not meet the market needs outweighs the risk of failing to analyze every possible usage model, run every possible test case, or follow every step in the defined delivery process. This is particularly true in cases where changes to existing systems must be quickly understood, analyzed, and enacted. This kind of flexibility, or agility, in delivery is becoming an essential element of enterprise software delivery.

The past few years have seen wide adoption of agile software development approaches in many parts of the software industry. Driven by demands for more software more quickly, organizations studied the practices in use by high-performing teams to see how they could be replicated. Those high-performing teams tried to shake off the overly constraining processes that they believed were hampering innovation and creativity. From this emerged a series of principles for agile development, most famously captured in the "Agile Manifesto," and a series of development practices that encapsulate those principles.[1]

Briefly stated, the approach to agility can be defined as follows: "An iterative and incremental approach performed in a highly collaborative and self-organizing manner with just the right amount of ceremony to frequently

---

1. See www.agilemanifesto.org.

produce high quality software in a cost effective and timely manner which meets the changing needs of its stakeholders."[2]

Captured in this rather dense definition are several concepts that are essential to the spirit of agility:

- Activities necessary to adhere to process rules, governance, and conformance (broadly defined as *ceremony*) should be kept to the minimum necessary for the context of development.

- Focus on quality is consistent and continual, with early definition of testing criteria, constant test execution, and clear validation of test status.

- Interaction and collaboration among the team is fundamental and must be made as rich and simple as possible to ensure high-quality communication.

- Changes are expected and demand clear visibility, early intervention, and rapid response.

- Stakeholders and customers have a critical ongoing involvement in the project.

- Frequent delivery of working software is essential and is the primary means of understanding and measuring progress.

A majority of the work around agile software delivery has focused on the software development area, with new approaches and techniques for accelerating coding and testing, understanding requirements changes, and coordinating code-test-build activities. Several available books and papers provide overviews of agile development processes, techniques, and best practices [58,59], but a broader perspective on agile software delivery is also important. Organizations are now shifting their thinking toward applying agile approaches in all aspects of their enterprise software delivery.

In this chapter, I analyze that broader view of agility. After considering the changes in thinking about enterprise software delivery that agility requires, I focus on the ways in which this agility can be scaled and adopted in an enterprise software delivery organization.

---

2. This is the definition used by IBM and captures many of the ideas of agility commonly described. Of course, many variations exist in the literature.

5.2 Rethinking Enterprise Software Delivery

Over the past few decades, important advances in enterprise software development have enhanced the productivity, quality, and effectiveness of enterprise software delivery organizations. But the current challenges in enterprise software delivery have forced organizations to rethink aspects of how they perform their task. They've recently focused attention on three fundamental observations:

- The value a business derives from an enterprise system is frequently not clearly understood in relation to the investment in the development and maintenance of that system.

- Enterprise systems undergo constant change, both during their design and construction (as the true needs and necessities of the system become better understood) and after delivery (when end users start to exercise the system). The ability of these systems to evolve is a core quality that is poorly addressed in principle and expensive to support in practice.

- Most costs in enterprise systems delivery occur after a system's first release to production, with substantial rework, changes, and continual evolution of capability over a long period of time. Yet much of the attention and investment in many enterprise software delivery organizations is focused on detailed descriptions of a system's initial requirements and an expectation that software delivery will be "built as defined," fielded into production, and then slowly evolved and updated.

5.2.1 From Software Development to Software Delivery

As summarized in Figure 5.2, the change in perspective characterized as a move from software *development* to software *delivery*, affects several dimensions. A software delivery perspective focuses on the following concepts and practices:

- *Continuously evolving systems.* Enterprise software undergoes a continual process of change. Traditionally, the goal is to optimize the development of the first release of the system. But the critical phase comes after first release. This evolution should be the focus of attention, and investment should be placed in techniques that support and encourage software to evolve.

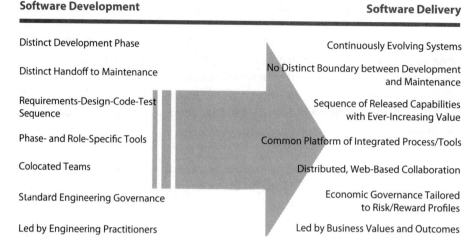

Software Development	Software Delivery
Distinct Development Phase	Continuously Evolving Systems
Distinct Handoff to Maintenance	No Distinct Boundary between Development and Maintenance
Requirements-Design-Code-Test Sequence	Sequence of Released Capabilities with Ever-Increasing Value
Phase- and Role-Specific Tools	Common Platform of Integrated Process/Tools
Colocated Teams	Distributed, Web-Based Collaboration
Standard Engineering Governance	Economic Governance Tailored to Risk/Reward Profiles
Led by Engineering Practitioners	Led by Business Values and Outcomes

Figure 5.2 *The contrast between a software development and software delivery perspective*

- *Blending of boundaries between development and maintenance.* A clear distinction is normally made between development and maintenance, often involving organizational, process, and cultural implications for "handing off" the system into maintenance. With an evolutionary view of software delivery, the distinction between these two activities is blurred to the point that development and maintenance are just two aspects of the same need to create and deliver the system.

- *Sequence of released capabilities with ever-increased value.* A development view operates from the understanding that after a deep analysis, the requirements for a system are signed off and development of the system begins with the goal to "fulfill" those requirements and place the system in production. But the reality in many systems is that requirements emerge and evolve as more is discovered about the needs of the stakeholders and as understanding of the delivery context grows. A more realistic approach to delivery views the system not as a number of major discrete releases but as a continuous series of incremental enhancements with increasing value to the stakeholders.

- *Common platform of integrated process and tools.* The siloed delivery approach is usually supported by processes and tools that are optimized for each silo. This occurs because most organizations define processes and acquire the tools individually, function by function, with little thought for the end-to-end flow of information and artifacts. A delivery view recognizes the predominance of the interoperation of these processes and tools to optimize enterprise system value.

- *Distributed web-based collaboration.* Teaming and teamwork is a focus within functional areas for a development approach. A delivery view defines the team more broadly, recognizing that stakeholders in software delivery may vary widely in function, geography, and organization. Technology support to include all those stakeholders in team activities is essential. While a variety of collaborative, web-based technologies have emerged in recent years, many organizations have deployed them in an ad hoc way and invested little in concerted approaches to adopt them across their enterprise software delivery organization.

- *Economic governance tailored to risk/reward profiles.* To manage software development, most organizations use a collection of processes, measures, and governance practices that focus on development artifacts such as the software code, requirements documents, and test scripts. A delivery view moves the focus of governance toward the business value of what is being delivered, aiming to optimize features delivered and time to value of delivered capabilities, increase burn down of backlogs of new requests, reduce volatility of systems, and sustain velocity of delivery teams.

- *Business value and outcome led.* Many enterprise software delivery organizations have prided themselves on their technical skills and the depth of their knowledge in technologies for software development and operations. These are vital to success. However, at times, this emphasis on development has created the perception in the broader organization that the enterprise software delivery organization is constantly in search of the latest technology solution with little regard to where and how such technology investments help the business achieve its goals. A focus on software delivery gives greater emphasis to the business value of those investments and creates a more balanced view of investment.

This change in thinking radically alters the way an enterprise software delivery organization approaches its task. A delivery perspective encourages styles of software delivery that move away from the early lock-down of decisions (to reduce variance in software projects) toward controlled discovery, experimentation, and innovation.

5.2.2 The Basis for Agility

The growing interest and literature in agile development practices has been the primary source for much of this thinking. Drawing from the practices of high-performing teams, a philosophy of software delivery was defined that was captured in four clear statements of principle in a "Manifesto for Agile Software Development," expressing the importance of the following:[3]

- Individuals and interactions over processes and tools

- Working software over comprehensive documentation

- Customer collaboration over contract negotiations

- Responding to change over following a plan

The repercussions of these beliefs have been profound, and we've seen a great deal of subsequent analysis and activity in defining new processes, methods, and tools that support these beliefs. The summary of the implications for large-scale software teams shown in Figures 5.3 and 5.4 illustrate how such agile thinking has altered the approach to enterprise software delivery.

In Figure 5.3, a waterfall-style software delivery approach shows how increasing knowledge of the system context is obtained through stages of requirements and analysis before construction, test, and delivery activities can take place. In addition, these activities are largely executed in sequence, with little opportunity for overlap. The involvement with (and hand off to) operations staff occurs once the system is complete. The automation platform that supports these activities is optimized to each set of functions in a collection of largely discrete tools.

In Figure 5.4, the agile approach, unlike the waterfall approach, recognizes the evolutionary nature of the development and delivery tasks and aims to involve all project staff in decision making as early as possible. While it's not an option to *avoid* essential design and delivery tasks such as requirements management or testing, the approach overlaps these tasks so that they occur concurrently, with the involvement and cooperation of the whole team throughout the lifetime of the project. Consequently, the automation platform must consist of tools and services that facilitate and support common teamwork, with specific attention to collaborative interaction, visibility and status management, and coordinated planning.

The agile delivery approach seeks to shorten the time to delivery through optimized concurrency, early visibility into problems and blockages, reduced late

---

3. See www.agilemanifesto.org.

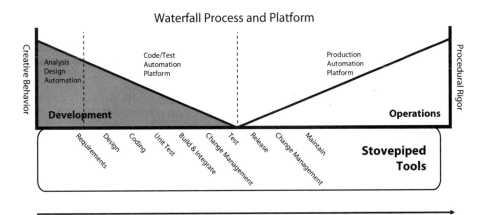

Figure 5.3 *The implications of agile thinking on enterprise software delivery—*
A waterfall perspective

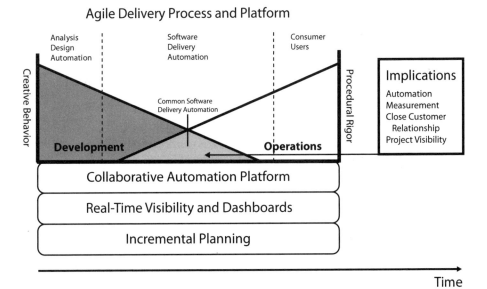

Figure 5.4 *The implications of agile thinking on enterprise software delivery—An agile*
perspective

rework through continuous feedback, and greater cooperation at all stages. To this
end, a core necessity is a common software delivery automation capability. This
capability is essential because agility is possible only when the following is true:

- High-bandwidth communication and coordination among teams is supported to realize the distributed collaboration that is necessary.

- Decision making is based on real-time information on current status.

- Early insight into problems allows quick diagnosis and immediate intervention through continuous measurement and transparency into individual, team, and project progress.

5.2.3 The Focus for Agility

Agile thinking has galvanized several important ideas relevant to enterprise software delivery. Consequently, an agile project views itself differently, placing emphasis on the following elements:

- *Collaboration.* Agile approaches focus on less paperwork and more on conversations across the team and with actively involved stakeholders.

- *Quality.* Agile practices encourage inclusion of test activities as early as possible in projects and continuously execute tests to maintain quality.

- *Evolution.* Agile projects create loosely coupled, highly cohesive architectures and frequently refactor to keep them that way.

- *Working software.* Agile projects monitor progress based on what they can prove actually works, instead of focusing on designs and descriptions of what should or could be produced.

- *Individual and team flexibility.* Agile team members are "generalizing specialists" who are often experts in some area but may perform many tasks on a project and work for the good of the team.

5.3 Agility at Enterprise Scale

Many of the ideas and approaches toward agility in enterprise software delivery are self-evident to the individuals and teams involved in the projects. Many would argue that they represent no more than years of accumulated common-sense techniques that distinguish high-performing teams from the rest. However, less clear to the broader organization is how to scale and manage agile practices as part of a concerted effort of improvement across their integrated supply chain for enterprise software delivery. Here, we'll look at three dimensions of the scalability of agile approaches. The first examines the context in which agile practices are applied. The second dimension describes the key scaling factors and their impact on agility. The third dimension reviews rollout and deployment issues that can limit the adoption of agile approaches in practice.

5.3.1 Agility in Context

As with a majority of aspects of enterprise software delivery, the context in which ideas and approaches of agile thinking are applied can have significant impact on their utility and value. Although the key principles may remain consistent, their application in practice can vary widely. Organizations must understand the complexity of the particular enterprise software delivery environment in which agile thinking will be applied.

As illustrated in Figure 5.5, it's useful to highlight the context for agility in two dimensions: *organizational drivers* and *technical/regulatory drivers*. Through these dimensions, we can understand the implications of increasing complexity on how agility is applied in practice.

At the bottom left of the diagram, where the organizational and technical/regulatory aspects are least complex, we typically see colocated teams with small numbers of developers building applications of limited complexity and minimal deployment risk. Many of the initial agile approaches began in this context, and techniques such as *extreme programming* find their majority of use in this context.

As shown in the middle of the diagram, increasing complexity forces teams to address additional concerns:

- Larger team sizes requiring more coordination and transparency into planning and progress

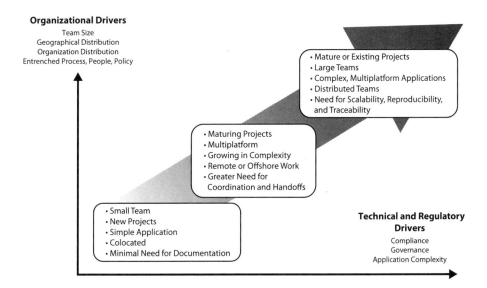

Figure 5.5 *The context for agile delivery in two dimensions*

- Distributed teams supported by remote access, outsourced partnerships, and varied access to artifacts and system knowledge

- Complex or mission-critical applications requiring more attention to analysis, architecture, and testing procedures

- Multiplatform deployment environments often requiring more extensive and rigorous testing, management of multiple variants, and enhanced support mechanisms

As shown in the top right of the diagram, in the most complex situations, teams face an increasing number of issues:

- Very large team sizes, teams of teams, and more complex management structures forcing additional attention on coordination and management and creating an increasing need to standardize best practices to avoid reinvention and miscommunication across artifacts and processes

- Distributed and global development, requiring attention to many technical, organizational, and cultural issues as the teams interact to cooperatively deliver the solution

- Compliance needs for domains in which regulatory controls require audits based on process conformance and regular collection of development information from multiple data sources

- Very complex applications that may include safety-critical or mission-critical components and hence require complex test environments, dedicated test teams, and careful attention to analysis and architecture properties (e.g., recovery, fault tolerance, security monitoring)

In short, complexity issues in enterprise software delivery can have significant impact on the adoption of agile approaches. Agile strategies must be evaluated, tailored, and perhaps combined with traditional approaches to suit the particular context.

5.3.2 Agile Scaling Factors

Examining in more detail this need for adaptation, I'll discuss eight key factors that have major impacts on the scaling of agile approaches, as illustrated in Figure 5.6:

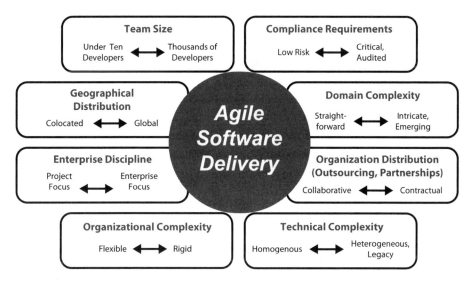

Figure 5.6 *Key factors in agile scaling*

- *Geographical distribution.* For teams that are distributed in several locations, a primary challenge is the need for close, frequent interaction and collaboration. Short delivery cycles typical of agile projects force close cooperation across the team. Clearly, complexity surrounds the technical aspects required to connect the team in meaningful ways. Additional complexity includes the challenge of managing a common team approach in light of the various distances, time zones, work hours and labor laws, holiday schedules, and so on.

- *Compliance requirements.* The agile principle of focusing attention on working software rather than documentation is challenged when that software will be controlling a power distribution network or embedded in a medical device. In such situations (and many others) there are explicit, mandatory compliance issues that require various documents to be produced and maintained, periodic audits of practices, and clear traceability between a specified feature, its implementation, and its executed tests. Agile delivery methods cannot ignore or subvert this documentation. Finding the right balance of effort is, of course, critical.

- *Technical complexity.* Systems that are very complex in scope can be difficult to understand and manage in practice. They require a great deal of up-front analysis to define their correct behavior and sophisticated analysis and verification to ensure they function correctly. Agile approaches seek to create working code early, involve stakeholders frequently, and keep noncoding activities to the bare minimum. Such objectives must be balanced against the reality of the application system being produced.

- *Team size.* The classic approach to agility uses small, colocated teams. However, larger enterprise software systems require larger teams. One approach is to break those systems into smaller segments and divide the teams into "teams of teams." This approach increases the flexibility within agile teams but also increases the coordination challenges across those teams. Choosing and implementing an appropriate organization structure for enterprise software delivery is a critical early decision that can have profound consequences for the rest of the project.[4]

- *Enterprise discipline.* Different organizations will assume different approaches toward control, management, and reporting in their enterprise software delivery organizations. Some aspects of the approach are a result of the operating domain (e.g., industry and government regulations, laws, and guidelines). However, the culture and history of the organization are equally important. Management teams introducing and scaling agile approaches must take such elements into account as they come up against common perceptions and norms and even the local political structures.

- *Organization distribution.* As organizations engage in more complex supply chain arrangements with partners, it's likely that projects will be delivered with resources from different companies. Such companies may be partners in one area of the business while competing head-to-head in other areas. Agile approaches encourage close, frequent, open cooperation among the teams, with high levels of transparency. Organizational distribution can severely limit what is feasible or what is advisable in this regard.

- *Organizational complexity.* We know that the biggest factor in the success of most projects is the people involved. Their specific experience, skills, and attitudes bring a lot to the character of and approach to the project. The need to recognize individuals and team dynamics is a major principle of agile approaches. This is very positive when a team is motivated, flexible, and highly skilled. But individuals and team dynamics can also be a major roadblock when scaling agile practices to teams that have a twenty-year heritage of skills, feel overwhelmed by the new techniques, and are suspicious of increased transparency and personal responsibility.

---

4. One of the common sayings in enterprise software is that "you ship your organization"—the way you organize individuals and teams will undoubtedly have significant impact on the structure and effectiveness of the system delivered.

Successful adoption of agile approaches requires that they adjust to these situations and take such personal factors into account.

- *Domain complexity.* There are several implications for selecting the appropriate agile approach that depend on characteristics of the domain in which the enterprise software is being created and delivered. There may be less emphasis on managing technical and delivery risks in domains that are relatively stable and well understood than in domains where experimentation and innovation is needed to encourage a stable set of requirements to emerge. Highly complex domains (e.g., industrial device control, satellite image analysis) may also require specific attention to modeling, analysis, and verification techniques to comprehend, analyze, and manage domain knowledge.

These factors force adjustments in important areas to the practical realization of agility at scale. They encourage a disciplined approach to the scaling of agile techniques.

My experience with several large enterprise software delivery organizations suggests that agile approaches can be successful in almost every kind of development team and in almost all organizations. Each situation has its own specific needs and variations, yet the basic core agile principles can provide significant results when applied with care and with realistic expectations. Surveys and studies in enterprise software delivery support the view that adoption of agile approaches is seeing major uptake in many domains and that the scale of adoption is continuing to increase. One survey showed that 60 percent of respondents believed they were using agile techniques, in teams of up to two hundred people, with more than 70 percent of those teams distributed over two or more sites.[5]

To summarize the practical aspects of scaling agile approaches, I make several observations of critical success factors drawn from my personal experience.

5.3.2.1 Observation 1: The Roles Most Challenged by Agile Approaches Are Those of Executive Managers, Product Managers, and Project Managers

Interest in and excitement about agile approaches is common in many enterprise systems organizations, and the majority of organizations have some experience with applying agile techniques in small teams or in limited categories of projects. The benefits of an agile approach are easily positioned for those in a development and delivery role. However, to a large degree, agile approaches focus attention on development aspects of enterprise systems delivery and have

---

5. www.infoq.com/news/2008/05/agile-adoption-survey-2008.

paid little attention to the needs of those in management roles. Agile methods such as Scrum and XP are described frequently in terms of the reduction of unnecessary controls on developers and testers, and they introduce new development roles such as *Scrum master* and *product owner*.

However, executive managers and project managers can often feel rather lost by the introduction of agile techniques. In reality, it's not unusual for a certain tension to arise in which developers perceive agility as an excuse to avoid burdensome management practices and ignore long-term planning in favor of shorter cycles and continual replanning. Management may therefore view this attitude as dangerous and chaotic, as it may be perceived that it reduces their insight and diminishes their role in managing the projects. A typical anecdote told by managers goes like this: project managers working with agile development teams ask product owners for plans but can obtain no clear view of a project outside of the current iteration or sprint—often only a few weeks away—with the comment "We don't do long-term planning because we're agile."

As a result, great care must be taken to help each of the management roles understand how agile approaches will affect them, how their role will evolve, and how planning and management activities support and adjust to an agile approach. Often, new management techniques are required to improve management of agile projects. For example, as project managers and product owners work in agile projects, they may need support in learning how to write requirements in terms of epics and stories, improving their approaches to item backlog analysis and prioritization, and acquiring more accurate estimation techniques using story points and velocity for systems that will undergo significant evolution.

Rather than reinforcing the divisions between the management and delivery roles, agile teams can be a catalyst for including these roles in new ways. For example, in one large electronics company, the scaling of agile practices using Scrum methods was struggling to get management support. Delivery teams found a way forward by working more closely with product managers to leverage their skills within the team. The product owners had always had a significant role in defining and managing new versions of consumer products to the market. They had very well-developed skills in feature prioritization, value analysis, and market assessment. Rather than being considered "outside" the main software delivery team, these product owners were found to be critical players in backlog analysis, sprint planning, and complex priority analysis. Including them in the software delivery teams throughout the project life cycle had the dual benefit of improving the delivery cycle while gaining important advocates within the company's management community.

5.3.2.2 Observation 2: Plan at Multiple Levels and
Adopt a "Measure and Steer" Approach to Agile Planning

More broadly, agile projects must use a different set of techniques for planning software delivery. Specifically, planning must take into account multiple levels of needs and operate on an understanding that the plan is a current snapshot of tasks and deliverables that will evolve as the project delivers more capabilities toward its stated goals.

First, in terms of *what* planning is necessary, several agile methods discuss planning approaches on the level of development teams and projects (sometimes referred to as *two-level planning*) but say little about how those ideas measure up to high-level planning needs. My experience suggests four levels of planning must be addressed:

- *Enterprise level.* Traditional planning approaches provide a global strategic view of the organization's business objectives, key performance indicators (KPIs), resource usage, and so on. Such planning depends highly on historical data that is amenable to different forms of analytics and comparison against benchmark data, analyst studies, and industry norms. Executive management and strategists in the company have a need to understand clearly what impact, if any, agile practices will have at this level. For example, with one global system integrator (SI), major concerns around cost management and outsourcing were driving strategic decisions concerning resources. Broader scaling of agile approaches was effectively blocked by these managers, until a detailed study was carried out on the impact of the SI-specific agile delivery model on the offshore delivery approaches they were using as the basis for key business decisions.[6]

- *Portfolio level.* At any one time, most enterprise software delivery organizations are engaged in a wide variety of projects, programs, and initiatives. While planning must occur on each of these individually, often the more difficult aspects of planning concern the interactions and impacts across these efforts. Such projects are often grouped into a portfolio of activities, which is managed as a whole in terms of resource usage, return on investment, business value, technical investment, and prioritization. Agile approaches can cause risk and uncertainty in portfolio-level planning. For example, in one large retail organization, portfolio planning aimed to establish pooled resources, matrixed approaches to using people on projects, and flexibility for moving people between projects. However, the

---

6. In fact, to be even more blunt, this organization found that the benefits of using a very structured, mature, CMMI level 5 offshore software delivery team was lost when the introduction of agile practices into the onshore project management team lead them to act in an immature, CMMI level 1 way.

agile project initiatives that were being scaled up had a very strong principle of dedicating resources to projects. This clash of cultures resulted in several roadblocks. It was essential to discuss these differences in philosophy with both parties and gain a clear understanding of the way forward.

- *Project level.* In the most straightforward cases, projects are easily identifiable in terms of collections of teams contributing to the project's success. But for many enterprise software delivery organizations, projects vary greatly in size, complexity, and organizational structure. Project management plays a critical role in controlling and managing the delivery of systems across these organizational structures. Projects that consist of collections of teams that have little shared experiences or techniques frequently pose challenges for project management. An obvious example is a situation where large enterprise back-office applications on mainframes have been in place for many years and supported by the same team for most of that time. The team will have well-established methods of working and a long history of delivery success. Team members often react defensively when a new team appears professing support for agile approaches to build new capabilities that must integrate with that back-office system. Special attention must be given to planning and delivery in these mixed-mode projects, often with additional support for working with both teams to gain a common view of plans and progress against those plans. In particular, vary careful attention is needed to align team interactions for systems delivery when there is a mix of projects using both agile and nonagile delivery techniques.

- *Team and individual levels.* Enterprise delivery organizations typically have a lot of experience in agile planning for individuals and teams. They have learned how to gain greater insight into project status and progress by planning based on epics and stories, estimating time using story points and "ideal days," and measuring using metrics such as velocity, burn down, and technical debt. While retraining using such approaches has been effective, a problem remains. Many managers of teams inappropriately use such measures to compare and contrast individual and team performance and make false abstract summaries from the lower-level data. For example, the agile practices in one large software product company insisted on transparency for all individual and teamwork item lists and backlogs, together with detailed accounts of time taken on each activity. This is very much in line with the agile principles of honest interaction, and it aids whole-team thinking and planning. However, it soon became clear that project managers and executives had been using this data to rate and rank individuals and teams based on their daily performance, using criteria that had never been discussed with those teams. The result was a period of confusion and hostility in which the individual and team-level planning approach effectively collapsed. Some level of normality returned only after a period of discussion and education on agile planning and measurement.

Second, in terms of *how* to plan, experience shows that traditional planning approaches do not easily fit with agile projects. The basis of planning for most organizations is a detailed list (more or less fixed) of requirements against which a work breakdown structure partitions the tasks that are estimated and managed using a set of Gantt charts. This approach is widely understood and well supported by project planning tools and best practices, and is the basis for status reporting and governance procedures in many organizations.

Unfortunately, this approach has very limited flexibility when confronted with evolutionary delivery styles such as agile development. Many organizations find a basic conflict between the need for stability and control with traditional planning techniques and the push toward increased flexibility, continual replanning, and late decision making in agile planning methods. The simple analogy is that traditional planning is based on a philosophy of *aim-and-shoot*, while agile planning is more about continual *measure-and-steer*.

Addressing these different viewpoint requires making a clear, explicit set of decisions about how agile projects will be planned, managed, and reported. Additional awareness training and education is essential to help the organization understand the broader impacts of agile planning.

5.3.2.3 Observation 3: Don't Use Agile Methods for Everything; Match Those Practices to Project Characteristics to Optimize Success

When asked where agile approaches do and do not fit, I'm tempted to respond simply that agility is right for every project. Certainly for all projects, the broad agile principles provide valuable insights and techniques when interpreted intelligently and in context. However, I've learned from experience that in practice it is essential to limit the scaling of agile approaches to projects with properties that are well matched to the characteristics of agility, at least when establishing new practices in a complex organization undergoing significant change.

In Figure 5.7, I've summarized project properties via a number of dimensions with respect to how well those project properties align with the agile ideals. For simplicity, the diagram shows three basic categories of projects: maintenance, process improvement, and business innovation projects. For each of these, I list a series of properties that generally pertain to projects in that category. Business innovation projects mesh well with the agile approach. Here, we typically see an evolutionary approach to requirements, flexibility and frequent replanning, and a drive for incremental delivery of new capabilities. These properties clearly align with most agile approaches, and the application of such techniques can readily take place.

	Maintenance	Process Improvement	Business Innovation
Project Type	Repeated, predictable	Understood, variable scope	New, exploratory
Requirements	Fixed, clear	Variable, clear	Emergent
Key Management Metrics	Cost	Time	Quality
Governance Risk	Low	Medium	High
Primary Sourcing	Offshore or outsourced	Mix of offshore and onshore	Onshore
Contract Type	Fixed price	Time and materials	Results, value
Development Method	Waterfall	Iterative	Agile
Collaboration	Low, fixed handoffs	Medium, fixed handoffs	High, variable handoffs
Project Length to Release	Long (>3 months)	Medium (1–3 months)	Short (<1 month)

Figure 5.7 *A simplified analysis of project properties*

In the other two categories, *maintenance* and *business improvement projects*, the adoption of agile approaches is more difficult and brings a greater risk in scaling agile within an enterprise software delivery organization. Their properties make the mapping of agile methods much more complex. This does not mean that the use of agile approaches is impossible. Rather, such a mapping requires greater care. Training needs may be increased, and additional piloting is usually necessary. Many enterprise software delivery organizations implement a staged approach to scaling agile approaches, with the initial phases clearly targeted at projects with a greater affinity to the agile concepts.

5.3.2.4 Observation 4: Adapt and Harden the Agile Process as the Project Gets Closer to Delivery

An important lesson from many of my experiences with scaling agile practices is that the agile process does not stay consistent throughout the lifetime of a project. The normal pattern I've observed is that governance and control elements of the process increase as the project moves toward formal delivery milestones. In practice, projects often need a discrete point at which they move into a more constrained period where important *hardening* activities take place (e.g., finalizing tests, obtaining conformance sign-offs, completing documentation).

This evolution of an agile approach is illustrated in Figure 5.8. Here we see a high-level representation of the agile delivery approach used in the enterprise software delivery organization for a large financial services company. Management has distinguished three clear phases of a project life cycle that categorize the sprints or iterations.

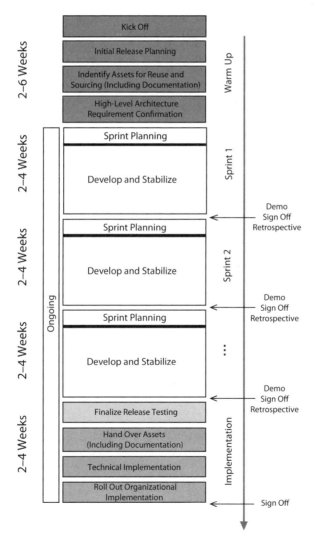

Figure 5.8 *An example of a modified agile delivery process*

In the early phase of the life cycle, the initial sprint is defined as a *warm-up* phase. In this phase, the objectives of the project are clarified, initial architectural principles and assets are agreed upon, and common communication channels for the project are established. Then a series of ongoing sprints implement the key capabilities of the system, following practices typical of agile methods. In the final *implementation* phase of the project, time is dedicated to activities such as handover of assets, training of system users, and documentation completion. Two additional aspects are worth highlighting:

- There are explicit sign-off activities at the end of each sprint. These involve demonstration of capabilities to stakeholders and agreement on progress made, reinforcing the iterative nature of the process. These formal reviews play an important role in cementing the relationship between the business owners and the enterprise delivery teams and are critical for subsequent project auditing and compliance exercises.

- As the project evolves, restrictions on development increase. Initially, these take place through increased scrutiny in sign-offs, greater attention to performance metrics, and explicit inclusion of mandatory nonfunctional requirements in the later sprints. However, additional practical restrictions are typically introduced as the project proceeds. For example, as delivery deadlines approach, the teams may restrict who is allowed to initiate a new work stream, kick-off builds, or reprioritize work item backlogs.

In understanding the process described in Figure 5.8, it's important to remember the context in which it is applied: in this example, it was a highly regulated banking environment with a risk-averse culture. Hence the additional governance and control steps in the process bring a level of coordination that was viewed as essential for broader acceptance of agile techniques within that setting. Other approaches to agile process hardening may be more appropriate in other domains where a different set of pressures exist.

5.3.3 Scaling Rollout of Agile Approaches

Adopting any new ideas at scale requires explicit attention to rollout and transition activities. A key consideration for any change in approach toward enterprise software delivery is to plan that change within the confines of the organization's need to continue its tasks while adopting new techniques. Much of the existing literature and best practices for managing successful technology transition can be applied to scaling rollout of agile approaches. My experience working in a number of large-scale agile practice rollout situations has led me to focus in several areas.

- *Define an appropriate organization to manage the rollout.* An essential starting point for agile practice rollout is to determine how it will be governed and managed. An appropriate organizational structure is necessary. A general scheme I've found useful is shown in Figure 5.9.

    As illustrated in Figure 5.8, the rollout of agile practices is itself viewed as a project that requires a project manager overseeing areas of strategy, methods, tools, organizational improvement, and piloting. The context and broader vision is provided by an executive steering committee to align the rollout with the broader company-wide activities, a design authority to govern how the agile practices impact existing operational rules and practices within the enterprise software delivery organization, and a reference group composed of the senior practitioners that both provide direct feedback on day-to-day issues and act as champions for the change across the organization.

    We see this general scheme for governance enacted in different ways, depending on the context of use. For example, in an agile delivery rollout with a large financial services company, the goal was to move the enterprise software delivery organization of almost two thousand people to adopt agile practices over a two-year period. This represented a significant shift in mindset, techniques, and delivery practices. While careful attention was placed on each aspect of this governance structure, particular attention was given to building early pilot successes, creating a small team

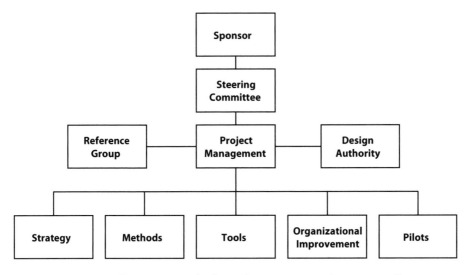

Figure 5.9 *A general organizational scheme for governing agile practice rollout*

of high-profile champions as a reference group, and investing significantly in organizational improvement through education and coaching.

- *Implement the rollout as a series of "waves of change" around carefully selected pilot projects.* To effectively make changes, you need an approach that encourages early success and builds incrementally toward broader institutionalization of those successful changes. To support this approach to scaling agile practice adoption, two techniques are particularly important.

  The first technique structures change in "streams" and delivers that change in "waves." That is, we typically see a set of areas where we must act to support agile practice rollout. Then we identify some of these areas as essential to scale agile delivery rollout. For example, in a large enterprise software delivery organization, we may choose to focus on areas such as education, methods, tooling, and infrastructure as they relate to agile practices. Each area will have different levels of maturity and different needs. Hence we consider these the streams of effort, and we plan change as a series of waves of change that package a number of activities in each stream aimed at increasing the capabilities and maturity in these areas.

  The second technique for agile delivery rollout defines a customized piloting scheme to optimize early success and provide a clear focus on major organizational characteristics. For example, in one recent agile delivery rollout scenario, we created a questionnaire that captured pilot project selection criteria in a simple, usable form. This was the basis for prioritizing potential projects for inclusion in pilot activities based on the organization's needs and context. In addition to focusing on characteristics such as project size and scope, the questionnaire paid particular attention to areas believed to be high risk for broader rollout of agile delivery in the organization. This ensured the following:

  ○ At least one pilot project included some degree of globally distributed team members.

  ○ At least one pilot project included multiple teams in a team-of-teams structure.

  ○ At least one pilot project involved cooperation with one or more internal or external vendors.

  ○ The pilot projects addressed different platform technologies in use across mainframe and distributed systems.

  ○ The pilot projects addressed different kinds of project styles (e.g., new development, extension of existing systems, business improvement tasks, maintenance and fixes).

- *Focus attention on improving practices.* In several different agile delivery rollout scenarios, we placed a great deal of effort on identifying and prioritizing the practices that are important to the organization. Agile delivery rollout efforts experience significant roadblocks when they become too focused on specific techniques and tools, rather than staying centered on improving the practices important to the organization. It's far too easy to place all the attention on the details of implementing a technique or deploying a new tool, thus losing track of the overall practice improvement that it's intended to support.

  A simple practice framework can help here, as illustrated in Figure 5.10. Here we see a core set of agile practices in the center, with several categories of additional practices surrounding it. I've found that early

Figure 5.10 *A practice framework for adoption of agile delivery*

efforts must address the core practices to gain a shared understanding and a common approach in those areas. Without that, a lot of adoption and rollout efforts will prove very inefficient. For example, for an organization that lacks experience in iterative delivery techniques, the jump to an evolutionary approach is a large one. It will demand a great deal of attention and support. Similarly, it's very difficult to increase flexibility in delivery when there is no attention to bringing the team together or when integration and test activities are relegated to a second-class status.

In this practice framework, it is essential to define and agree upon the key elements of the practice with the organization and place appropriate priority and measures on improvement. I've found that we need to explicitly define several dimensions of each practice:

○ *Key concepts.* What does this practice mean, and how should it be interpreted in the context of this organization?

○ *Work products.* Which artifacts are critical for this practice, and how will they be created and maintained?

○ *Tasks.* What are the most important activities and use cases for the practice?

○ *Guidance.* What best practice advice and heuristics are useful for the practice?

○ *Measurements.* What are the key measures for this practice, what is the current baseline, and what benchmarks can be used to assess current status in this practice?

○ *Tool mentors.* How can automation be applied and which tools have been configured to support this practice?

Based on this approach, the organization can create priorities around the areas for improvement. Practices are adopted incrementally based on a measured plan for improvement that is well understood across the organization.

• *Adopt a clear and automated set of performance metrics.* It is natural that an agile delivery adoption approach is supported by metrics and measures that help to understand status and progress against a series of objectives. However, defining and measuring agile adoption remains a particularly challenging task in rolling out these approaches at scale.

The area of metrics and measures is an important and complicated challenge for any enterprise software delivery effort. Much attention has been turned to this topic in recent years, due to the greater pressures for cost control and efficiency in enterprise software delivery. A great deal can be applied from this work in the context of agile delivery roll-out. However, in practice, the most critical first steps are simply to sort out what *could* potentially be measured, what *can* actually be measured, and what *is readily* measured. Too often, we see agile delivery adoption programs that include sophisticated measuring schemes for an organization that has little history or context for those measures. Or we see extensive manual efforts to gather data from unreliable sources that produce dashboards of information for decision making highlighting trends of questionable validity. The result is that such schemes become abused and discredited.

Instead, a much more pragmatic approach to agile delivery adoption is usually more effective. An example, illustrated in Figure 5.11, shows a simple three-level measurement approach used with one large banking organization to understand their agile delivery adoption.

As illustrated in Figure 5.11, the goal of the agile delivery adoption scheme was to address three basic questions:

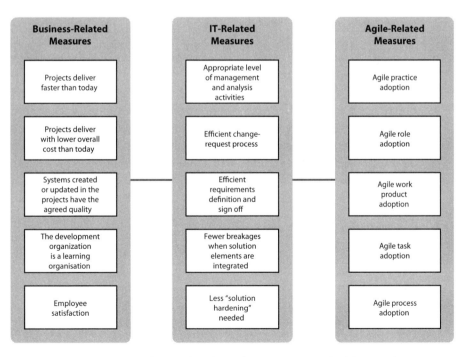

Figure 5.11 *An example of a simple scheme for measuring agile delivery adoption*

o *Are we meeting the business objectives?* The original business objectives for the agile delivery program raised expectations with executive management that the enterprise software delivery organization would be faster, cheaper, and better. Simple quantitative measures were agreed upon with those managers to understand those objectives and manage their expectations from the program.

o *Are we seeing the benefits in software delivery we expected?* Within the enterprise software delivery organization, KPIs gave a high-level view of the status and progress. The agile delivery adoption program was aligned with those KPIs to ensure that its contribution was well understood.

o *Are we agile?* Individuals and teams in the organization who were already involved in some agile project efforts had their own view of what they wanted from the agile delivery program. Continual assessment through surveys and qualitative approaches took place to understand how the agile delivery program was proceeding.

Through these kinds of approaches, a constant monitoring of the health of the agile delivery program takes place. These measurements can be used as the basis for early decision making, and they provide visibility into the program for all those involved.

- *Effectively educate and support different roles.* Any major change in the enterprise software delivery organization must be supported with education, training, and ongoing support (via coaches or consultants).[7] Many approaches are possible: using online- or classroom-based techniques, through specific coaching sessions or in-project support, employing external consultants or using in-house experts, and so on. Each organization will make its own choices based on its context and experiences.

  However, from recent agile delivery projects I've been involved in, I highlight two often overlooked dimensions that I believe provide value in this context:

  o *Vary the education and training by role.* Perhaps this seems obvious, but I've found that careful attention to the needs of certain roles within the organization is required. For example, in one situation, agile practice training was very advanced for practitioners and was under way for project managers, but the resistance to supporting large-scale

---

7. Here I also would like to emphasize the distinction between education (as a way to inform and understand) and training (as a way to change practices). Both are important, but they are different activities.

rollout was coming from a lack of executive management understanding. Little attention had been paid to discussing agile practices adoption with key personnel in critical functions such as contract management, human resources, and financial planning. Basic understanding of agile approaches for these roles was important because the broad adoption of agile practices was starting to have an impact on individual performance assessment, hiring decisions, and the approach to defining contracts between departments.

- ○ *Vary the education and training by project type.* In many enterprise software delivery organizations, we see clear distinctions among project categories, such as maintenance projects, mainframe projects, and online channel projects. While a core set of education and coaching may be broadly appropriate, there will undoubtedly be requirements for specific topics to be addressed with different people working in these project categories. For example, in one enterprise software delivery organization I worked with, the mainframe software maintenance project teams significantly resisted agile practice adoption. Closer investigation showed that the external consultants providing education and support for those teams were very skilled in the latest agile methods for web-based systems but had very little background, understanding, or experience in the challenges of maintaining business mission-critical applications on mainframes. The mismatch of cultures led to very poor results.

5.4 Examples of Large-Scale Agile Adoption

Any large-scale adoption effort requires careful attention to planning, management, and delivery. This is particularly the case with the introduction of agile delivery practices. While there is a growing demand and grassroots movement in many delivery teams to adopt agile approaches, some organizations have the perception that introducing these techniques in enterprise software delivery contexts will reduce their ability to govern and manage the delivery of systems.

Here I'll provide two examples of large-scale adoption of agile practices taken from real-world experiences. For these examples, I've steered away from the usual agile case studies that focus on how small teams of coders have seen success using agile methods such as Scrum and XP. Many such examples can be found in the available literature. Rather, I focus on enterprise software delivery issues where agile approaches have been adapted within software supply chain management and software factory contexts. In addition, two further detailed case studies with significant attention to enterprise-scale agile delivery can be found in later chapters of this book.

5.4.1 Agile Supply Chain Management at ABC Bank

ABC Bank is a large worldwide financial institution with a diverse, widely distributed IT organization. In an attempt to efficiently manage rapid growth at ABC Bank, the IT organization created substantial software delivery centers for major parts of its software development and delivery activities and located those software centers in Latin America, Europe, and Asia. This approach was aimed at reducing fixed IT costs and increasing flexibility to adapt to customer demand. While there were benefits, the growth of this model proved challenging for the following reasons:

- *Lack of governance to control project progress.* Across the organization, different teams were using different governance mechanisms, not connected, with progress measured during informal weekly meetings.

- *Poor communication due to different time zones and locations and cultural and political differences.* Not all team members were fluent in English, and due to different time zones, many discussions were inconclusive or had to be postponed for days.

- *Inadequate planning and change management procedures.* Projects were subcontracted using a fixed-price model, and there was little flexibility to negotiate changes or modify initial planning.

- *Mismatches between user expectations and the real outcomes.* End users were not involved in requirement analysis or reviews, and there were many rejected requests and conflicts across the main stakeholders.

- *Poor infrastructure for remote access and lack of a common asset repository.* Distributed teams were not notified when new versions of the common architecture framework were released, and a lot of rework had to be done to adapt these changes at the last minute.

- *Unclear information sharing and privacy rules.* Integrating components from different providers raised many issues with privacy and security, often as a result of unclear ownership for cross-provider activities.

To recover from this situation, ABC Bank explicitly focused on looking at this distributed organization from the perspective of an agile supply chain. The organization underwent changes to its development processes and infrastructure, and a common collaborative delivery environment to improve communication and coordination across the supply chain was implemented. The first wave of changes introduced a set of agile practices that would improve flexibility and visibility into how each of the distributed centers contributed to the overall supply chain. This required changes in several areas:

- *Organizational changes* took the form of the creation of a new software factories project office in charge of negotiating and managing subcontracted projects.

- A *common infrastructure* was established based on a central repository, accessed from external locations using standard Internet connection protocols. This central repository was used to share and integrate information across the teams.

- *Governance dashboards* produced data and reports that showed the progress of individuals, teams, and software delivery centers to assess their performance. This central governance dashboard was updated automatically with project information in real time, allowing the enterprise to keep external developments under control and to reduce meeting and travel costs.

- *Planning and change management processes* were adapted to augment traditional waterfall software development processes with agile techniques (based on Scrum) to enable faster response to changing demands.

- *Confidentiality* was addressed by identifying every critical private data element that the company had, isolating it from subcontractor access, and explicitly granting permissions for common assets to be shared with subcontractors via a central register of shared artifacts (e.g., common architecture components).

Figure 5.12 shows a view of a management dashboard derived from those in use at ABC Bank. Progress in each of the different delivery centers can be shown in such dashboards to allow more efficient, flexible decision making about resource allocation, work item reprioritization, and redistribution between the bank's different delivery centers around the world.

Implementing these agile management changes was not easy and caused political and technical conflicts inside ABC Bank and across the supply chain. However, as a result of this transformation, the enterprise was able to adapt to the new software delivery model and to benefit from the reduction of fixed costs and increased flexibility into their development activities across their delivery centers. Thanks to the governance dashboard, they are now able to measure the status and progress of each delivery center, penalizing or terminating the contracts of those with less-efficient delivery.

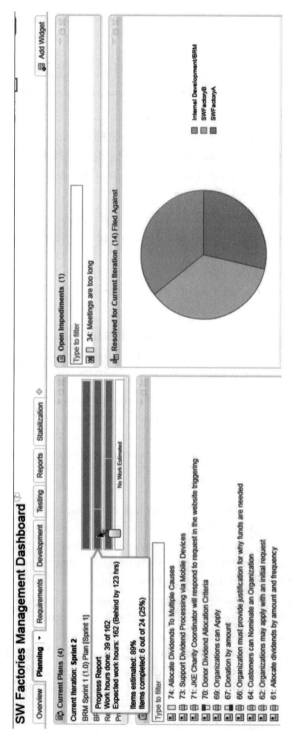

Figure 5.12 *Software factories governance dashboard*

5.4.2 Enterprise Agile Testing Services at XYZ

XYZ is a European software services and consulting company, specializing in software development and testing services. Among the company's most important concerns are efficiency and quality of delivered services and a repeatable lean approach to software delivery. To that end, XYZ has standardized many key practices and has obtained a capability maturity model integration (CMMI) level 3 certification.

As part of its global strategy, XYZ offers expertise and services in software testing and provides a catalog of services to its customers, as follows:

- Services to assure the quality of the work-products generated in each phase of the software development life cycle, reducing defects across phases

- Providing the role of facilitator between the different actors in the quality assurance (QA) process to objectively assess quality practices and review project milestones

- Advising on quality processes and practices, including assessing deliverables and designing appropriate test and support processes to increase quality

The total quality focus of XYZ's engineering and QA teams encourages agile practices throughout the software life cycle, aligned with the rules and constraints associated with CMMI. An agile software delivery approach is important for XYZ because it encourages the early project involvement of testers and other quality-focused roles, highlights the transparency of delivery progress with well-defined metrics, and makes quality management a high priority throughout the project life cycle.

To realize its enterprise agile approach to testing services, XYZ decided to set up several large European delivery centers and adopt a software factory delivery model for its quality-focused services. It refers to these as *agile software testing factories*.

In line with traditional agile principles, the basis for its agile software test factories is an infrastructure supporting close cooperation across the software testing teams and an automation framework that efficiently executes test-driven scripts. Underlying this is a supporting foundation of software configuration management, build management and continuous integration practices, and agile project management. These core capabilities are fully integrated with specific testing services to manage the test plans, execute tests, and assess test coverage in light of the project requirements.

A streamlined agile software testing factory infrastructure is the cornerstone of the XYZ approach. This solution, augmented with additional tools for developers or test engineers in their day-to-day work, offers the integrated capabilities that ensure the delivery of quality solutions to XYZ's clients in an agile delivery approach aimed at the following goals:

- Close ongoing cooperation with the client

- Transparency in the testing process

- Continuous improvements to delivered quality in a series of short increments

As illustrated in Figure 5.13, the testing factory services were automated by a suite of integrated tools, covering several process areas of CMMI. The need for supporting geographically distributed teams and roles (project management office [PMO]), test manager, test engineers, etc.) was also critical. A series of customized processes were designed, resulting in the following:

- *Templates* to specify test cases and test scripts to define automated or manual tests

- *Automation* of building and continuous integration process and regression testing or other quality standards, such as those encouraged by CMMI

- *Visual dashboards* to monitor the state of the projects, delayed activities, open versus closed defects, metrics of coverage, productivity of the team, and so on

Figure 5.14 shows an example agile software testing dashboard that is used to share testing progress with the client organization, provide basic feedback on progress and results, and ensure that the testing teams all share a common understanding of the current testing project status.

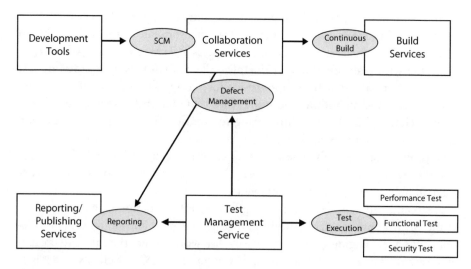

Figure 5.13 *A simplified view of the agile testing factory solution architecture*

Figure 5.14 *A dashboard from XYZ's software test factory*

In summary, we see that an enterprise agile approach to testing and quality is a critical part of XYZ's strategy. As a result of this initiative, XYZ has successfully increased the efficiency of their processes, improving the productivity of their key testing factory in Europe. This solution is now being introduced at test factories across the XYZ organization.

5.5 Conclusions

The need for greater flexibility and the increased pressure on time to market are driving many organizations toward development techniques that optimize their team interactions and their connection with stakeholders. The resulting agile development approaches are being widely discussed and seeing broad adoption across the software industry.

In this chapter, I provide a broad view of agility as it applies to enterprise software delivery. In particular, I focused on how agility at scale can be realized, providing practical guidance for adapting agility in complex enterprise software delivery organizations. Much more has yet to be experienced, understood, and analyzed to improve the adoption of agile approaches in large-scale enterprise software delivery.

Chapter 6

Software Quality

Chapter Summary

Software quality factors are important early targets for improvement and represent critical indicators of success in global enterprise delivery. I propose a broad view of software quality that encompasses the complete enterprise software delivery life cycle. A particular focus in quality is on testing services; I explore how and why software testing factories are frequently a core element of a global software delivery organization. I observe the following:

- A broad view of quality is critical in applying agile techniques to enterprise-scale delivery organizations.

- A global supply chain view of enterprise software delivery emphasizes the synchronization and hand off points in the supply chain as critical places to assert and verify quality objectives are being met.

- Organizing test activities in well-defined software test factories is an efficient model that offers many benefits to organizations seeking to specialize skills or to outsource noncore services.

- New software testing factory models are emerging that are optimized for globally distributed teams and support flexibility and agility in software delivery approaches.

6.1 Introduction

We're all aware of highly public examples of software quality failings, such as those in which businesses have lost millions of euros/dollars, governments have been unable to collect taxes or deliver essential services, and military organizations have exposed damaging information. In extreme cases, software quality failings have led to injury or death. (For an interesting list of well-known software failures, see Charette [60]). Many reports determine the general quality of enterprise software to be low (based on almost any scale you wish to use). The pressure to improve the quality of the delivered systems is ever present.

But quality costs. The evidence shows that the major portion of enterprise software delivery budgets is spent on improving the quality of those delivery systems [61]. Typically this expense accrues during the stages immediately before hand off into production in an attempt to fix errors that have been introduced during the software's earlier design and construction. In fact, the National Institute of Standards and Technology (NIST) reports that as much as "80 percent of development costs [are spent] on identifying and correcting defects."[1]

The costs of fixing poor quality have been analyzed in some detail. We have a wealth of history that tells us that the later we discover an error, the more it costs to fix it. Detailed analyses of a wide variety of systems result in similar findings. As summarized by Capers Jones [2], the cost of fixing a defect increases dramatically throughout the life cycle:

- During coding and unit test activities, it costs $25 per defect.

- While integrating code as part of the build activities, it costs $100 per defect.

- As a result of formal system and acceptance testing activities, it costs $450/defect.

- After delivery to the customer, it costs $16,000/defect.

Consequently, testing serves a critical role in improving software quality. All enterprise software delivery organizations invest in a plethora of testing processes, tooling, and best practices. However, the challenges of delivering quality software systems do not begin or end with testing. Correct functional behavior is simply one way to view a system's quality. We must take a broader view of quality to discover why those systems frequently do not meet the expectations of their users, are difficult to operate, are expensive to change, and cannot adapt to new operating environments.

---

1. www.nist.gov/director/planning/upload/report02-3.pdf

From the perspective of enterprise software delivery, the pressures on quality are intense and the areas requiring attention are numerous. According to one report from the former chief information officer (CIO) of a large insurance company,[2] the main software quality problems in large, multiplatform, multilanguage applications were the following:

- *Lack of documentation.* Few usable documents exist, and they are poorly maintained. This slows down changes and increases errors in making updates to software.

- *A tangle of interconnections.* Complexity is evident in all aspects of how the software operates and interrelates. In the worst cases, no one has a complete view of some of the key software solutions in production.

- *Inadequacy of testing.* Testing is often initiated too late in the cycle and is incomplete in its coverage. Also, the software solutions are becoming so complex that it's impossible to understand how to test them adequately.

- *Lack of quality measures.* Maturity in measuring quality remains very low. Current simple measures of quality are inadequate and misleading.

- *Lack of expertise across application silos.* As a consequence of system complexity, few people understand how the software solutions interoperate, how changes to them affect the business, and where investments in improving them will deliver the most benefit.

Complicating the situation still further is the move toward globally distributed and organizationally distributed delivery of enterprise software solutions. As teams cooperate across geographic and organizational boundaries, the challenges for ensuring high quality increase. For example, long distances between teams make some technologies for coordination unusable due to latency and bandwidth issues. Cultural and language differences make shared understanding of key concepts unreliable, and legal and contractual barriers make transparency and visibility into some key delivery processes impossible.

As a result of this rather damning view of software quality in enterprise software delivery, many organizations are making significant efforts to view quality differently and make improvements. In this chapter, I examine software quality in the context of global enterprise software delivery organizations involved in complex supply chains. After discussing a broader look at

---

2. Comments from Paul Camille Bentz, former CIO at AGF-Allianz and Paribas, as reported in "Boosting Software Quality in Insurance IT Systems," IT-Expert report, March 2010, distributed by CAST Software.

software quality, I focus on the challenges of testing, introduce the concept of the software testing factory, and highlight specific concerns in the area of security. I conclude with some real-world examples to illustrate these ideas more concretely.

6.2 A Broader View of Software Quality

While most attention is focused on testing activities, a broader view of software quality is essential to address the concerns typical of today's enterprise software delivery organizations. If we examine where and how errors occur in enterprise software, we see that there is an important distinction that must be made between where errors are *injected* and where they are *found*.

As shown in Figure 6.1, an examination of data from a large number of enterprise software delivery projects directly contrasts where errors are injected into the software with where they are found. Almost two thirds of the errors are a result of requirements and design problems, misunderstandings, and omissions, while more than 80 percent of error discovery occurs in acceptance testing or once the software is placed into production.

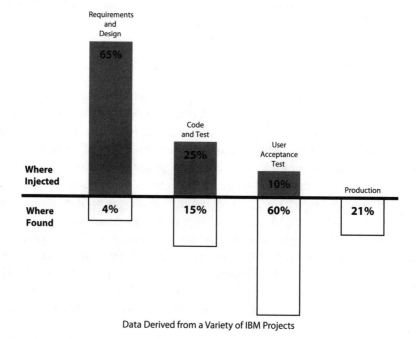

Data Derived from a Variety of IBM Projects

Figure 6.1 *A comparison between fault injection and fault discovery (derived from data from a variety of IBM project experiences)*

These data lead to the conclusion that a priority in making software quality improvements should be to increase investment in techniques that reduce early fault injection, while optimizing the later life-cycle activities of user acceptance testing and postproduction that help identify, communicate, and repair the errors found. Four primary approaches to achieve these improvements prove effective:

- *Automating repetitive tasks within the enterprise software delivery life cycle, thus saving labor costs.* Initial attention is on later stages of the life cycle, where most of the costs occur. Focus areas are build automation, test automation, and configuration management.

- *Discovering more defects earlier in the life cycle, thus reducing the repair costs.* Often the problems occur as a result of simple misunderstandings, poorly communicated changes, and lack of consistency in applying checks. Focus areas are requirements management, code scanning, and formal modeling and analysis.

- *Closer alignment between customers, business analysts, and engineers.* Cooperation across these different disciplines is frequently weak, with separate approaches to information management and governance. Focus areas are greater stakeholder involvement in all aspects of projects, richer requirements elicitation and analysis, early prototyping, and business process simulation.

- *Lowering the risk and decreasing the variance of software projects.* Much of the chaos and frustration in enterprise software delivery starts with poor estimates, little attention to ongoing risk management, and wide variance in measurements. Focus areas are expanded project management and tracking, software process standardization, consolidated reporting and business intelligence, and reusable asset libraries.

By investing in these focus areas organizations, we can achieve improvements in enterprise software delivery quality. Equally important is to take an end-to-end view of quality to optimize quality across the life cycle.

6.2.1 End-to-End Quality Management

An end-to-end view of software quality requires the institutionalization of common processes, methods, and tools across an enterprise software delivery organization. Consistency in key communication and collaboration activities, supported by objective metrics, helps to increase return on investment across a project portfolio. This benefit is mostly visible during the testing activities, where costs are highest and where value to the organization can be demonstrated more quickly through earlier release of higher quality software.

Confirmed in several studies, this end-to-end approach is the basis of improvement frameworks such as the Software Engineering Institute's (SEI) capability maturity model integration (CMMI) activity, which advocates a series of levels of maturity that improve efficiency and increase predictability. Much of the attention with the use of CMMI has been focused on the steps necessary to achieve these so-called levels of maturity. But in looking at results from large enterprise software delivery organizations applying CMMI, we see that visible benefits from this improvement in maturity are derived from the end-to-end quality view that the CMMI promotes. We've often seen poor estimation and planning lead to unrealistic targets that increase project pressure, encourage shortcuts, and lead to mistakes. The result is extensive rework, increasing the pressure on the compressed project schedule. Better estimation and planning practices coupled with improved change management promoted by the CMMI can result in a big reduction in this unnecessary rework. Enterprise software delivery organizations categorized as CMMI level 1 have reported that rework can constitute up to 50 percent of their development effort. By achieving higher levels of maturity, projects set better expectations on the project schedule, detect schedule slippages much earlier, and hence avoid producing excessive defects when projects are racing to complete tasks with unrealistic timescales and resources. With increased maturity comes an increase in the knowledge base and experience of the organization, further improving planning and estimation. Once automation of key activities is introduced, the benefits of consistency and visibility are magnified, and the importance of a broad software quality view becomes apparent.

Figure 6.2 illustrates the key activities across the enterprise software delivery life cycle that directly contribute to improved software quality. While each activity individually provides value, the importance of the end-to-end view is the recognition, support, and automation for connecting these activities to provide a more holistic approach to software quality.

6.2.2 Assessing the Health of Enterprise Software Delivery

At certain points in time in the lifetime of an enterprise system, an assessment of the health of the enterprise system is necessary. This necessity may be the result of some discrete event (e.g., a major system failure, a new project proposal with significant impact on existing systems, or a decision whether to retire an existing system). But it may also be the result of an accumulation of experience that shows a negative trend in the enterprise system (e.g., too much effort

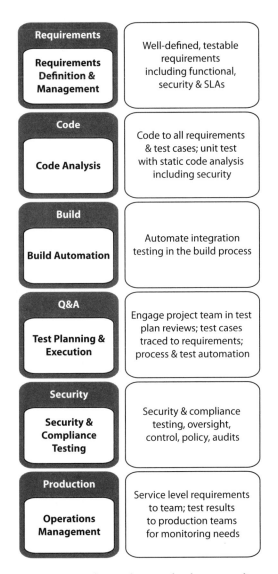

Figure 6.2 *Key activities in an end-to-end view of software quality*

to maintain, unpredictable system behavior). Typically at these times it's necessary to perform some form of health assessment on the enterprise software system to gain a more accurate understanding of its current status.

For assessment of large codebases, automated analysis techniques are possible, where code scanning and analysis algorithms execute across that codebase and provide data concerning the code size (e.g., lines of code, function points, and components), complexity (e.g., code structure, interfaces, and call graphs), and coding style and consistency (e.g., use of common conventions and comments). Many inefficient and problematic coding practices can also be detected and reported.

However, code-level analysis is only one dimension of an enterprise system's health. Broader analyses of the system are also possible. For example, several techniques pioneered at SEI allow organizations to perform software risk analyses [62] and software architecture assessments on existing enterprise systems [63]. In these approaches, a structured breakdown of quality attributes is provided that serves as a summary of the primary characteristics of the systems and software that contribute to the overall system health. Then a series of questions is defined that help to extract data that is converted into meaningful indicators of the current status of each quality attribute. Further insights are possible by comparing data obtained from analyses across several similar systems. Such approaches can offer important diagnostic techniques in maintaining the quality of large-scale systems.

As illustrated in Figure 6.3, these diagnostic techniques can aim to uncover different kinds of information that is useful in learning more about the system to inform decision making. Specifically, by focusing on different "quality

Heath Factor	Description	Value
Understandability	Ease with which new team members can become productive with this application	Helps when recruiting new people, moving applications to new departments, or in preparing to outsource to an external team
Changeability	Effort required to make changes and additions to an application	Improves speed of fix and release of an application, and may be critical in determining reuse or repurposing of an application
Performance	Having a clear understanding of operating parameters and effectiveness in performing key actions	Allows usage of an application to be aligned with the operating characteristics of the application, and helps determine impact when usage needs change
Robustness	Adaptability of an application to failures and errors in its design, use, or operating context	Reduces expense in costly fixes when errors occur, and increases an application's adaptability to new environments
Security	Confidence in the application when subjected to various kinds of misuse or attack	Reduces risks in using the application in mission-critical situations
Size/Complexity	Analysis of the technical dimension of an application based on many factors, including its scope, the difficulty of the domain it covers, the amount of functionality it provides, the range of platfoms on which it operates, and so on	Helps in understanding likely maintenance costs as these typically are largely a factor of size/complexity of an application

Figure 6.3 *Various health dimensions of enterprise software* [3]

---

3. Adapted from *Assessing Application Development Like the Rest of the Business*, CAST Software, 2007.

attributes" or "health factors" of the enterprise system, we can place business value on assessments against the health of those attributes.

While analyzing the health of a specific enterprise system provides useful information, an assessment of the enterprise software delivery organization itself is equally important. In many cases, the quality of the enterprise software is a direct reflection of the organization's activities, practices, skills, and morale. Appropriate assessment methods are needed to understand the organization's health, to relate that to the status of the enterprise software for which it is responsible, and to propose areas on which to focus to see future improvements.

Various questionnaires and assessment techniques are commonly used as the basis for assessing enterprise software delivery organizations. These are based around a set of improvement practice areas and supported by benchmark data to pinpoint where changes are likely to have the most benefit. An example of such an approach is illustrated in Figure 6.4.

Figure 6.4 illustrates a health assessment framework that highlights practice areas for improvement by linking those practice areas to operational objectives aimed at accomplishing business needs. Various metrics and measures can be used on an ongoing basis to ensure that progress moves toward an expected outcome [64].

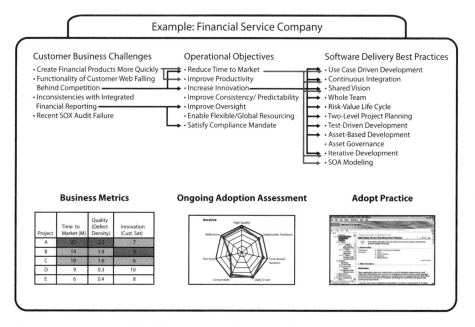

Figure 6.4 *An example health assessment framework for enterprise software delivery organizations*

6.2.3 The Keys to Continuous Software Quality Assurance

In short, software quality in enterprise software delivery requires a broad perspective. Underlying this key theme are the three important elements of enterprise software delivery: collaboration, automation, and visibility:

- *Collaboration.* Streamline communication across the project life cycle, coordinate test planning, and ensure effective communication of changes to all parties.

- *Automation.* Improve operational efficiency in the management of activities and assets, test utilization, coverage, and validation.

- *Visibility.* Improve decision making (particularly in the pressure to move software quickly into production), ensure ongoing analysis and process improvement, and achieve greater predictability based on historical data.

6.3 Quality across the Software Supply Chain

The software supply chain poses additional challenges for managing and improving quality in enterprise software delivery. The nature of the supply chain implies that geographic and organizational distribution of projects must be handled effectively. I'll discuss how these challenges are commonly addressed in the context of the three key dimensions that characterize a supply chain approach: collaboration, automation, and visibility.

6.3.1 Collaboration

Coordination of changes is perhaps the most difficult challenge in managing software quality in a distributed enterprise software delivery supply chain. The geographic and organizational barriers across the distributed team can mean that even the most straightforward change requires a variety of hand offs, approvals, and validations. Without careful attention, the elapsed time between a change request and its execution can easily extend into many days.

Consider the scenario illustrated in Figure 6.5, based on the experience of a global industrial company. Here we see how two distributed groups collaborate in managing change.

In this example, a group in the United States and a group in Europe must interact to plan, manage, and execute the change. The submission of the change request initiates collaboration in the three milestone categories of plans, implementation, and releases. Once there is agreement around the plan, the implementation

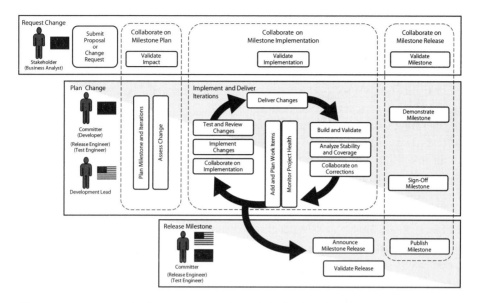

Figure 6.5 *An example change scenario for a globally distributed team*

involves multiple work items that may be spawned by that request, each requiring changes to be enacted, tested, reviewed, and signed off. Finally, the overall request can be tested and signed off, and the completion can be recorded.

Complexities can arise in each step of this relatively straightforward process. Such complexity increases with the likelihood that multiple organizations are involved in the change. Consequently, collaborative procedures and practices must be well defined and universally agreed upon. Automation across these interactions is essential to ensure smooth communication, record relationships between artifacts, govern and control access to intellectual property, log ongoing activities, and so on.

6.3.2 Automation

Many forms of software quality analysis that take place throughout the life cycle of enterprise software delivery involve repeated, exhaustive analyses to verify that the system meets particular needs and objectives. Consistency, rigor, and completeness are essential properties of those software quality approaches. Unfortunately, these are not well handled by manual, human-centric activities. Errors, inconsistencies, and omissions can easily occur. As a result, automation proves particularly important to ensure enterprise software delivery quality.

Furthermore, the processes involved in testing large-scale enterprise systems can be very complex. A great deal of effort is spent understanding aspects such as which components of a system to include in a build, how to assemble that build and deploy it to a set of target machines, which tests should be run against that particular configuration of the system, how to log the results, and so on. For example, consider the process shown in Figure 6.6. This is a simplified view of how one large software services company views the build and test process for its products.

In Figure 6.6, we see that when a new build is initiated, it may require installation and testing on several machines, each configured for a specific combination of operating system and database that the software supports. A large collection of test cases is then run, and the results of that test execution is then delivered. In an initial manual approach to this process, a great deal of time was spent in areas such as installing builds on machines (several hours per build per machine), configuring test hardware and executing all test suites (often several days per test configuration), and collating the results for distribution (several hours). In each of these areas, automated build and test management technologies can be applied. They can reduce the manual effort significantly, so that the whole process can execute in less than one day and can do so repeatedly and accurately.

Again, a distributed supply chain increases the need for such automation. In addition to management of these build and test automation steps, with

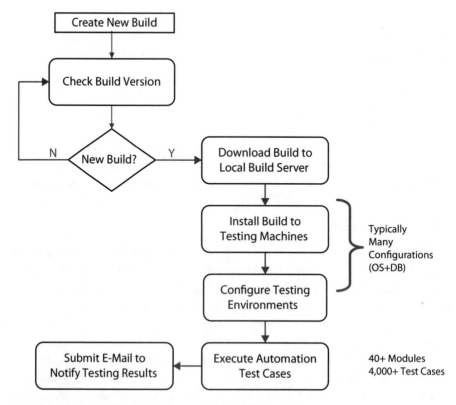

Figure 6.6 *A simplified view of an example build and test process*

organizationally distributed scenarios, additional code scanning, data management, and security analysis aspects are vitally important to maintain confidence in the assembled system and to guarantee essential properties of the delivered results.

6.3.3 Visibility

The broad nature of software quality across the enterprise software delivery life cycle makes obtaining a clear appreciation for the quality status of an enterprise system particularly difficult. Organizations rely on manual reports, log files, and status indicators gathered from a myriad of sources. From these data, they attempt to make an analysis that helps their ongoing decision making. With the complexity of supply chain dynamics, obtaining an accurate real-time picture of progress and status in the software quality of a system becomes even harder.

One interesting approach to software quality management and visibility is to view enterprise software delivery from a business optimization and analytics perspective. This perspective considers the vast array of data generated and maintained across the enterprise software delivery life cycle as a rich source of information that can be analyzed, correlated, and reviewed. A software quality dashboard is one key concrete result of this viewpoint. The various data sources are analyzed, and cross-sections of that data are surfaced in viewlets or portlets that can be used to populate an integrated dashboard displaying that data in a variety of meaningful forms. An illustration of one of such software quality dashboard is shown in Figure 6.7.

The example of a software quality dashboard shown in Figure 6.7 is used for tracking and managing an enterprise software system for a commercial software product company. Different kinds of software quality information are displayed in an easily understandable form, including defect arrival rates (categorized in different ways), defect fix latency, test coverage against requirements, and planned versus actual defect discovery by life-cycle phase. Such dashboards greatly increase management visibility into the software quality process and help managers utilize resources to fix emerging failure patterns before they become overwhelming.

6.4 Software Testing Factories

The changing pressures on enterprise software delivery have led to many advances in software delivery approaches. Important changes have taken place in areas such as agile development, lean thinking, and model-driven code generation. But in the area of software quality, the basic approaches to software testing have been slower to evolve. The primary approach remains a traditional model that involves dedicating large numbers of full-time testing staff to projects,

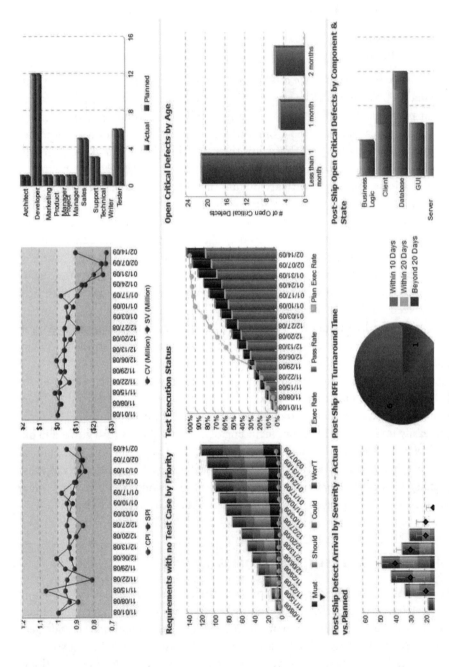

Figure 6.7 *An example software quality dashboard*

use of expensive enterprise testing tools, acquisition of large amounts of infra-structure to validate all possible deployment configurations, and so on. More recently, however, organizations have made efforts to curtail the heavy expense and cyclic nature of many of the testing and quality management aspects. Initial approaches have involved pooling testing staff and resources across collections of projects and departments to share costs and smooth the resource loading on test teams. More recently, organizations have broadened this approach to allow variable staffing, using specialist quality assurance (QA) consulting companies to supply talented and experienced help for specialized needs and to augment resources during peak periods.

The natural extension of these approaches is to separate large parts of the test and quality management process into a more factory-oriented model: the software testing factory. The goal of a software testing factory is to provide a highly organized facility that performs various tests using standardized frame-works and processes with well-trained test professionals. The scope and deliv-ery of those testing capabilities can vary based on several factors. It's helpful to distinguish between different kinds of specialized software testing factories and the more general software testing factories. As illustrated in Figure 6.8, a

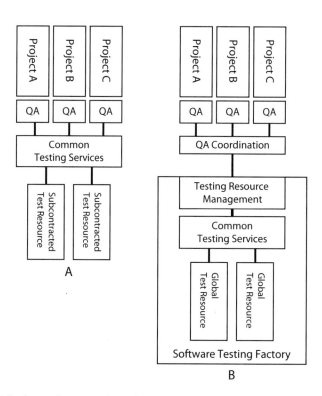

Figure 6.8 *The basic elements of a software testing factory*

software testing factory identifies and externalizes common testing capabilities and practices with the goal of optimizing their effective use.

As shown in diagram A on the left side of Figure 6.8, a typical enterprise software delivery organization executes a number of projects, each investing in its own specialized QA capabilities. Quite often, some level of common testing infrastructure and services may be pooled across projects, and subcontractor resources may be used to augment capacity or to provide specialized skills. However, a natural evolution of this approach in many organizations, shown in diagram B on the right side of Figure 6.8, is to separate testing services in a (semi-)independent unit. This allows the software testing factory to optimize its resource usage and to apply a global sourcing strategy for maximum flexibility in cost and capacity planning. It also creates the possibility for outsourcing the software testing factory in part or in whole.

In many organizations, the software testing factory offers specialized services for specific kinds of testing, analysis, or validation. These specialized software testing factories focus on several areas:

- Performance and load testing (using preconfigured dedicated server farms)

- Security testing (running a battery of security scans and ensuring frequent updates to include checks for the latest reported operating system flaws and hacker trends)

- Compliance testing (providing analyses and certifications of compliance against government and industry standards)

Operationally, the software testing factory collaborates with the individual projects to perform work on their behalf. An example of a specialized software testing factory is shown in Figure 6.9.

Figure 6.9 depicts the operational workflow for a specialized software testing factory for a global system integrator (SI). The SI has created several specialized software testing factories for different kinds of testing needs. One of these, illustrated in Figure 6.9, serves a large group of clients who are deploying enterprise solutions based on the SAP packaged applications. Such packaged applications are large, complicated enterprise systems, and they play a core function in an organization. These applications contain a large number of features, divided into a number of business areas. Typically such packaged applications are heavily customized and extended during deployment, and they must be carefully tested and validated before their release into production. However, deep, specialized skills are frequently needed to validate the correct operation of these packaged applications. Such skills are expensive and difficult to find. In this context, a specialized software testing factory approach becomes very attractive.

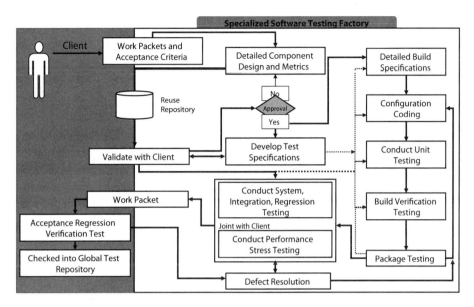

Figure 6.9 *An example operational workflow for a specialized software testing factory*

In this example of a specialized software testing factory, the client of the SI and the software testing factory agree to a set of work packets and acceptance criteria to initiate the complete testing process. The software testing factory executes a complete set of tests on the system and returns the results to the client for their review.

While many kinds of specialized software testing factories have emerged to meet different needs, the concept of a specialized software testing factory is still expanding. Hosting a complete virtualized testing facility is now possible, driven by greater availability of high-bandwidth networks, cheap data storage, and fast servers. The result is the emergence of general software testing factories. These can perform wide varieties of software quality functions as services to client organizations. The advantages they offer to their clients is that they create specialized work centers where high levels of particular testing skills are matured, they maintain extensive databases of analytical data to improve the quality of their testing, and they invest in research to advance their testing practices to be more predictive, accurate, and efficient.

From an organizational and financial viewpoint, software testing factories are being created within organizations as a way to pool costs across a series of departments and lines of business. Additionally, a separate testing industry is also emerging in which SIs and third-party companies are creating independent software testing factory offerings that can be used by a variety of clients. Furthermore, costs can be further reduced by locating software testing factories in locations where there is greater access to skills and lower labor rates. Consequently, many organizations have made major investments in software quality improvements by deploying global software testing factories in locations such as India, China, and Latin America.

As illustrated in Figure 6.10, the use of independent software testing factories provides the opportunity to create different business models for the delivery of testing services. Initially, the role of software testing factories was viewed from a staff-augmentation approach based on reducing costs. Now that role is evolving and software testing factories are viewed as centers of excellence in important areas of software quality delivery. Ultimately, the evolution of the role of the software testing factory is toward a utility view of testing as a service that can be readily acquired on a pay-per-usage model or a results-based scheme.

6.5 Security

The increasing importance and visibility of enterprise software has also raised the expectations on those systems with regard to security, privacy, and compliance. In particular, a raft of government legislation in recent years now demands that enterprise software does not just work correctly but that it does so without making itself vulnerable to illegal access and that it can provide proof that good practices were followed in its development and delivery. While a full analysis of the implications of these demands on enterprise systems delivery is outside of the scope of this book, I highlight two important areas: (1) code scanning and (2) web access and compliance testing.

6.5.1 Code Scanning

There is a long history of code scanning solutions that can be used to improve quality in enterprise software (e.g., see [65,66]). With such approaches, sets of

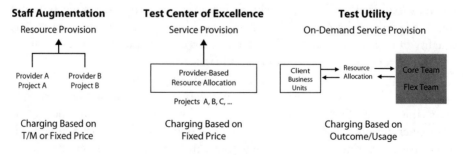

Figure 6.10 *Evolution of the software testing factory*

rules encapsulate mandatory checks or best practices and can be run periodically (e.g., at the end of specific phases or on every code check-in to the source code repository). Different forms of scanning and code analysis can be applied:

- *Code reviews.* These analyze the code to ensure compliance to coding best practices, to ensure adherence to well-known design principles, or for common performance patterns. They also may look for specific aspects of importance to some systems, such as code globalization.

- *Structural analyses.* These examine the code using pattern analysis to enforce good coding patterns and to highlight poor practices (e.g., interclass dependency, cyclical dependencies, hubs).

- *Software metrics reviews.* These gather information about the code, including core sizing (counting lines of code), complexity metrics, and more complex dependency and maintainability metrics.

- *Data flow analyses.* These look for errors in coding logic that lead to resource leaks, memory leaks, and mismanagement of user-interface objects.

6.5.2 Web Access and Compliance Testing

An important addition to the categories of code analysis that are required today involves ensuring that web-facing applications meet web compliance standards and cannot be compromised. With the growing importance of Internet-based access to enterprise software, ensuring software quality must include additional analysis of web-facing systems for compliance and security based on best practices, regulatory requirements, and internal organizational policies [67]. At least three areas are critical:

- Web quality testing to ensure that web-facing functionality operates effectively (e.g., in multiple browser technologies or on handheld devices) and delivers a positive user experience

- Web privacy testing to meet regulatory compliance standards that are in place in many domains (e.g., HIPPA, COPPA, SOX, Safe Harbor).

- Web accessibility testing to ensure websites are available to those with disabilities and comply with regulations and best practices for ease of use to all potential users.

The challenges in these areas are particularly difficult to address in software supply chain delivery models [68]. These regulations and best practices are complex to understand and interpret, have many ramifications on software development and delivery, and can be very dynamic in nature. Many organizations now have chief security officers dedicated to defining the security policies for the enterprise software delivery organizations and interpreting how those policies will be enacted and enforced.

In multiorganizational approaches to enterprise software delivery (e.g., where some aspects of the software development have been outsourced) there must be a clear agreement on how all organizations will operate with regard to security in delivery of those systems. Enforcing security across the delivered systems remains a very difficult challenge, where technology aspects must align with complex political and legal demands. This is an active area of ongoing discussion and debate in most enterprise software delivery organizations.

6.6 Conclusions

Enterprise software delivery organizations are challenged with balancing the need for delivery of quality software with their goals for efficiency and time to market. This chapter highlights a number of key dimensions of this challenge with respect to industrialization of enterprise software delivery. In particular, I emphasized that industrialized approaches improve quality through their focus on the following:

- Automation of repetitive costs to save labor costs

- Earlier identification of defects to remove them from expensive late-stage repair cycles

- Improved communication across delivery teams and between business and delivery groups

- Repeatable use of common components and processes to improve predictability

Chapter 7

Governance, Measurement, and Metrics

Chapter Summary

I review governance, measurement, and metrics topics from the perspective of the global software supply chain. I discuss traditional metrics and measurement approaches, and I focus on the question of effective governance for globally distributed enterprise software delivery teams. I draw the following conclusions:

- Traditional software metrics and measures are a useful starting point for governing the global software delivery process but are insufficient.

- Managing the global software supply chain has required a new measurement focus that is particularly explicit in outsourcing scenarios where both outsourcers and outsourcees have developed new ways to evaluate and track performance.

- Dashboards summarizing critical measures, often correlated across teams or displaying historical trends, are an essential tool for governing the global enterprise.

7.1 Introduction

Success in enterprise software delivery requires effective management across the enterprise software delivery organization and across the entire enterprise software supply chain. Effective management ensures that the organization understands how it uses its resources, enables it to report effectively on its status against agreed targets, and guides coordination of the network of interconnected activities toward a common purpose [21].

A clear governance approach supports management in carrying out its daily tasks. Two aspects of governance are particularly important [68]:

- Establishing chains of responsibility, authority, and communication

- Establishing measurement, policies, standards, and control mechanisms to enable people to carry out their roles and responsibilities

The need for good governance stems from the need for organizations to make effective decisions and communicate them appropriately. Whether the decisions are large in importance and broad in scope (such as initiating a major improvement program across the organization) or more confined (such as approving a software component upgrade for release into production), the organization must have clear approaches for making decisions and implementing structures that support better decisions going forward.

At the heart of any management approach is information with which to govern and make decisions. The information, drawn from many sources, supplies a basis for understanding where the organization currently stands, how it got there, and what steps can be taken to move forward. As illustrated in Figure 7.1, governance of the enterprise software delivery organization involves using information such as performance measures to compare the organization's current activities with the planned objectives and to make any necessary adjustments to bring those activities into line.

Any measures and metrics approach in enterprise software delivery entails a clear understanding of the economic basis for the activities of software development and delivery. This domain has received some attention over the past years, notably with the work of Barry Boehm [20] in the context of traditional waterfall-style projects. More recent work by Walker Royce [69,70] has extended Boehm's ideas into the areas of iterative and agile delivery practices, providing a significant basis for considering measurement-based governance approaches in a global software supply chain.

In this chapter, I explore key aspects of the governance of enterprise software delivery. I begin by considering which measurements and metrics are useful,

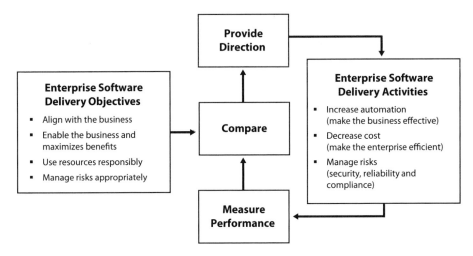

Figure 7.1 *Key elements of governance in enterprise software delivery*

and I discuss how those measures can be used. Providing several examples, I then focus on governance and measurement across the software supply chain.

7.2 Measuring Enterprise Software Delivery

All enterprise software delivery organizations define metrics and keep measurements on their status and performance.[1] Drawing from a variety of tools and data sources, the organization maintains dashboards and produces reports that help in running its business. Typically this metrics gathering and analysis scheme involves extracting data from multiple tool repositories to warehouse in a central metrics repository, defining rules and heuristics from different metrics analysis sources, creating different styles of reports appropriate for a number of roles within the organizations, and so on. Each organization differs in terms of the kinds of metrics of value, the ease and frequency with which the data are collected (e.g., how much automation of data collection is used), and the depth of analysis to which the data are subjected.

Figure 7.2 shows a typical situation for enterprise software delivery organizations. In this example, I show the approach to metrics gathering and reporting used in the enterprise software delivery organization for a large insurance company. Here we can see that there are many kinds of data coming

---

1. Intuitively, we define *metrics* to be what we decide to measure and the *measurements* to reflect the values of those metrics for a given context at a particular point in time. However, in this chapter, I use the terms *metrics* and *measurements* rather informally

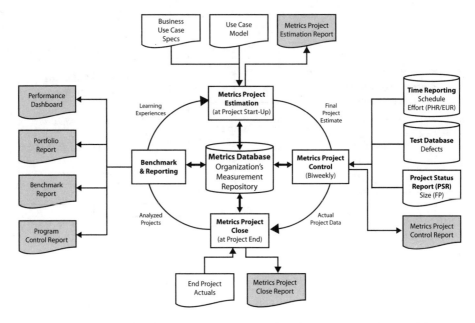

Figure 7.2 *An example of the metrics scheme used in the enterprise software delivery organization for a large insurance company*

from project-monitoring tools containing resource data, billing information, and time-sheet data. These are correlated with information on project plans, software changes, and defect trends. Benchmark data are used to analyze the measures to look for trends and patterns of significance. Finally, a wealth of reports and dashboards extract information and make it visible to users.

Many organizations struggle to implement a meaningful metrics program across their software delivery organization. The heart of the problem in enterprise software delivery is neither in obtaining a list of metrics to measure nor in obtaining data related to those metrics. Rather, the challenge lies in knowing which metrics are more meaningful in a specific context and how to use those metrics to change the way an organization performs it tasks. Here I focus on four areas as they relate to enterprise software delivery:

- What kinds of metrics to keep

- Who can see and use those metrics

- How to evolve the metrics that are kept

- How to use those metrics to improve performance

7.2.1 The Use of Metrics

Everyday we all use a variety of metrics to control and manage our lives. From the amount and type of food we eat, to the programs we watch on television, and many other areas, we use these metrics to make decisions and organize what we do. The same occurs in our working lives. In enterprise software delivery, we find that the metrics we choose to keep say a great deal about what we value and how we govern key processes. I highlight several important aspects of this connection between values and chosen metrics:

- *One cannot control what one cannot measure.* It's often said that without clear measures, the decisions we make are little more than educated guesswork. In other words, when we choose a set of metrics, we are explicitly or implicitly stating which parts of the enterprise software delivery process and organization we wish to control and which we do not.

- A *well-chosen set of metrics clarifies the goals of the organization.* Human nature dictates that the identification of metrics has the effect of galvanizing behavior toward improvement of those metrics; the mere fact that someone chooses to measure something immediately has an impact on what is being measured.[2] Conversely, a poor set of metrics obscures the goals of the organization, particularly when the organization decides to measure a wide range of elements with unclear relationships and interdependencies.

The classic view of metrics is that they are gathered to benchmark and rank individuals in an organization. However, in my experience, this is the *least* useful way to view the role of metrics. I believe a more valuable use of metrics is at the level of the enterprise software delivery organization. Here the metrics can be used not to monitor individual behavior but to improve processes. In this way, the metrics track organizational progress and improvement.

Hence what we measure not only becomes important to the organization but also has important implications on the individuals, teams, and projects in the enterprise software delivery organization being measured. We can separate three different contexts for the measures: private to individuals, private to teams, and public to all. While many metrics are possible, a sample of typical metrics commonly used is illustrated in Figure 7.3 (derived from several sources including [71]).

In Figure 7.3, I illustrate common software metrics for enterprise software delivery organizations at the levels of the individual, team, and organization.

---

2. This is known as the *Hawthorne effect*; see http://en.wikipedia.org/wiki/Hawthorne_effect.

Individual	Work items performed Effort spent on delivered artifacts Productivity Code covered by unit testing How many defects found by unit testing How many defects found by peer reviews
Team	Work items executed or triaged Number of requirements and their delivery status Requirements volatility Amount of software produced Workload distribution Planned and actual delivery milestones Planned and actual staffing variance Number of defects found by integration and system testing Number of defects found by peer reviews Test coverge of code and percentage of tests passed
Organization	Overall project delivery time Planned schedule and actual performance Planned budget and actual performance Variance between planned schedule/resources and actual performance Defect density of shipping software into production Frequency and severity of customer support issues

Figure 7.3 *Examples of software metrics at the individual, team, and organizational levels*

Although these metrics are important indicators to the organization, they must be handled with care with respect to their use, particularly across the three levels. Note that in some senses, data may be considered private within that level:

- *Private to individuals.* Some kinds of measures can be used by individuals to monitor their own personal performance but may be open to misinterpretation when used externally. For example, there is controversy over how we measure individual productivity within enterprise software delivery organizations and how such data should be used. It's very reasonable, for instance, to create daily reports for everyone in the organization on the work items handled, source lines of code changed, e-mail messages sent, and so on. However, direct interpretation of these data to compare individuals may be misleading, as the context for each individual's activities can vary significantly.

- *Private to teams.* Team progress and status must be clearly monitored to optimize the success of a project. Often teams will have a good shared understanding of those metrics that are most meaningful to them and help them plan more effectively. Those metrics may have meaning within a team sharing the same objectives and within the same working context;

however, they may quickly lose their value across teams with very different characteristics. So while a base of common team metrics may be necessary across the organization, each team must be free to augment them with metrics that are meaningful to their context and needs and to revise them as the team matures and the project evolves. Again, due to this variation in context, care is needed in team-to-team analysis with such metrics.

- *Public to all.* It's important to use organization-wide metrics to understand the status and performance of organizations, teams, and individuals. Organizations need an accurate reading of the organization's performance both historically and with respect to peer organizations in their relevant markets. However, any sharing of these metrics will be more effective if they are commonly understood and used for positive reinforcement rather than for punitive purposes.

7.2.2 Measurement Maturity

Perhaps the most obvious question for an enterprise software delivery organization is "What should we measure to assess status and improve governance to ward our goals?" Unfortunately, no single definitive answer can be given. The different context of each enterprise software delivery organization makes such generalities impossible. However, what we can do is provide guidance and heuristics that make the choice of metrics more obvious and meaningful.

The first element of providing guidance for the choice of metrics is to recognize that the choice and complexity of metrics that are useful are dependent on the organization's maturity in terms of metrics-driven governance. Where there is little history of metrics-driven governance, a simpler set of metrics is typically more appropriate. In this regard, more structured software process maturity models such as the capability maturity model integration (CMMI) and the infrastructure technology information library (ITIL) both offer focus areas for software metrics (e.g., the key practice areas [KPAs] of the CMMI) and guide the depth of analysis that is appropriate (e.g., in line with the five maturity levels of the CMMI).

I have personally been involved in many efforts to define metrics programs in enterprise software delivery organizations over the years. One of the main challenges has been to match the measurement aspirations of the managers with the reality of the software delivery practices in place. Inspired by the lessons of these more formal maturity models, we can take a simpler, more intuitive approach that distinguishes four categories on metrics maturity in an enterprise software delivery organization:

- *Measure what you can.* If few metrics are collected and used in any organized way, the first step is simply to understand what is easily measurable and to begin to collect these data to build a baseline for decision making. For example, many enterprise software delivery organizations will have greater automation and control in later parts of the life cycle, such as build, test, and deployment. Efforts at establishing a common approach to metrics gathering and reporting in these areas are likely reasonably advanced, and quick progress can be made by focusing here. A long list of useful metrics is available and many tools will assist in compiling and coordinating such data.

- *Measure what you value.* The next level involves focusing on metrics that give a clear indication of what is important to the organization and can tie into the corporate goals. For example, if the company believes its future depends on accelerating market innovation, it would be useful to focus attention on metrics in the enterprise software delivery organization that correspond to this aim (such as measuring the project velocity, the number of new features delivered in each release, the number of projects transitioned from research into production, the education level of new hires in the organization, etc.). If instead the company wants to focus on product stability and quality in production, a different set of metrics would be necessary (such as measuring postship defects detected, support calls from customers, percentage of code covered by automated regression test cases, etc.).

- *Measure what drives behavior.* At the next level, the enterprise software delivery organization can optimize metrics toward those areas where changes in behavior are necessary. This approach uses the metrics to change the way individuals and teams prioritize their activities. For example, if the enterprise software delivery organization wishes to reduce duplicate effort across projects, then metrics that optimize product-line architectures and reuse can be highlighted (such as measuring architectural complexity of systems, complexity of interface dependencies, adherence to common platform usage, etc.). Exposing this information allows increased attention to these metrics and encourages positive actions to impact the measurements.

- *Measure what optimizes results.* At the highest levels, with the advantage of experience in measurement and a history of data from a variety of projects, it's possible to improve the statistical analysis of projects and become more predictive about key properties with less variance. This helps in optimizing activities toward greater efficiency. For example, where the enterprise software delivery organization has a long history of change management for an enterprise system, optimized use of offshore software testing factories can be very effectively driven by historical data on code churn, defect densities, and change turnaround times. Key indicators concerning the quality and performance of the system can then be monitored and maintained more readily.

7.2.3 Measurement and Improvement

A particularly critical use of metrics is to drive improvements in the enterprise software delivery organization and the systems for which it has responsibility. In this case, the important step is to closely tie the metrics to defined practices within the organization that can be targets for improvement. Typically we see improvement objectives mapped to a collection of measures that allow the enterprise software delivery organization to monitor the current status and tune specific practices in an attempt to influence those measures.

A practice-based approach to measurement is important to many organizations looking to adopt a longer-term improvement approach to their systems and software delivery activities. Most notably, this approach gives the organization the framework by which improvement goals can be tied to a set of measures that explicitly highlight the key indicators to be monitored and establish a value chain from those measures to practice areas in the organization where investment and reprioritizations will improve results.

For example, as illustrated in Figure 7.4, an enterprise software delivery organization has decided to focus attention on four quality attributes related to reducing effort in software and system test areas. For each quality attribute, a collection of metrics has been chosen as the primary indicators for that quality attribute. Measures for each of these can be taken on a periodic basis to understand how the status of a quality attribute is evolving. The way to affect those measures is by focusing on a number of practice areas to change the

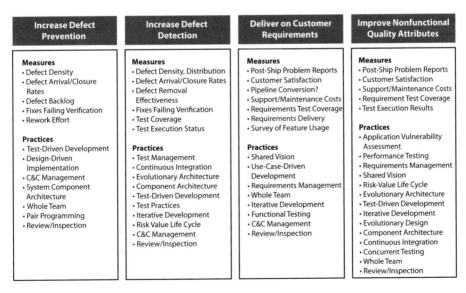

Increase Defect Prevention	Increase Defect Detection	Deliver on Customer Requirements	Improve Nonfunctional Quality Attributes
Measures • Defect Density • Defect Arrival/Closure Rates • Defect Backlog • Fixes Failing Verification • Rework Effort **Practices** • Test-Driven Development • Design-Driven Implementation • C&C Management • System Component Architecture • Whole Team • Pair Programming • Review/Inspection	**Measures** • Defect Density, Distribution • Defect Arrival/Closure Rates • Defect Removal Effectiveness • Fixes Failing Verification • Test Coverage • Test Execution Status **Practices** • Test Management • Continuous Integration • Evolutionary Architecture • Component Architecture • Test-Driven Development • Test Practices • Iterative Development • Risk Value Life Cycle • C&C Management • Review/Inspection	**Measures** • Post-Ship Problem Reports • Customer Satisfaction • Pipeline Conversion? • Support/Maintenance Costs • Requirements Test Coverage • Requirements Delivery • Survey of Feature Usage **Practices** • Shared Vision • Use-Case-Driven Development • Requirements Management • Whole Team • Iterative Development • Functional Testing • C&C Management • Review/Inspection	**Measures** • Post-Ship Problem Reports • Customer Satisfaction • Support/Maintenance Costs • Requirement Test Coverage • Test Execution Results **Practices** • Application Vulnerability Assessment • Performance Testing • Requirements Management • Shared Vision • Risk-Value Life Cycle • Evolutionary Architecture • Test-Driven Development • Iterative Development • Evolutionary Design • Component Architecture • Continuous Integration • Concurrent Testing • Whole Team • Review/Inspection

Figure 7.4 *An example set of quality attributes, measures, and practices for an enterprise software delivery organization*

organization's behavior. For each quality attribute, a set of focus practice areas is defined. These can then be the subject of improvements in new processes, additional resources, increased automation, and so on.

7.3 Managing the Global Software Supply Chain

In the last few years, the enterprise software delivery organization has become more globally distributed in nature and involves a variety of different companies in a complex network of relationships:

- To improve flexibility and manage costs, most enterprise software organizations have engaged staff from external companies to augment their resources.

- To standardize common business processes, they have acquired packaged applications and popular industry software platforms.

- To find the necessary skills and manage risk, they have engaged system integrators (SIs) and specialist third-party companies to outsource some of their tasks.

In some respects, these arrangements can be thought to have simplified the governance tasks. For example, when standardizing on a large packaged application to handle all customer relationship management capabilities, the maintenance and upgrade of those capabilities becomes the package vendor's responsibility. However, on closer inspection we see the move toward integrated software supply chains has increased the pressure on enterprise software delivery organizations with respect to governance and control. I'll indicate why this is the case by focusing on several dimensions of these software supply chain measurement challenges.

7.3.1 Governance in Outsourcing

One of the most interesting areas to consider involves how to measure and manage outsourcing relationships. Cost-efficiency pressures have led many companies to engage in outsourcing, with a majority using multiple outsourcing partners for different parts of their business. Unfortunately, in many situations the potential financial benefits from outsourcing different aspects of their enterprise software delivery activities have not been fully realized. Among several factors at play, Cohn and Young describe many experiences where the responsibility for this failure can be placed directly on governance and management issues with outsourcing [72]. They believe the roots of the problems are due to several factors:

- Outsourcing decisions are made independently by different groups in the company, without a clear, holistic governance strategy. For example, many such decisions are based almost entirely on cost reduction and are made by executive and financial management with little insight into the technical implications of the decision.

- Multiple sourcing activities are contracted individually, often by different parts of the enterprise software delivery organization, and without a clear understanding of the management of relationships and interdependencies between the services delivered. Decisions that may be considered optimal in one area of the business (e.g., software testing) may introduce challenges in other areas (e.g., deployment management).

- Misunderstandings arise from the way economies of scale and standardization of delivered services are realized in the organization. Accomplishing planned savings may require significant change to business practices and related IT services to introduce those standards across the organization. Where this is not possible, the costs quickly rise and the timetable for seeing the benefits grows.

- A lack of recognition that the outsourcing contract is not a sufficient basis for ongoing management is prevalent. The contracts that are signed with the outsourced company contain elements that define the governance of that outsourcing arrangement, often in the form of a service level agreements (SLAs). However, many assume this is all that is required for governance, and they don't recognize the need for additional active management and control of the outsourced activities and artifacts.

- Outsourcing relationships are viewed as purely contractual events where the goal is getting the most service for the lowest price. This does not support viewing the arrangement as a partnership that requires building ongoing relationships, creating a dialogue, building trust between those involved, and maintaining ongoing interactions to improve the relationship over time.

- There are false assumptions that the outsourcing arrangement will be carried out in a steady state without the need for constant monitoring in light of business changes. Expectations and success criteria will likely not remain constant through the life of the project. Little consideration is typically given to such change and evolution of the relationship between outsourcer and outsource.

- There are overexpectations that the organization's existing internal governance and controls can be applied readily to the outsourced activities. Unfortunately, this is frequently not the case, and additional reporting and management approaches are necessary.

Cohn and Young reach the conclusion that governance of these multivendor supply chains is the most important critical success factor and that the basis for this governance must be well-defined measures. Whether based on cost or not, any outsourcing should include a complete statement of work and expectations. This way, the partnership will include clear objectives that should be measurable.

7.3.2 Metrics and the Software Supply Chain

As organizations create software supply chains, they require dashboards that provide a summary of the metrics they use to understand status, assess progress, and adjust their plans. We can make a distinction between the views required by the outsourcer and the outsourcee.

7.3.2.1 From the Perspective of the Outsourcer

The outsourcer frequently looks at the outsourcee as a "software delivery factory." In such cases, three kinds of metrics are important to monitor:

- *Project and resource view.* In adopting a software factory approach to delivery, a primary goal is to have clear insight into the use of resources across a wide variety of projects, programs, and initiatives, with the aim of increasing the flexibility to rebalance the resources as needed. The resources may reside in local teams, reside in remote teams, or be delivered by third parties. In addition, a variety of contracts, agreements, and working conditions may govern parts of the organization. A number of different kinds of metrics must be available to the enterprise software delivery organization to allow it to make more informed choices on optimal resource use. Figure 7.5 shows an example of a global enterprise software delivery organization's dashboard for managing projects and resources. Here we see that products are aligned against a series of business and financial metrics. The top chart (bubble chart) shows the degree of a project's advancement against its delivery objectives (x-axis), the variance the project has on its schedule (y-axis), and how much money is being spent on the project (e.g., for capital headcount, contractors, discretionary money), represented by the size of the bubble and the project health (white, gray, or black). With this one chart, an entire portfolio can be

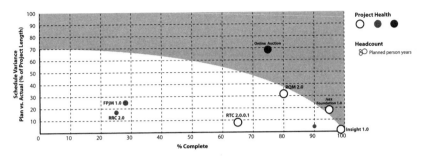

Segment	Product	Revenue Year to Date (M)	Revenue % of Plan	Pipeline (M)	Release	eGA Plan	eGA Outlook	eGa Plan Outlook	Headcount (PY)	Project Health	Overall Profit Margin	Overall Market Share
Application Lifecycle Management (ALM)	Jazz Foundation	75.7 ▼	96% ▼	87.9 ▼	Jazz Foundation 1.0	May 28, 2009	Jun 12, 2009	15 days	52 ●	71% ●	●	△
					Online Auction	Mar 31, 2009	Jul 7, 2009	98 days	118 ▼	50% ▼	▼	▼
	RTC	75.7 △	99% ●	109.6 ●	RTC 2.0	Jun 15, 2009	Jun 19, 2009	4 days	12 ●	90% ●	●	△
					RTC 2.0.0.1	Sept 22, 2009	Sept30, 2009	8 days	72 ▼	86% ●	●	●
Governance Solution	Local Point for Project Management	29.1 ●	93% ●	84.2 △	FPjM 1.0	Oct 15, 2009	Nov 17, 2009	33 days	60 ●	74% △	●	●
	Rational Insight	108.7 ▼	98% ▼	162.7 △	Insight 1.0	May 26, 2009	May 26, 2009	0 days	40 ●	83% ▼	▼	●
Quality Management (QM) Solution	RQM	35.2 △	112% △	79.6 ●	RQM 2.0	Jun 15, 2009	Jul 31, 2009	46 days	56 ●	89% △	●	△
	RRC	35.2 ●	83% △	45.1 ▼	RRC 2.0	Nov 4, 2009	Nov 24, 2009	20 days	32 △	85% ●	●	▼

Figure 7.5 *An example dashboard for project and resource management in an enterprise software delivery organization*

viewed. The table below the bubble chart shows more detailed information in a tabular form. Here, we can see trends over the last day, week, or month (user-selected by the indicator located to the right of each number).

- *Work item view.* In a software supply chain, one of the most important aspects of governance is managing the variety of different incoming change requests from many stakeholders. The outsourcer is responsible for managing a myriad of categories of incidents, requests for new features, planned upgrades, emergency fixes, contract changes, and so on. Generally we can refer to any of these requests as a work item. A complex process of analysis and distribution may be required simply to determine what is involved in executing a work item, who needs to be involved, and how the process for its completion is monitored and signed off. Metrics are required that help the outsourcer to understand the current status of all work items and to identify trends and patterns in these data. An example work item view is shown in Figure 7.6. Here we see how the enterprise software delivery organization in a large bank monitors all work items across its software factory of multiple service providers. All open work items can be displayed in selected categories, such as their priority, the systems they impact, the responsible organizational units, the time outstanding, and so on.

- *Delivery view.* The ultimate goal, of course, is for the enterprise software delivery organization to bring new systems into production in a controlled and effective way. The delivery view of metrics is essential to understand how components delivered by multiple suppliers can be assembled and managed into production with minimal risk. Often the outsourcer has responsibility for final test and validation of all delivered elements of the system. Therefore metrics that assess the overall quality of the system and its readiness for deployment must be available. The example in Figure 7.7 shows a delivery view used by the enterprise software delivery organization in a large insurance company. This view helps assess the progress of key components and monitors the health of builds that bring together those components into a running system. With this view, problems can be identified and the originating component owners can be notified.

7.3.3.2 *From the Perspective of the Outsourcee*

From the perspective of the outsourcee organization (provider of components and services), metrics are used to make sure the organization is as efficient as possible in the execution of its tasks. Clearly the outsourcee will invest a lot of effort in metrics that support effective resource management and billing. Many systems are available that allow the outsourcee organization to manage time sheets, project tracking, and hours billed per project. However, attention is also needed to make sure the quality of delivered software is high and that the outsourcee is meeting the conditions of the SLA under which it is employed. Trending information is particularly critical to anticipate future problems.

An example of a high-level dashboard for an outsourcee organization is shown in Figure 7.8. Here we see important metrics that indicate schedule variance, defects of delivered systems in terms of warrantee agreements, and trending data across a variety of quality factors.

As shown in Figure 7.8, the outsourcee organization can select and examine a variety of data on the projects it manages for different clients. For example, the menus in the center of the dashboard provide choices to filter the information displayed based on the geographic location of the client, categories of projects (e.g., financial services, communications, distribution), and different kinds of work (e.g., new development, enhancements, maintenance).

7.4 Examples

Here I'll show two interesting examples from the wide variety of governance processes and mechanisms in use by enterprise software delivery organizations.

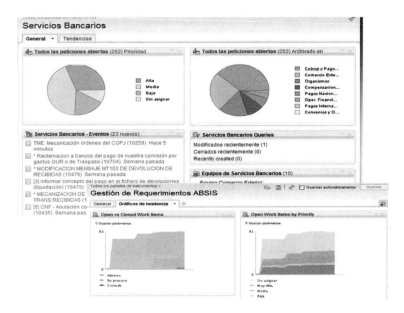

Figure 7.6 *An example work item view for the enterprise software delivery organization for a large bank in Spain (shown in the local language)*

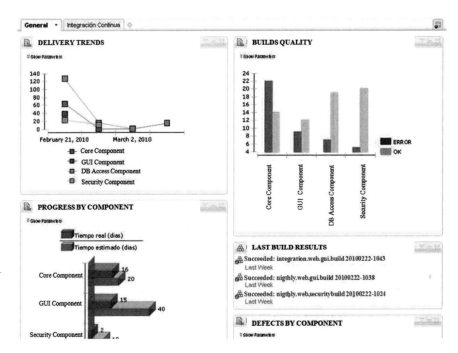

Figure 7.7 *An example delivery view for the enterprise software delivery organization in a large insurance company in Spain*

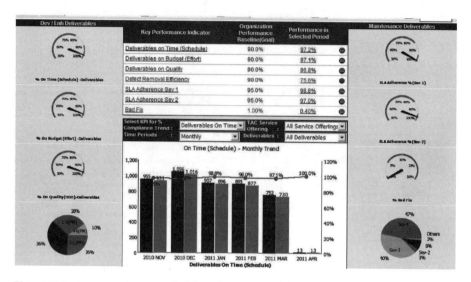

Figure 7.8 *An example status dashboard maintained by an outsourcee organization*

One example is drawn from IBM Rational's software delivery approach and the other from a large bank's management of its major software supplier.

7.4.1 Product Porfolio Management at IBM Rational

IBM Rational employs over two thousand people who are responsible for delivery of a wide collection of software products. It makes use of a variety of measurement and management approaches as the basis for its governance.

In Figure 7.9, I illustrate the wide variety of software measures that IBM Rational considers valuable to manage. This represents a collective view of all the potentially useful metrics to the organization. In particular, the measures are slotted into four main categories, depending on their role: project health, customer quality, development quality, and strategic health. Together these four categories provide an executive dashboard for management decision making. For each specific product development activity, a selection of these metrics in each category is agreed upon and a baseline set of measures is established. Subsequently, the overall health of the product is assessed in relationship to historical data and trends derived from the baseline.

7.4.2 Supplier Management at a Large Bank

A large European bank has outsourced major portions of its enterprise software delivery capability to several key suppliers. Effective management and governance

Project Health	Customer Quality	Development Quality	Strategic Health
• Defect Backlog	• Transactional Survey	• Defect Backlog	• Sales Plays
• Defect Density	• PMR / Call Rates	• Test Escapes	• Partner Enablement
• Defect Repair Latency	• Critical Situations	• Functional Test	• Support Enablement
• Build Health	• Cost of Support	Trends	• Technical Enablement
• Project Velocity	• Installability	• Critical Situations	• Sales Enablement
• Staffing Actuals	• Enhancement SLA	• System Test Trends	• Localization
• Process Timeliness	• Useability	• S-Curve Progress	• MCIF Index
• Milestone Status	• Consumability	• Automation	• Competition
• Severity Analysis	• Perceived Performance	Percentage	• Integrated into Story
• Security Vulnerabilities	• Scalability	• Customer Test Cases	• Scalability
• Static Code Analysis	• Integrations with Other	• Consumability	• Green Threads
• Requirements Met	Products	Scorecard	• LCM
• IPD Timeliness	• User Experience / Doc	• Defect Latency	• Pipeline/ Multiplier
	Time to Resolution	• Quality Plan	• Revenue
		Commitments	
		• Test Coverage	

Figure 7.9 *The overall executive dashboard containing candidate IBM rational metrics*

of those suppliers requires insight into the status and history of delivery with respect to several critical success factors agreed upon with each supplier as part of the original SLA.

Figure 7.10 illustrates a dashboard that summarizes the critical success factors to use as the basis for decision making. There are three main areas. The first dashboard (*critical activities*) describes exceptional events or indicators that are worthy of special attention. These may need immediate action or indicate the impact of recent decisions. The second dashboard (*quality of service*) shows several operational service quality indicators related to current delivery quality for agreed services as specified in the various contracts with suppliers. The third dashboard (*management indicators*) describes management indicators that are both technical and financial in nature and relate to preidentified improvement areas that require constant attention.

7.5 Conclusions

Success in any activity requires effective decision making based on clear indications of status and progress. In enterprise software delivery, it is essential that governance practices make use of accurate, timely data that support the goals and objectives of the organization and drive behavior toward a meaningful

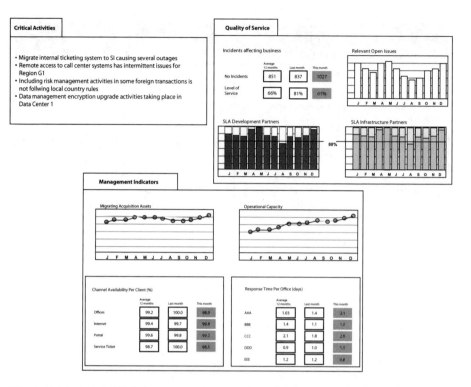

Figure 7.10 *A simplified governance dashboard used for managing a key software supplier in a large bank*

result. Three critical points pertaining to the management and governance of enterprise software delivery are as follows:

- Early intervention prevents disputes and reduces costs in enterprise software delivery. Successful early intervention requires constant feedback with respect to historical results and industry benchmarks.

- Metrics are an important aspect of reinforcing and motivating desired behavior in enterprise software delivery. Choosing what to measure can be as important as deciding what to do with those measures.

- A supply chain approach to enterprise software delivery increases the need for adequate dashboards that provide insight into supplier progress and status. Dashboards are essential for industrialized approaches to enterprise software delivery.

Chapter 8

A Case Study in Agile-at-Scale Adoption at Danske Bank

Chapter Summary

I present a detailed case study in agile-at-scale adoption. I explore several real-world issues in the deployment and rollout of agile techniques in the context of the global enterprise software delivery organization supporting Danske Bank, and I describe key lessons from these experiences. The case study illustrates several important points:

- The move toward more agile practices is one of many steps in an organization's transformation and must be blended with other ongoing improvement efforts.

- There is no "on/off" switch for a global enterprise, and any process or practice improvement must adapt and evolve in the context of the organization's characteristics, heritage, politics, and plans.

- A tooling and automation platform is an essential component of a scaled approach to agility to support coordination of the teams, automate integration between tasks and metrics collection, and visualize current status and impact of changes.

- Scaling issues, such as training, education, and migration, have major impact on adoption, thus requiring a systematic focus and approach.

8.1 Introduction[1]

The banking and financial markets are under increasing pressure to be competitive, respond more quickly to change, and be more transparent in their governance practices. In a fiercely competitive market, Danske Bank is finding that it must realize synergies from a period of active acquisitions and mergers, solidify its market value by strengthening weakly positioned services in key customer segments, and enhance customer satisfaction in comparison to key competitors in several key market areas.

Danske Bank is the largest universal bank in Denmark and the second largest in Scandinavia, managing over $500 billion in assets. It's part of the Danske Bank Group, offering a wide range of financial services, including insurance, mortgage finance, asset management, brokerage, and real-estate and leasing services. Danske Bank is responsible for almost 5 million retail customers and more than 2 million active Internet customers and has almost 200,000 corporate, public, and institutional clients. As a result, it has more than 21,000 employees, who are responsible for more than 600 branches across 15 countries.[2]

Over the past decade, the business climate has pushed Danske Bank toward a more global approach to banking. Consequently, Danske Bank has expanded into other countries, including acquisitions across Scandinavia, Finland, and Ireland, with more than ten acquisitions over the past twenty years.

The enterprise software delivery organization for Danske Bank is tasked with timely and efficient development and delivery of quality end-to-end solutions to the different business areas (and through them to the customers of Danske Bank). That organization currently has an annual budget of about $400 million, allocated to developing new solutions as well as to maintaining and delivering the existing portfolio of solutions (excluding infrastructure-related costs).[3] As summarized in Figure 8.1, about 70 percent of the people are located in Denmark, 20 percent are located in India, and 10 percent are external contractors. Up to 80 percent of this budget is used for maintenance efforts, and the remaining 20 percent is used to fund new systems and delivery projects.

A variety of main platforms and technologies are used in Danske Bank for enterprise software delivery:

---

1. Further aspects of this case study are discussed in Brown [73].

2. These, and subsequent figures, are based on public data issued in 2011.

3. All infrastructure and operations activities are provided separately by a partner as part of a strategic outsourcing contract.

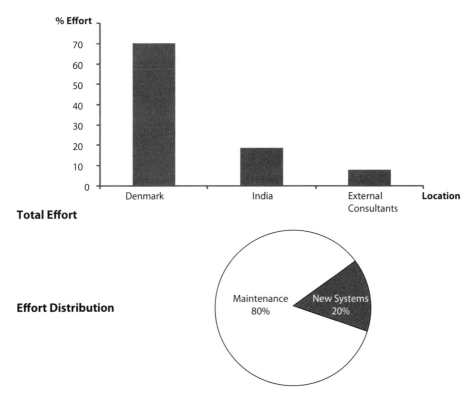

Figure 8.1 *Total effort dedicated to Danske Bank's enterprise software delivery organization*

- Transaction processing on zOS (CICS/DB2)

- Front-end (Internet/intranet) on Windows (Microsoft operating systems)

- Business intelligence solutions on Windows (MS SQL Server with IBM information server for extracting, transforming, and loading data)

- Selective (and limited) use of commercial off-the-shelf solutions

The enterprise software delivery organization is responsible for a large portfolio of systems, with more than 50,000 applications and many hundreds of concurrently executing projects to add, update, or decommission those applications. Those applications are implemented in a variety of technologies and programming languages: CICS/PL1 (55 percent), CICS/Cobol (25 percent), J2EE (5 percent), and Microsoft VisualBasic/C# (15 percent).

In recent years, increasing the level of process maturity in the development organization has been a key focus. As a result, development projects in Danske

Bank are now consistently able to achieve capability maturity model integration (CMMI) level 2 compliance. The stated goal is to achieve CMMI level 3 compliance within a couple of years.

8.2 Motivation for Change

While the increased level of process maturity in the enterprise software delivery organization has enabled projects to deliver solutions of a higher quality and with a higher degree of predictability, there is still room for improvement. Industry analysts and other third parties have performed a number of analyses and health-check studies in recent years. They've identified a number of potential areas of waste and inefficiency. Specifically, the following symptoms were observed:

- General symptoms
  - Delivering new/improved solutions to the business areas takes too long. Currently, the average calendar time used by projects to deliver a solution exceeds twelve months.
  - Solutions are too expensive to develop and maintain, particularly in comparison with industry benchmark figures for the financial sector. In the future, the current solution development and delivery must be provided with less cost than today.

- Enablement symptoms
  - There is further potential for automating manual and time-consuming tasks across the software development and delivery life cycle, particularly as it relates to build, test, and release management.
  - Greater standardization and simplification of delivery would be achieved through additional reuse and consolidation on a smaller number of architectural patterns and components.

- Discipline-specific symptoms
  - Extensive and excessive management and analysis activities are often undertaken to enable a firm up-front commitment to a project's scope, deadlines, and resourcing.
  - The change-request process is cumbersome and time consuming, which leads to business analysts overspecifying the project scope to ensure

everything is included up front. When changes occur, the effort to manage their implementation is too large.

○ Requirements definition and requirements sign-off processes are too lengthy.

○ Integration of the different solution elements is infrequent and done late in the project life cycle.

○ A considerable "hardening period" of the solution is needed just before and just after release in order to achieve an acceptable level of quality.

8.3 The Focus on Adopting an Agile Approach

Faced with these challenges, Danske Bank decided to launch a series of strategic programs aimed at making measured improvements in several areas. By focusing on the highest revenue-generating aspects of the business, the primary objective was to achieve a substantial improvement in efficiency in the development effort, with the following goals:

- Provide solutions to the business within short release cycles (less than twelve months but typically achieving releases every three to four months for more agile projects).

- Increase delivery flexibility to change scope as required with minimal impact on schedules and commitments.

- Manage project risks through earlier identification of problems and easier mitigation of risks.

- Deliver higher-quality solutions at a cost that is the same or lower than previously seen.

- Expand the sourcing options for projects to allow an increased use of offshore resources.

Following a number of internal reviews, it was decided to leverage a wide variety of improvement practices and to concentrate attention on emerging agile practices. The concepts and principles of agile software development were well known to Danske Bank. In previous years, the bank had initiated several efforts involving a number of agile methods and had contracted a limited amount of coaching and external consulting. A handful of projects openly described their approaches in terms of agile processes and techniques. A small but growing grassroots agile community had been formed. This was beginning to gain visibility and influence in the organization, particularly among influential groups of users across the enterprise software delivery management team. The challenge, then, was not *whether* agile approaches should be used but *where* and *how* agile approaches could be applied in a more controlled way to the greatest benefit of Danske Bank.

To help with this task, Danske Bank defined a focus for its agile adoption efforts by creating a shared *agile adoption charter*. This charter outlined a series of focus areas (dos and don'ts) to clarify how agility would be scoped and interpreted at Danske Bank. From the organization's viewpoint, an agile project at Danske Bank should focus on the following:

- Delivering a potentially shippable (part of a) solution after each sprint and after each release

- Self-organized and highly disciplined teams

- Collective ownership of project results by team members working across multiple disciplines

- Close and ongoing collaboration with the business (represented by the product owner)

- Continuous improvement through meaningful measures

The previous Danske Bank experiences with agile development had raised some troubling concerns for people in the organizations, who perceived that agility was simply a lack of governance and a way to avoid burdensome reporting practices. It was therefore also essential to be clear on what an agile project at Danske Bank should *not* focus on:

- Working without a plan

- Producing no documentation

- Neglecting to do analysis and design

- Having no process for managing change

- Avoiding managing risks, stakeholders, or suppliers

- Not adhering to common Danske Bank standards, terminology, and work products

8.4 The Danske Bank Agile Delivery Process

Based on these needs, the basic approach at Danske Bank was to build on best industry practice to create an agile delivery process that adapted well-known agile development methods to the Danske Bank context. As illustrated in Figure 8.2, the organization defined a set of layers of concern with different scope and focus.

As shown, there are four layers of concern to the agile delivery approach at Danske Bank:

- *Scrum.* The core development ideas of the agile delivery approach in Danske Bank are drawn from the Scrum approach [11]. The limited existing experiences at Danske Bank mostly involved use of Scrum in small development projects, so it made sense to leverage those experiences and use the main terminology from Scrum as the basis on which to build. Hence the Danske Bank agile approach reuses the familiar ideas of backlogs, sprints, Scrums and the new roles of product owners and Scrum masters, and so on. This also allows the opportunity for Danske Bank to use a wide range of existing training materials and external consultants.

- *OpenUP and XP.* The core ideas of Scrum are augmented with the broader view taken by OpenUP [74] and XP [75]. These approaches introduced a

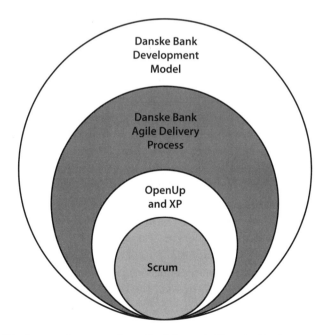

Figure 8.2 *The layers of concern for agile delivery in Danske Bank*

perspective based on agile practices that extend beyond development and into the broader software delivery life-cycle areas. In addition, this enabled easier adoption of agile ideas for those in Danske Bank who have a history with the rational unified process, already widely deployed in the organization [14].

- *Danske Bank agile delivery process.* The customization and packaging of the agile delivery process for Danske Bank was given its own identity (including a logo, graphics, and posters). This encapsulated the specific choices of concepts, processes, and terminology for agile delivery, expressing them in a familiar vocabulary and making them more readily identifiable to the wide range of stakeholders around Danske Bank who would be involved with the enterprise software delivery organization.

- *Danske Bank development model.* The final concern was to align the agile delivery processes with the preexisting delivery model in use at Danske Bank. Not only were many projects already in flight using existing development approaches, but also many new projects would be a blend of traditional and agile approaches. A clear relationship to the existing delivery approaches was essential.

The resulting Danske Bank agile delivery process was a balance of innovative agile techniques within the context of the traditional concepts and practices widely understood and in use in the organization. In this way, the Scrum-based ideas of backlogs and sprints form the core of the agile delivery process, but it's extended in the Danske Bank delivery model to include broader elements of the software delivery life cycle.

More specifically, surrounding the well-known agile techniques of backlogs and sprints at the core of the Danske Bank delivery approach is a further layer of product backlogs that help specify and define a product release. Then, at the outmost layer, a set of project ideas captured in a project charter create the managed definition used by project management for project tracking.

A specialized process-authoring technology was used to formalize the capture, validation, and delivery of this broad process. This technology eased process authoring to ensure all elements had been captured effectively and consistently and allowed validation for completeness and compatibility with the existing Danske Bank delivery processes. An example of the Danske Bank agile delivery process is shown in Figure 8.3.

The result of the use of the process-authoring technology, as shown in Figure 8.3, was a detailed process that extended the bank's existing development process and was delivered in a user-friendly common format for sharing across the organization. This level of detail proved to be invaluable in bringing common terminology and concepts to everyone involved in the program.

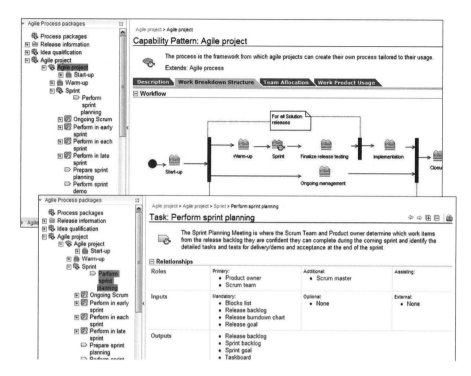

Figure 8.3 *An example of the Danske Bank agile delivery process*

8.5 Implementing an Agile Delivery Process Workbench

Automation and support for the Danske Bank agile delivery process is essential to improve efficiency, ensure consistency, and enable broad rollout to the distributed organization. The Danske Bank enterprise software delivery organization already had in place a fairly complete (and complex) tooling platform for software delivery. As illustrated in Figure 8.4, this platform already addressed several key areas of concern in software delivery (shown in the white boxes).

Many potential candidates for additional tool support are possible. However, in line with the incremental adoption and rollout philosophy at Danske Bank, a simplified approach to automation was sought. The primary addition for supporting the Danske Bank agile delivery process was found to be a collaborative application life-cycle management (CALM) workbench to automate team interactions and provide additional visibility into the projects and their progress [46]. The most critical additional automation targets were determined to be around work-item management, continuous integration, and visibility via dashboards. These were the central coordinating elements that would ensure

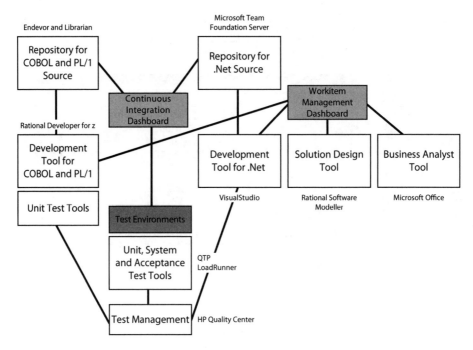

Figure 8.4 *Key areas of automation in the Danske Bank enterprise software delivery organization*

the teams worked together effectively, communicated in real-time on the primary delivery artifacts, and improved process transparency to plan more effectively and quickly intervene when problems arose.

The rapid interactive nature of the Danske Bank agile delivery process encouraged particular attention on areas of interteam collaboration and communication. Hence the bank implemented the rational team concert CALM workbench. This has resulted in the following:

- A lightweight team management platform that coordinates team members across the geographically distributed organization

- Multiplatform support to match the heterogeneous development and delivery technologies at Danske Bank

- Open interfaces and a simple integration approach to ease interconnection of the currently deployed tools

- Support for agile techniques, particularly a clear alignment with Scrum practices

8.6 Piloting the Danske Bank Agile Delivery Process

Designing and executing an effective piloting phase proves particularly important in any organizational change. For the Danske Bank agile delivery process, the pilot approach was carefully designed to gain as much feedback as possible across a range of different delivery scenarios and to use the feedback to adapt the agile delivery process.

The most important initial choice was not to "invent" pilot scenarios but to select pilots from real projects that were planned or in early stages of delivery. The primary characteristics for suitable pilot project selection were defined in five key areas:

- Project team characteristics

- Project and task characteristics

- Business engagement

- Delivery or maintenance engagement

- Stakeholder involvement and commitment

A formal process of selection was conducted across different business divisions. Candidate projects were not difficult to find, as many different groups around the Danske Bank organization had early agile development experiences or had previously expressed interest in trying out agile techniques. Narrowing the field, additional criteria were used to help the organization select pilots that would represent a broad set of experiences. The pilots were filtered to ensure the following:

- Pilots covered different kinds of project types and tasks (e.g., new development, extension of existing systems, maintenance, etc.).

- At least one pilot project included some degree of globally distributed team members.

- At least one pilot project included multiple teams.

- At least one pilot project involved cooperation with one or more internal and/or external vendors.

- Pilot projects covered a variety of different technology delivery platforms.

The selection and execution of eight pilot projects involving more than a hundred people took place over a nine-month period, with continual monitoring and adjustment to the Danske Bank agile delivery process as a result of ongoing feedback and analysis. The main lessons from the pilot activities are summarized here:

- The start-up activities for pilot teams proved to be complex and challenging. The first pilots gave very poor feedback on the initial support they received. This resulted in a great deal more investment in coaching, education, and task transition in the early pilot stages.

- The key new role in many pilots was the product owner. This role was pivotal in providing a bridge between the development and project management teams. Having the right person perform this task (based on skills, mindset, and attitude) and effectively customizing his or her training proved essential.

- The pilot teams had a great deal of trouble moving from a schedule-driven activity view of their work to one focused on work items (stories) and tasks. For many people, this shift in thinking proved difficult to adopt. Additional specialized training and coaching was introduced in this area.

- Project planning and estimation were radically altered, and estimation using story points rather than function points per hour required guidance and practice.

- Establishing the right levels of transparency into the pilots was difficult. It was important to allow the pilots some privacy to learn and experiment, but receiving management information and status summaries quickly became a priority.

- Traditional project management involving artifacts such as work-breakdown structures and Gantt charts needed reinterpretation to include the agile practices of backlog management, reprioritization activities, and the impact of sprint retrospective activities. This was a big step for many in the organization, where traditional project accounting practices had been in place for a long time.

- The enablement concept needed to be very well structured to provide the right information to the right roles at the right time. The effort required here was initially underestimated. An expert in organizational improvement was brought into the team to help redesign the enablement approach in a more structured way.

- The pilots were initially defined and managed in isolation, but the expected value of the agile approach was intended to be reflected across the organization. After some readjustment, common terminology and work products were defined across all project types. This was critical for realizing synergy and providing flexibility across the pilots.

- Effective rollout to the offshore teams in India was essential to demonstrate the wider applicability of the agile delivery process and to understand the impact of an offshore model on the techniques. Some reorganization of the global teams needed to be accommodated, and additional training for offshore resources was expanded.

8.7 Measuring Success

During the pilot phase, a key challenge concerned determining the best ways to measure the improvements expected from the Danske Bank agile delivery process. As in most organizations, in Danske Bank, the theme of measurement and metrics is both complex and politically charged. Deciding on an appropriate measurement scheme is essential but comes with many challenges. The decision in this case was to adopt a simple, three-dimensional approach to probe answers to three key questions:

- Is agile being adopted?

- Are the agile practices working?

- Are we seeing real business results?

This scheme was based on a range of experiences in other organizations adopting agile approaches.

As illustrated in Figure 8.5, two kinds of measurement were used for the Danske Bank agile delivery process: *business-related* and *agile-related*. The business-related measures were intended to be clear signals to the business owners that the adoption of an agile process was helping to deliver more, higher-quality software more quickly. The agile-related measures were to be used within the agile projects and by the enterprise software delivery organization to manage and govern those projects.

In addition, an informal survey approach for periodically checking on the agile team "pulse" was found to be particularly useful in regard to fine-tuning the agile delivery process. Although this is a relatively simple and limited mechanism to monitor status of the projects, it gave immediate feedback if the projects were beginning to experience unnecessary challenges and issues, as shown in Figure 8.6.

Figure 8.6 shows a simple summary of an agile team pulse for a Danske Bank agile delivery project. Behind each of the practice areas indicated is

	Business Related	**Agile Related**
Cycle Time Reduction	Time spent from project initiation to delivery of first increment Time spent from project initiation to project closure	Sprint velocity Blocking work items
Quality	Defects (severity 1 and 2) in production per 100 FPs	Defects trend
Continuous Optimization	Process maturity level	Adoption of agile practices
Productivity	Function points per man year	Sprint burndown chart Release burndown chart

Figure 8.5 *The measurement schema used for the Danske Bank agile delivery process*

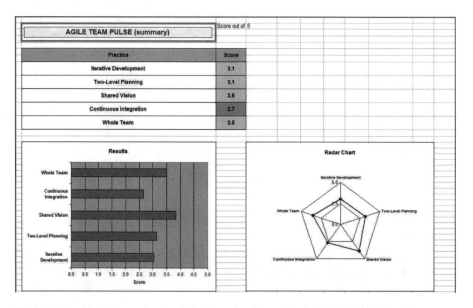

Figure 8.6 *A summary of an agile team pulse for a Danske Bank agile delivery project*

a detailed survey and analysis that allows greater insights into the current team perceptions.

8.8 Rollout Principles

The pilot projects were the initial steps in a broader adoption of agile delivery practices in Danske Bank. The rollout was aimed at taking an accelerated approach to introducing agile practices as broadly as possible throughout the enterprise software delivery organization. Given the characteristics of Danske Bank and its history, several important rollout principles were established.

First, the organization decided to prioritize system maintenance projects ahead of new development projects while acknowledging that there would be a certain window of opportunity for projects to switch into new practices (e.g., once a project was approved and about to be initiated or during transition of the project from delivery into production). Given the high investment in maintaining existing systems, the target distribution was to have two-thirds of the projects adopting the agile delivery process to be system maintenance projects.

Second, agile practice rollout would be carried out across the organization and not focused too heavily in one area or department. This broad approach would not only gain wider experience of the adoption but also limit risk and resource bottlenecks that can occur with overconcentration in some groups.

Third, the experience from the pilots clearly suggested that "agile readiness" and competences should be a primary determinant of when to introduce the Danske Bank agile delivery process into a project. Without an agile mind-set and required skills present among all (potential) participants and stakeholders, the risks of failure increase dramatically. Similarly, essential coordination with other ongoing initiatives that affect the project must be taken into account.

A broad and accelerated rollout of the Danske Bank agile delivery process required a clear model for taking on new projects and supporting their transition to the new practices. The rollout model consists of a set of enablement "trains" that start on a periodic basis. A number of "tickets" are available for each train, and obtaining a ticket requires that the project passes the readiness gate. Subsequently, a series of criteria determines if the project is ready to take its place on the next agile delivery process enablement train. If the project is considered ready, a seat on the train is made available and detailed planning for introduction of the Danske Bank agile delivery process can begin. If not, then an action plan is created to help the project prepare for revalidation.

Perhaps the most critical step in the rollout approach for the projects is carrying out the initial enablement activities. As a result of the pilot experiences, a well-structured approach to enablement was established.

As shown in Figure 8.7, the structured enablement program for new projects that enter the Danske Bank agile delivery process covers the life of the project from start-up through to delivery and provides support for each of the roles needed with clear measurement activities to assess progress through the process.

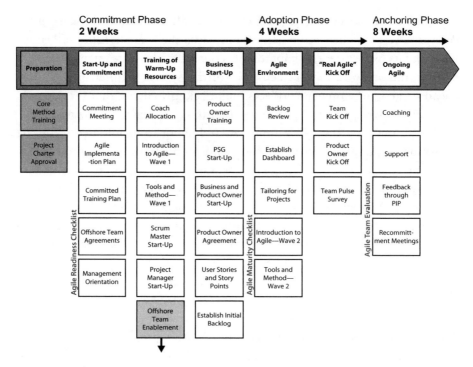

Figure 8.7 *An example of the structured enable approach for the Danske Bank agile delivery process*

8.9 Lessons Learned

From the initial eight pilots, a broad rollout of the Danske Bank agile delivery process is now taking place. At the time of this writing, more than three hundred people were actively engaged in delivering projects at Danske Bank using this agile delivery process, with plans for more than eighty new projects and more than five hundred new people to be enabled and productive in these approaches over the coming year. The main lessons from this rollout experience are summarized as follows:

- *Progress requires strong management support.* Given the financial and political pressures that exist, the work would have struggled for success without visibility and support the rollout received from the chief information officer (CIO) and his team.

- *Intensive coaching and support for new projects is essential during the first six months.* Cutting corners in these areas is very easy, but the long-term implications are severe.

- *Taking a broad view of enablement and awareness is essential.* In particular, training must be specialized for the development teams, business stakeholders, and management executives. Awareness training for upper-level management must also be included.

- *Commitment to the adoption and rollout is critical.* Addressing ongoing challenges will require a level of faith and a determination to succeed.

The focus of the agile adoption approach at Danske Bank has been on simple, incremental, and structured delivery. While in practice the adoption has not been easy, it has been effective. Several lessons have been learned:

- The challenges related to adopting agile approaches are well known; however, interpreting those approaches in a specific organizational context remains challenging.

  ○ The relative importance of these challenges and how they should be addressed is different for each organization. Careful customization is required.

  ○ Piloting is the best way to identify where to focus. Choose the pilots carefully and use the feedback wisely.

- Automation helps address some of the most important challenges in scaling the rollout of agile delivery in a geographically distributed organization. A common collaborative agile workbench was an essential platform for teams to communicate and coordinate activities.

- A structured enablement concept allows for large-scale deployment of a common agile delivery process in a complex, multiplatform, multiproject context.

8.10 Conclusions

Greater flexibility and time to market are driving many organizations toward development techniques that optimize their team interactions and their connection with stakeholders. The resulting agile development approaches are being widely discussed and seeing broad adoption across the software industry.

In this case study, I examine a broad view of agility as it applies to enterprise software delivery. In particular, I describe how agility at scale can be realized, providing practical guidance on adapting agility in complex enterprise software delivery organizations. This detailed illustration has emphasized many key factors in scaling agile practices for enterprise delivery.

As with many enterprises, Danske Bank has made a major commitment to agile delivery practices as a primary way to deliver more effective enterprise systems to its business stakeholders on a more frequent basis. Furthermore, the focus for Danske Bank has been to address the challenges it faces across all aspects of software delivery, including both maintenance and new software development efforts. Agile practices have been found to be effective across this spectrum of activities.

The results have been very positive. The initial eight pilots were able to show improvements in productivity and quality of delivered systems. They worked more closely with their business stakeholders and created an atmosphere of mutual trust that increased their effectiveness. Rollout of the approach across the organization is in flight. More than three hundred people used the Danske Bank agile delivery process by the end of 2010, and this figure was expected to double within the next twelve months.

Chapter 9

A Case Study in Global Software Product Delivery at IBM Rational

Chapter Summary

I examine the software delivery experiences in a highly distributed enterprise software delivery organization. Providing a historical perspective that documents the improvements in enterprise software delivery performance over a five-year period, I describe the specific agile practices and tools adopted by the IBM Rational product delivery organization and assess reasons for productivity and quality improvements. Key elements of the improvement include the following:

- A revision of development practices to create more stable, high-performing teams with practices that encourage and support strong team interactions

- A focus on a flexible delivery process that emphasizes prioritization and analysis of the impact of what is being delivered over blindly following the details of an out-of-date plan

- Explicit coordination of multiple teams to deliver integrated features and capabilities that address the customer's needs

- Increased integration and automation across critical delivery activities to avoid waste and provide real-time information on progress

9.1 Introduction

IBM is a global computer products and services company with annual revenue of almost $100 billion. One of six brands in IBM's Software Group, Rational focuses on system and software delivery for IBM's clients. With its origins in software configuration management and software modeling tools, Rational was acquired by IBM in 2003 and has expanded its areas of concern to provide tools and technologies that support all aspects of the software delivery life cycle, including project planning, requirements management, code delivery and management, testing, security analysis, and application delivery.

The Rational software delivery organization consists of over two thousand practitioners[1] in a variety of locations around the world, responsible for a portfolio of more than a hundred products. The wide distribution of these practitioners, illustrated in Figure 9.1, is a consequence of a global strategy to engage resources wherever the skills are available (with certain specialties in short supply), decisions to use offshore locations to reduce cost (including recent trends to increase its labs in China and India), and the organization's history (including a variety of acquisitions and restructuring events).

The integrated product delivery (IPD) process governs the overall context for software product delivery in IBM. The IPD is a management system designed

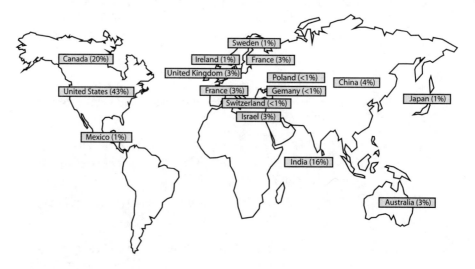

Date from the start of 2011

Figure 9.1 *Global distribution of the Rational software delivery organization*

---

1. The term *practitioner* denotes all those involved with software delivery related tasks but excludes sales, marketing, and other support personnel.

to optimize the development and delivery of successful products and offerings in IBM. As illustrated in Figure 9.2, the basic approach of the IPD is to create a meaningful product context for ensuring that projects address market needs in delivering solutions that will bring value to customers and revenue to IBM. The IPD is the basis for governance and management of all software delivery projects.

9.2 Status and Motivation

Over the past decade, pressures on enterprise software tools vendors have increased. For IBM Rational, the constant cost and efficiency pressures typical of many software domains have been augmented with particular challenges, such as the following:

- Increased competition from offerings of open-source software development tools producing highly innovative capabilities developed and supported by large worldwide communities and available for use at zero cost[2]

- Rapidly evolving software delivery practices, including the push toward more frequent, incremental delivery approaches; self-service administration; and interface-level transparency to integrate and adapt software to local needs

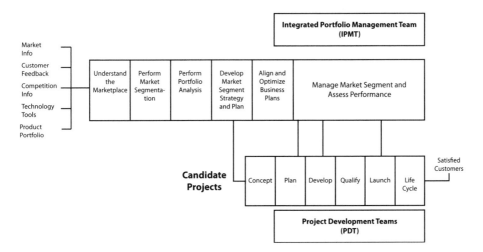

Figure 9.2 *The main elements of the IBM IPD process*

---

2. There is a deeper discussion over whether open-source software is really zero cost. It's free to download, but other factors must be taken into account if that software is to be adapted, integrated, deployed, and maintained.

- Greater use of system integrators in many domains of software delivery as the primary contractors for developing, delivering, and supporting enterprise software

- Technology shifts in software delivery from mainframe to distributed to virtualized platforms (including the current moves toward cloud-based delivery infrastructures)

- Proliferation of handheld devices and other end-user access technologies, with the effect of substantially changing users' data and service access profiles and accelerating the demand for new kinds of capabilities better suited to these devices

These changes in the enterprise software delivery landscape have resulted in increasing need for massive innovation in the products being delivered. The enterprise software delivery tools from the early 1990s are quite removed in architecture, features, and performance from what the market demands today.

In 2006, Rational conducted a detailed analysis to understand its current situation in the market and plan its future directions. Among elements addressed in this review were current market position, product portfolio, and competitive analysis. The review provided a clear contextual view for Rational's strategic vision.

However, most disturbing was an analysis of the status of software delivery inside the Rational software delivery organization. As summarized in Figure 9.3, data collected from multiple sources revealed that the quality and timeliness of software delivery in Rational was not at acceptable levels to respond to the current market pressures and demands. Rational's growing portfolio of products, global distribution of teams, and lack of investment had taken its toll.

As summarized in Figure 9.3, measurements taken in 2006 showed that Rational software delivery was underperforming in several dimensions. Not only was delivery frequently late, but the pace of innovation in the products was slow, with long response times to requests for new features.

9.3 Goals and Objectives for Software Delivery in Rational

The result of the analysis in 2006 was to refocus Rational's software delivery organization on major areas for improvement:

- *Organize differently.* The typical project structure in Rational involved at least three different sites in at least two time zones. Supporting and

Metric	Goal	2006 Measurement
On-Time Delivery	65%	47%
Defect Backlog Months	3 Months	9+
Enhancements Triaged	85%	3%
Enhancements into Release	15%	1%
Customer Satisfaction Index	91%	88%
Beta Defects Fixed Before GA	50%	3%
Agile/Iterative Projects	25%	5%

Note: Goals are either internal IBM statistics or industry benchmarks.

Figure 9.3 *A summary of Rational performance in 2006*

reinforcing the global nature of the software delivery organization and enabling distributed teams to operate more effectively proved essential.

- *Develop differently.* Rational reexamined existing development styles with the goal of identifying optimizations in the approaches, while maintaining compliance to broader IBM standards. The organization aimed toward more flexible delivery approaches focused on increased visibility and improved time to market.

- *Deliver differently.* Greater cooperation was boosted across the delivery cycle, improving relationships across the development teams and with product management, support, and product strategy roles.

- *Measure differently.* To improve governance, Rational reviewed reporting and management systems to determine which metrics needed greatest attention and to understand how to provide more insight and transparency into the development and delivery process.

Among the series of different activities initiated, one centered on agility. Rational had experience and expertise from projects whose characteristics did not match the disappointing characteristics that were revealed by the analysis— projects that had excellent on-time delivery records, were leading in market innovation, and boasted high customer satisfaction with delivered quality. These projects had adopted and adapted emerging agile practices, and they were witnessing good results.

Seeking to extend those agile delivery experiences, Rational created a program with the following specific aims:

- Improve the response to the fast-changing software delivery environment.

- Reduce the large overhead costs for existing process management and control.

- Coordinate and share internal experience accumulated from successful projects, pilots, and experiments in agile delivery.

- Improve morale across teams where low quality and limited levels of innovation had become the norm.

- Drive increased levels of innovation in new product releases.

- Introduce the best practices for more agile delivery from external sources, notably as seen in several open-source communities.

- Reinforce and expand globally distributed development approaches.

Especially important for Rational was the need to be the pilot user for its own enterprise software delivery products. That is, the products that Rational produces should be the *same* tools, technologies, and processes that Rational uses to improve its own enterprise software delivery organization.[3] Simply stated, Rational decided it must become its own best reference for the tools and technologies it produces.

The result, under the name Rational Jazz, was an initiative that created a new vision in Rational for enterprise software delivery. It galvanized Rational around a software delivery platform with several distinguishing characteristics:

- Supports creation of integrated cross-functional teams

- Scales with the teams for projects of many different sizes

- Allows seamless sharing and effective tracking of information across teams, functions, and products

- Customizes the right tool for the job and the person

- Ensures loose coupling between the function-specific tools based on open web-based standards

- Enables custom integrations by providing stable REST-style application programmable interfaces (APIs) for function and data

---

3. Rational dubbed this "Drinking our own champagne!"

9.4 Introducing Agile Delivery at Rational

An important starting point in Rational was to revise the development practices in use across the software delivery organization. A majority of projects employed approaches that could be characterized as *waterfall* or *iterative-waterfall* in nature. That is, their primary organizational approach was to divide the project into a number of quite rigid life-cycle phases with serial relationships between phases. Some limited (and highly constrained) iteration was possible within phases, with the scope largely predetermined at the beginning of each phase.

By examining agile approaches in use within IBM and in other organizations, a more flexible approach to enterprise software delivery was defined and encouraged. The Rational agile delivery approach consisted of two dimensions: the development practices and the development process.

9.4.1 Development Practices

Agile projects at Rational support a different way of viewing the important practices and activities that take place in project delivery. As illustrated in Figure 9.4, the Rational agile delivery approach recognizes a network of practices that reinforce the commonly used techniques of high-performing teams.

As shown in Figure 9.4, iterative development remains at the heart of the Rational agile delivery approach. However, it's now liberated from the strict phase-based constraints of a waterfall approach and supported with additional

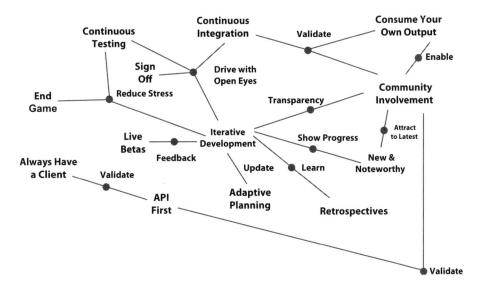

Figure 9.4 *A summary of Rational agile delivery practices*

practices that place those iterations in a more collaborative delivery context. Also, these practices operate in the context of several revised or new activities and organizational groupings.

9.4.2 Development Process

The development process provides a context in which the agile practices take place. IBM had significant experience in several projects that had adopted more flexible delivery approaches, most notably the Eclipse project.[4]

Eclipse is an open-source community focused on building an open-development platform composed of extensible frameworks, tools, and runtimes for building, deploying, and managing software across the life cycle. Originally set up by IBM in 1991, it is supported by several software vendors. The development process used by the Eclipse projects is based on agile practices, and it involves the coordination of globally distributed teams responsible for the delivery of a complex, highly interconnected platform of services.

The core Rational agile delivery process, which has come to be called the *Eclipse Way*, is primarily based on lessons from the Eclipse project. The basic process, as illustrated in Figure 9.5, involves a series of four- to six-week iterations composed of planning, development, and stabilizing activities. Each of

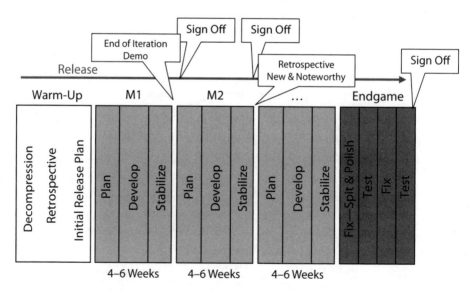

Figure 9.5 *A simplified view of the Eclipse Way, as used in the Rational agile delivery process*

---

4. See www.eclipse.org.

these iterations is completed with a demonstration of results followed by a sign-off. The postiteration retrospectives include summarizing the accomplishments with a new and noteworthy publication to publicize the results.

These iterations are preceded by a warm-up period that establishes the context for the release and creates the initial plans. They are terminated with an end-game period in which the release is hardened and ready for delivery.

9.4.3 Team Organization and Responsibilities

A particularly challenging aspect of the Rational agile delivery approach involved how to organize people into teams working on projects. Traditionally, Rational had very strong alignment around released products, and teams were clearly defined and identified by the products on which they worked. This organization was optimized to very strong product alignment but at the cost of flexibility, reuse, and integration of features across the product portfolio.

Following a series of different organizational experiments, the Rational agile delivery approach has moved toward an organizational structure in which projects are responsible for components that will be delivered, with teams focused on specific features that will be surfaced by those components. A team, therefore, is the most important organizational unit, and it has a defined set of responsibilities.

Figure 9.6 summarizes the core responsibilities of teams as they relate to the Rational agile delivery practices. Each team is self-organizing in terms of how it addresses these responsibilities according to the component features it's working on and the relationships it has with other teams.

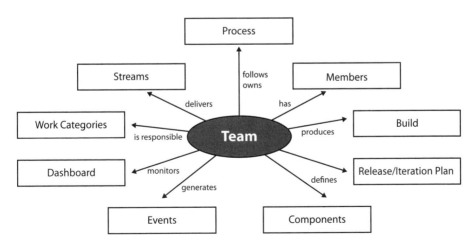

Figure 9.6 *A summary of team responsibilities in the Rational agile delivery approach*

When focusing on features, the nature of the relationship between teams becomes critical: they need to interact cooperatively to deliver the release of a product. Teams may hold different cross-team relationships. In the relationship summarized in Figure 9.7, one team is divided into a collection of teams that deliver a subset of features. Decisions on team structure are based on several factors, including the complexity of the features being delivered, team size, and geographic location of the team.

One important goal for agile teams is to minimize the artifacts for which they have responsibility. Previous experiences in Rational led to the conclusion that the artifacts managed should include only those that clearly add value to the project and are significant in ongoing validation and tracking activities. The list of artifacts that Rational agile delivery projects manage was narrowed down to the following:

- Plans
- Product backlogs
- Release plans
- Iteration plans
- Plan items, stories, and tasks

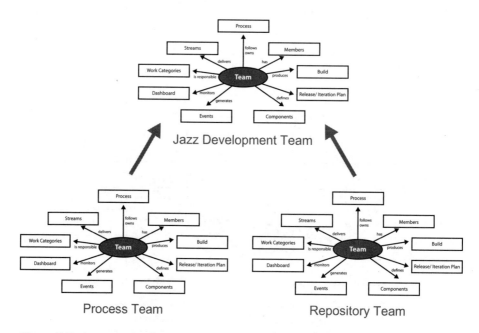

Figure 9.7 *An example of a cross-team relationship in the Rational agile delivery approach*

- Tracking descriptions
- Build status
- Adoptions
- Defects
- Enhancement requests
- Retrospectives

The relationships between many of these artifacts are summarized in Figure 9.8.

9.4.4 Planning

One of the most difficult transitions for any organization moving to more agile approaches involves the area of planning. Agile approaches are characterized by increased flexibility and constant reprioritization. These make traditional views of planning much less appropriate for agile projects.

In the Rational agile delivery approach, two levels of planning are managed. The first level of planning, *release planning*, has a coarse-grained focus and defines the specific rhythm of the release in terms of the themes and features for

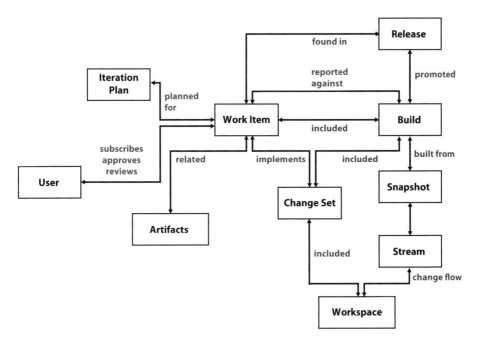

Figure 9.8 *Relationships between key artifacts in the Rational agile delivery approach*

the release and the number and size of the iterations. This level of planning is consistent across all teams that are part of the release.

The second level of planning, *iteration planning*, is more fine grained in scope and is concerned with the details of each iteration in terms of stories, tasks, enhancements, defects, and so on. Such plans are defined for each team and component.

As illustrated in Figure 9.9, plans are defined in terms of a collection of items that contains details of all aspects of the plan, including dates, risk, and status. Plan items are consistent across release and iteration planning activities.

9.4.5 Build and Build Management

A key central activity in the Rational agile delivery approach concerns build and build management. A core tenet of agile approaches holds that the health of a project is strongly aligned with the ease and frequency of individual, team, and system builds. The move to more agile approaches presupposes that a reliable, efficient way to create and manage builds regularly is in place.

In Rational agile delivery projects, the goal is to provide four levels of build management:

- Scheduled weekly integration builds that collect input from all teams working on a release as part of that iteration (stabilized until green, or approved)

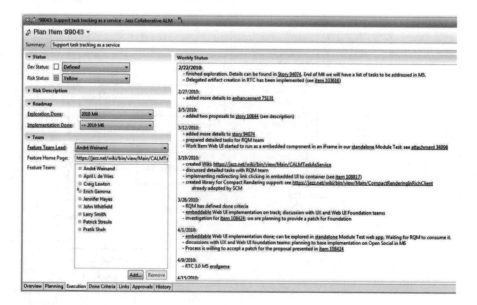

Figure 9.9 *An example plan item, as used in the Rational agile delivery approach*

- Continuous integration of the delivery streams in which changes are shared (rarely green)

- Continuous team builds that focus on the features being developed (always green)

- Developer builds that are used by individuals to validate local work (unmonitored)

The build management system is a critical part of the supporting infrastructure for Rational agile delivery projects. As illustrated in Figure 9.10, builds can be easily scheduled and run and the build status is readily accessible.

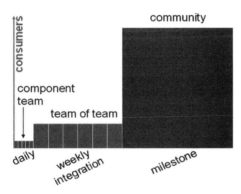

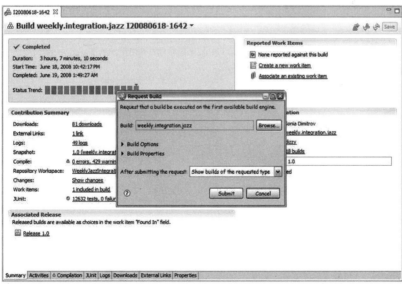

Figure 9.10 *An example of build management in the Rational agile delivery approach*

Ownership and management of the build system is a critical function. The "buildmeister" plays an important role in organizing, scheduling, managing, and authorizing the builds. An example dashboard for this role is illustrated in Figure 9.11.

While at the individual level anyone can perform local builds of the code for which they are responsible, at higher levels the builds require careful governance and monitoring (particularly as the release evolves toward its delivery dates). These controls are more essential when larger products are composed of a complex series of teams that are required to coordinate on the delivery of a release. Here the build management function plays a critical role. As illustrated in Figure 9.12, a comprehensive build management dashboard has a major impact on the coordination of those teams and is a clear indication of progress, weaknesses, and trends.

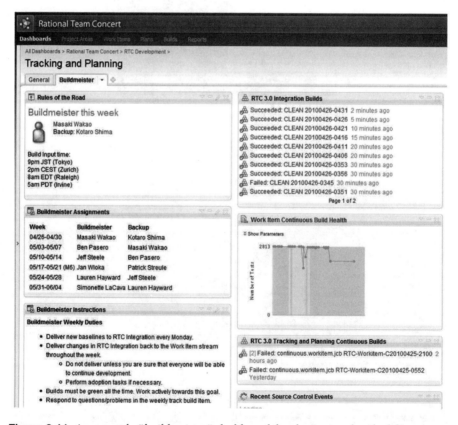

Figure 9.11 *An example "buildmeister" dashboard for the Rational agile delivery approach*

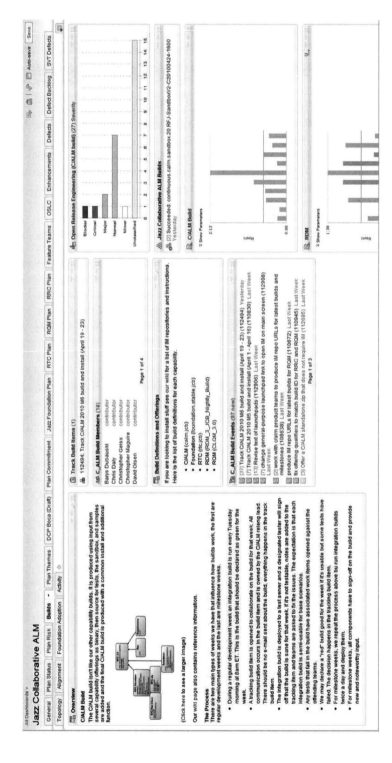

Figure 9.12 *An example of a complex build management dashboard in the rational agile delivery approach*

9.4.6 Retrospectives

The flexibility in the Rational agile delivery approach is based on reacting appropriately to changes in the context for delivery and to experiences that have been gained as the project progresses. During the retrospective parts of the project, the teams reflect on what worked and what didn't, seek to fine-tune the process, and may highlight actions and improvements that should be brought to the attention of the high-level teams.

As illustrated in Figure 9.13, clear records of retrospectives are essential to maintain a history of decisions during project execution and to function as a shared artifact that connects teams.

9.4.7 Transparency

One of the most surprising aspects of the Rational agile delivery approach has to do with transparency of the process. A couple early decisions were made with respect to transparency that proved to have a major influence on the projects: first, project status was globally made transparent with and across project teams, and second, project and team status were made visible to all external stakeholders.

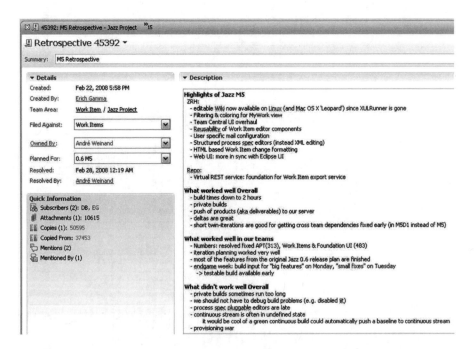

Figure 9.13 *An example retrospective record used in the rational agile delivery approach*

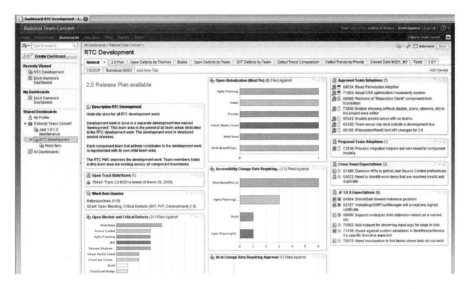

Figure 9.14 *An example release-level project dashboard in the rational agile delivery approach*

As illustrated in Figure 9.14, cross-team transparency involved a major effort to create open, customizable dashboards for understanding team status and progress. The Rational agile delivery approach makes complete, accurate information on the project status available in real time to all members of a project.

The availability of this project information had an interesting and unexpected effect. In addition to supporting cross-team awareness, these dashboards became the basis for sharing best practices and metrics, for highlighting improvement areas in teams, and for early identification of challenges and issues. The cooperation and interactivity of the teams increased dramatically, anticipation of possible problems led to early intervention, and wasteful status meetings were largely eliminated.

With respect to external transparency, as illustrated in Figure 9.15, complete access to all project team dashboards was made available over the Internet to any interested stakeholder.[5] While this decision initially caused a lot of internal debate and hand-wringing, the result has been overwhelmingly positive. The easy accessibility of information on the Rational projects is a critical part of how the organization shares information with clients, the basis for support interactions for direct submission of requests for changes, and used to create an interactive channel between the Rational labs and the clients they serve. Also, direct display of this information in a transparent fashion is an external

5. Accesible at www.jazz.net.

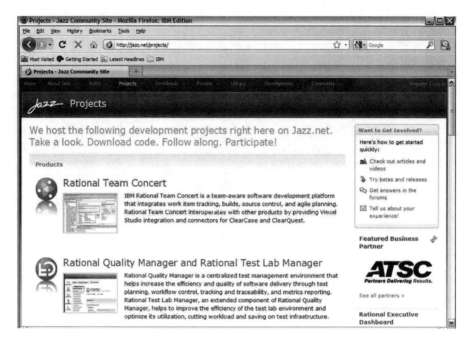

Figure 9.15 *An example external portal into the rational agile delivery approach*

demonstration of a set of best practices for agile adoption, and it's a clear demonstration of Rational's use of its own technologies.

9.4.8 End Game Tracking and Stability

An important challenge in agile development is to understand how the flexibility inherent in these approaches eventually gives way to stability in the release of a system. In the Rational agile delivery approach, the specific identification of an end-game activity serves to devote explicit attention to the tasks necessary to move an enterprise system into production. In particular, as illustrated in Figure 9.16, two important aspects must be addressed:

- *Visibility of status and trends.* The information needed to make decisions will grow as the release matures. Trending data becomes more critical and cross-team relationships and dependencies must be more easily visualized.

- *Hardening of the process.* As a release becomes more mature, a series of release candidates is created. They are aimed at establishing control of the baseline system and demonstrating a clear path to release stability. As

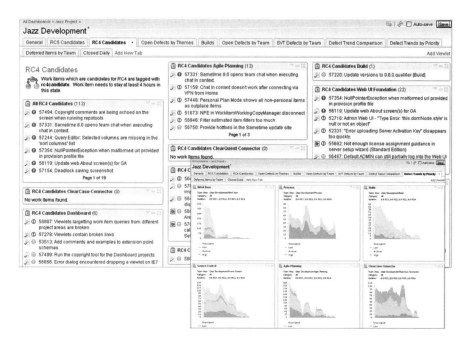

Figure 9.16 *An example trend dashboard in the Rational agile delivery approach*

the release candidates are produced, the agile process is adjusted ("hardened") to reduce flexibility. For example, hardening may include greater attention to code scans, additional sign-offs, restrictions on who can initiate new streams and builds, and so on.

9.4.9 Ongoing Management and Decision Making

Throughout the life of the project there will be enhancement requests, fixes, new requests for changes, resource reallocations, and so on. These must be handled in a responsive and meaningful way across the projects. In the Rational agile delivery approach, these changes are handled at two distinct levels.

At the project level, it's important to have a clear view of the current backlog and status for errors, requests, fixes, and so on. As illustrated in Figure 9.17, in the Rational agile delivery approach, a collection of dashboards shows this status information per product, per release, and per team. Each of these areas is accessible for detailed analysis and is traceable to individual work items allocated to individuals on teams.

At the portfolio level, management must have a clear view of how a set of projects relate to each other. To make informed decisions and trade-offs, project and portfolio managers must understand the financial, resource, and technical

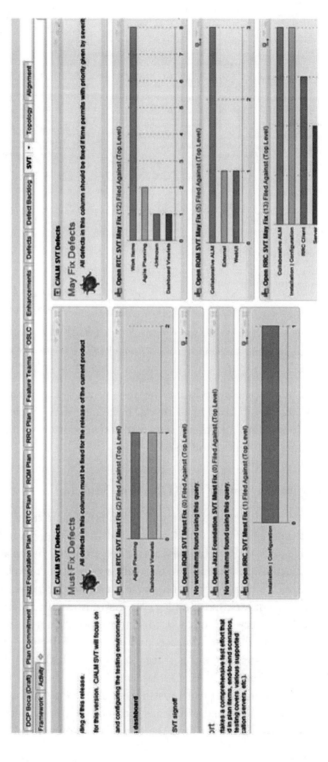

Figure 9.17 *An example system verification test dashboard in use in the Rational agile delivery approach*

relationships among those projects. Consequently, the project information is collected and analyzed in a shared repository using an analytics engine to provide data for decision making.

Figure 9.18 shows an example of the portfolio-level dashboards used by Rational portfolio-level managers to analyze projects and manage resources across the portfolio. The analytics engine allows different kinds of information to be warehoused (extracted from the resource management system, software development tools, project management tools, etc.) and allows a number of rule sets to be defined and run to obtain different views of these data. Several dimensions of project health can be viewed and related, with clear indications of where potential problems have arisen.

9.5 Results and Observations

The Rational software delivery organization launched a concerted approach toward agile delivery adoption in 2006, and it's been constantly upgrading and revising this approach from that time. The results of this effort, summarized in

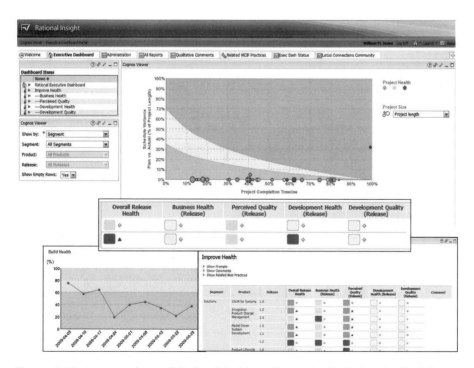

Figure 9.18 *An example portfolio-level dashboard in use in the Rational agile delivery approach*

Figure 9.19, show a remarkable improvement over the baseline situation observed in 2006.

While there were many influential changes and updates across Rational during this period, the significant improvements on software delivery performance from 2006 to 2009 are directly attributable to the change in the enterprise software delivery organization toward more agile delivery approaches.

Figure 9.20 illustrates the rapid uptake of agile delivery approaches in Rational, from a small number of projects and individuals in 2006 to more than a thousand individuals and almost fifty projects by the end of 2009. Perhaps most

Metric	Goal	2006 Measurement	2009 Measurement
On-Time Delivery	65%	47%	100%
Defect Backlog	3 Months	9+ Months	3.5 Months
Enhancements Triaged	85%	3%	100%
Enhancements into Release	15%	1%	21%
Customer Satisfaction Index	91%	88%	96%
Beta Defects Fixed Before GA	50%	3%	94%
Agile/Iterative Projects	25%	5%	78%

Note: Goals are either internal IBM statistics or industry benchmarks.

Figure 9.19 *A summary of Rational performance in 2006 and 2009*

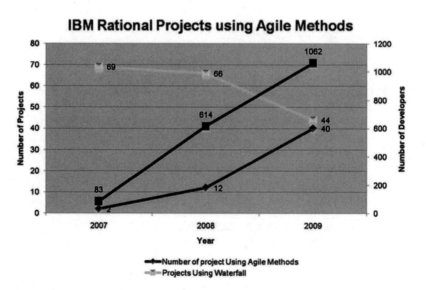

Figure 9.20 *A summary of Rational's use of agile methods*

significant of all, projects classed as primarily agile in nature are now at least as numerous as those that are primarily waterfall in nature. By early 2010, the Rational agile delivery approach was the dominant style in Rational.

The success of these approaches in Rational, aligned with others across IBM, has had a viral effect inside IBM Software Group and in IBM as a whole. The number of IBM users of the Rational agile delivery process, as delivered by the Rational Jazz platform, is now in excess of 60,000 practitioners. Similar results to those reported in Rational have also been observed and documented from groups such as the IBM Tivoli labs in Rome, Italy; the IBM WebSphere customer information control system (CICS) and MQ teams in Hursley, United Kingdom; and several of the IBM application assembly optimization teams in India and China.[6]

9.6 Conclusions

Rational is a large commercial software delivery organization with a twenty-year history of product delivery. It is a global organization with highly interactive teams responsible for a portfolio of interdependent solutions. To improve its performance, agile delivery approaches were considered essential to boost customer responsiveness, increase innovation, and reduce time to market. Rational substantially redesigned its overall delivery approach to incorporate its experiences in agile development in the Rational agile delivery approach.

The changes in Rational's own software delivery organization are essential drivers of Rational's products, tools, and technologies. Rational Jazz is a project and platform that has transformed how teams and individuals work together to deliver greater value and performance. Not only is it the basis for Rational's own delivery transformation, it is also now widely deployed across IBM and is the infrastructure for Rational's new generation of enterprise software delivery products.

---

6. These figures are taken from the end of 2011. The adoption and use of agile practices at IBM, supported by the IBM Rational Jazz platform, continue to grow.

Chapter 10

Lessons for Success in Global Enterprise Software Delivery

Chapter Summary

I summarize a number of the most prominent themes of the book. I provide a series of lessons for global enterprise software delivery based on the analyses in earlier chapters, and I explicitly challenge where and when those lessons can be applied, pointing out they may have limited value in specific contexts. I then compare what I've discussed in enterprise software delivery with similar approaches from other relevant domains and note the following:

- These practical lessons for global enterprise software delivery have great utility but are not a panacea for every ill, nor can they find ready use in every circumstance; they must be applied with thought and amended to the relevant context.

- Other domains, particularly in other engineering disciplines, have a rich set of experiences that we can leverage, such as those of global manufacturing, supply chain management, and so on.

- A number of large program failures can be examined where excessive, inappropriate, or unmanaged adoption of global software supply chain approaches have contributed to the failure. It's wise to be wary and take lessons from such experiences.

10.1 Introduction

Throughout this book I introduce a number of ideas, approaches, techniques, and examples that encourage the reevaluation of enterprise software delivery. Each can offer important improvements in delivery for those involved in software supply chains or those who confront challenges in global software delivery. However, it's essential that I also discuss the limitations and challenges of how to introduce them appropriately and provide a deeper understanding of the context for their use.

For global enterprise software delivery, a primary challenge concerns balancing the pressure to increase agility and flexibility to be able to change and adapt to emerging needs, on the one hand, with the pressure to ensure continued control, predictability, and governance to reduce risk and maintain efficient accountability in the use of resources, on the other hand. In previous chapters I examine this balance from several dimensions and describe techniques for how it can be established. Here I further examine this balance by analyzing the different factors that must be taken into account for practical success. The primary hypothesis I explore is that viewing enterprise software delivery through the lens of a global supply chain becomes valuable to a very wide set of contexts, offers critical insights into how such software delivery can be improved, and provides a useful framework for balancing agility and industrialization in enterprise software delivery.

I focus on four areas to examine this hypothesis. First, I refine the notion of *enterprise* to gain greater insight into how variations in the organization affect success in applying these approaches. Second, I raise a number of risks and limitations to the use of some of these ideas. In particular, I ensure that use of industrialized approaches can be introduced and enhanced in appropriate ways within specific organizational contexts. Third, I extract lessons from other domains, where industrialized, supply chain delivery models have been used for some time. Finally, I describe several small examples and illustrations of failures in global software delivery that we can learn from. I summarize the chapter with a high-level set of lessons for successful adoption of industrialized approaches to enterprise software delivery.

10.2 Revisiting the Enterprise

Previous chapters avoid any deep discussion of differences between enterprise software delivery organizations by using the term *enterprise* in a general sense to refer to any context in which there are multiple individuals and business units working together to perform a specified task or mission. This simplification enables me to focus attention on key themes that unify the messages explored in this book, avoiding too many distractions from the different variations in details of the approach and highlighting the general applicability of supply chain thinking across enterprise software delivery.

However, it is appropriate at this point to revisit the scope of an enterprise. Here I distinguish five categories of an enterprise and make a number of contextual comments concerning the applicability (or limitations) of the themes of the book as they relate to each category. This is not an exhaustive review of enterprise categories. Rather, I use this categorization to illustrate how the contexts of different enterprise scopes influence practical adoption of improvements in global enterprise software delivery.

10.2.1 Organizations Managing Front- and Back-Office Systems

Historically, the approach toward the role of computing and software in many organizations made a clear distinction between what came to be called *front-office* and *back-office* activities. Front- and back-office activities play distinct roles:

- The *front office* includes the capabilities and services that are made directly accessible to the clients of that organization. In a bank, these include opening an account, requests for account changes, and managing requests for new services. For a hotel chain, these are the functions related to a client reserving a room, changing reservation details, key management, and so on. In a hospital, the front-office activities include patient registration, diagnosis support, and treatment management.

- The *back office* supports the delivery of front-office services by offering the capabilities necessary for the organization to function effectively. Generally, the back-office functions include customer relationship management (CRM), human resource management (HRM), sales management, and so on. Additionally, in a bank this may include settlement and clearing activities. In a hotel chain this may include forecasting and booking consolidation. In a hospital this may include ordering drugs, scheduling doctors and nurses, and managing bed occupancy across several hospital wards.

Often classified as traditional *enterprise IT*, the management of the back-office functions is particularly important because it's frequently the primary determinant in the organization's efficiency and the major consumer of the enterprise organization's resources. Not only do we look at back-office capabilities in terms of the business, but we also see them as the cornerstone of software operations management for those organizations. Hence the back-office, or enterprise IT, function may include core functions such as data-center management, disaster recovery, backups and restoration, and so on.

There is a long history of management and measurement specifically aimed at the enterprise IT areas with the goals of standardizing and organizing these back-office activities for improved efficiency. Hence there is a strong affinity between the ideas of this book and traditional back-office software delivery.

In practice, back-office capabilities have been the clearest examples of software supply chain thinking, deployment of packaged applications, and the use of global outsourcing approaches to deliver software factories. The maturity of this approach in many organizations has led to strategic outsourcing of most or all back-office functions to third-party organizations. Many major corporations operate with large strategic outsource contracts in place and thus rely entirely on such third parties to deliver the capabilities they need to function on a daily basis [76].

10.2.2 Organizations Where Software Is the Business

In many companies, the traditional *enterprise IT* view of the software delivery organization, including the front- and back-office distinction, has been largely swept away. It's become impossible for these organizations to make any meaningful distinction between which services are affected directly by the client and which are not. As a result, it can be considered suboptimal to attempt to make that separation. This is the case in two distinct organizational situations:

- New businesses have emerged that rely entirely on software for their operation and delivery. Exemplified by Amazon and eBay, there are many recently created organizations that derive the entire business model, operation, and value from their software. With such organizations, there is little value in separating the capabilities they offer to the client, the services they deliver to allow that, how they support those activities, and how they work with suppliers and partners to optimize delivery of those services.

- Traditional businesses have created major operating channels that offer new capabilities to their clients. Initially this was the move from "brick-and-mortar" solutions in banking and retail companies toward Internet-based delivery of services (e.g., online banking at INGDirect and home shopping at TescoDirect). Now more and more organizations across many domains offer Internet-based solutions that augment their traditional businesses. The blend between traditional and Internet-based business is at times very clear (e.g., with completely separate organization, personnel, and infrastructure) but is now more frequently seen as an inherent component in the overall operating approach of the company (often accounting for the majority of investment and growth).

In these organizations, a dynamic and complex configuration of capabilities is necessary, with many different services that must be delivered by the enterprise software delivery organization. There is a continued need to offer traditional services that are necessary in any enterprise IT domain (such as CRM, HRM, and sales management) and to support effective operations (such as backup and recovery). However, significant investment in new capabilities is also required to support new delivery technologies (e.g., new mobile devices and their operating systems). Dedicated systems and resources must focus on security and fraud detection (e.g., to protect against viruses, Trojan horses, and phishing and to detect new kinds of attacks), and more attention must be directed toward partner ecosystems and supporting activities (e.g., through open application programmable interfaces [APIs] and service interfaces).

For organizations with a blend of traditional and new business activities, the integration of enterprise software delivery needs is particularly challenging. The new software-driven organizational aspects must work with the more traditional enterprise IT organization to deliver a complementary set of services. It's not unusual for changes and optimizations in one part of the organization to be implemented at the cost of creating additional challenges in other parts of the business. Careful consideration of the balance of these needs is critical.

In summary, software-driven organizations must address fast-paced changes and diverse business models with a balance that supports the organization's broader mission and function. These characteristics make supply chain thinking particularly relevant and valuable. It has become essential to develop views that allow companies to reassess the strategic importance of different parts of the business, use resources effectively across the supply chain, and employ outside organizations to deliver capabilities at lowest cost.

10.2.3 Organizations Where Software Is the Product

An extension of these ideas on the importance of software to many organizations is the specialization where software *is* the product. Many organizations create products that are delivered wholly as software to be executed on one or more platforms. Here are two common situations:

- *Niche software suppliers that support specific industry domains.* Some companies create specialist solutions in support of business processes and activities in that domain. Often their work is dominated by a specific platform, organization, or market. This affinity may largely dictate many aspects of the software, including the technology used, the pace of innovation, and the pricing and packaging of the software solution.

- *Software-dominant businesses where intellectual property is embedded entirely in software.* Many small and medium-sized enterprises (SMEs) have emerged that produce new capabilities entirely in software. The obvious example is in the games and gaming industry, where there are thousands of organizations producing innovative software solutions. But also, the pervasive use of PCs and handheld devices has opened up new business opportunities for many companies that do nothing except deliver software to their clients in domains such as education, entertainment, sports, and many more.

In all cases, the supply chain view has emerged as a viable way to look at how these organizations fit into a broader ecosystem. This approach helps them analyze the role they play and the contribution they make, encourages them to see their relationship with partners and competitors, and helps optimize their strategy toward the unique capabilities they bring.

The cost structure of software delivery today is such that many of these organizations are frequently distributed across several geographic regions, even though they may be small in size (between, say, ten and a hundred employees). A typical software delivery organization in this category may have a small design team in North America, several product management teams in Europe, and the majority of the development teams in Asia. These companies cannot manage and deliver quality software in a dynamic marketplace without careful consideration of many of the ideas presented in this book: collaboration, agile delivery, and clear visibility across the enterprise software delivery organization.

10.2.4 Organizations Where Software Delivery Is the Product

The complexity, unpredictability, and cost of enterprise software delivery have led many companies to use third-party organizations as software delivery agents. By outsourcing small or large parts of the software delivery tasks, the resulting enterprise software delivery organization is a blend of local and third-party resources. The promise of working in this way is that the company can obtain the specialist help it requires, have some amount of elasticity of resources, and obtain greater efficiency in the cost of delivery. This outsourcing also helps decrease the risk of a down market when staff cuts may be required to maintain profitability.

The third-party software delivery organizations tasked with carrying out this work must optimize around certain delivery capabilities that bring value to their clients (for which they can charge a premium) or deliver for lowest cost at acceptable quality (for which they can look to standardize and consolidate practices to repeatedly deliver to create the volume of business needed to make a profit). The result, as exemplified by system integrators (SIs) such as Accenture, CapGemini, Indra, and IBM Global Services, is a set of companies that must adopt product-line and software-factory thinking as a fundamental part of their delivery approach.

Such organizations typically offer at least three distinct delivery models to meet their clients' needs:

- *Project delivery.* Support for small-scale projects whose delivery time can be measured in hours or days. Typically, teams must be initiated quickly and become immediately productive. Working on fixed-price contracts, they quickly deliver some software-based solution to the client before disbanding and moving onto the next task. Speed, predictability, and consistent quality are the key to success in these projects.

- *Solution delivery.* For larger enterprise software delivery efforts, usually lasting many months, teams may be responsible for some components of a large system or augment local teams with specialist personnel. Frequently on long-term agreements or time-and-material contracts, the goal is to provide high value to the client through consistent performance and quality.

- *Strategic outsourcing.* When large parts of the enterprise software delivery function are outsourced, a structured approach is taken to construct semipermanent teams that can deliver greatest value in carrying out the role. Governed by a detailed contract and service level agreement, the goal is to meet that contract as efficiently as possible, making best use of the organization's global resources. Clear management against that contract is the key to all decision making, with cost efficiency directly aimed at meeting these service levels at the lowest possible cost.

While very different in nature, each of these delivery approaches leads the delivery organizations to adopt lessons from supply chain and software factory thinking as a way to improve performance and predictability and as central ideas of their cost management approaches. For internal efficiency, many such organizations create "centers of excellence" offering critical skills to the rest of the organization (e.g., in specialist software delivery techniques such as security testing or in domain-specific techniques such as safety-case analysis for real-time systems), and they use supply chain approaches to manage and control demand across those centers.

10.2.5 Summary

I've highlighted several important categories of enterprise. While each has its own characteristics, the importance of supply chain thinking can be demonstrated across these categories. However, the priority and interpretation of many of the specific techniques I've described is, of course, dependent on the context, and care must be taken in how these techniques are adapted to suit the specific circumstances.

10.3 Risks and Limitations

An essential part of any proposed set of changes to process and practices is to have a clear view of the risks and limitations associated with them. A global approach to enterprise software delivery is no exception. In this section I examine four important areas for concern: applicability to SMEs, the impact of organizational immaturity, how to maintain innovation in industrialized software delivery, and mitigation approaches across supply chain weaknesses.

10.3.1 Applicability to SMEs

It can be claimed that failure to manage enterprise system complexity is the single biggest reason that those systems so often fail.[1] But complexity has many dimensions and is a result of many factors. It may be that the domain being addressed is challenging to understand and model (e.g., domains such as avionics, biotechnology, telecommunications, and many others). Perhaps that domain is highly governed and requires extreme levels of transparency and reporting to be auditable (e.g., many financial management and health care domains). In many cases, the complexity is associated with the technology context in which the software operates, perhaps supporting an array of diverse platforms or requiring high levels of fault tolerance and self-correction due to instabilities that can arise in the technology as it is deployed.

However, most frequently the complexity arises as a result of scale. Many of the most complex enterprise systems exhibit that complexity because they address a broad range of capabilities, they are created by large teams of people, and they require diverse skills from several teams in different organizations to collaborate in their construction. Much of the work in software engineering over the past years has been aimed at understanding and managing these kinds

---

1. This claim was discussed in detail, for example, in Roger Session's writings, available at www .objectwatch.com.

of situations and controlling the complexity in the systems that are the result of such efforts.

The ideas I've discussed in this book are directed at managing the challenges that arise as the result of this complexity. Many of them are particularly effective in large-scale situations where the enterprise systems are the work of multiple teams from different organizations. But I believe that supply chain and software factory approaches also have an important role to play in SMEs. Specifically, I'll point to three areas where this thinking has relevance to SMEs:

- *The role an SME plays in the software supply chain.* Often the delivery of enterprise systems is highly dependent on SMEs for specialist skills and services. For example, a great deal of innovation in software is the result of small teams and organizations that can address challenging problems with new ideas and revolutionary thinking. Frequently this innovation is a critical differentiator as a component in larger systems. Therefore, it's essential for SMEs to understand the changes in supply chain thinking and technology that can affect their role and to develop their solutions with a clear knowledge of the context within which the solutions will be used.

- *Distribution and collaboration of teams.* As discussed earlier, even SMEs are now distributed across multiple locations. While the broader approaches to collaboration support may be overwhelming, informal synchronization across teams may be insufficient where team members are in different time zones, when insecure or high-latency infrastructure connects the team, or if they do not share the same cultural heritage. Hence regardless of an organization's size, some explicit forms of team collaboration infrastructure and practices will be necessary.

- *Interaction with partners.* It is tempting to think that supply chains and software factories are beneficial only in large enterprises. However, the economics of software delivery are such that many SMEs also use subcontractors, outsource activities to companies in other geographies, and use specialist technology suppliers. For SMEs the labor costs are by far the dominant expense. There are many situations in which one SME is in reality composed of a core team in Western Europe with small teams of developers in Eastern Europe, Asia, or Latin America. Understanding the dynamics of these diverse supply chains is an essential part of effective management regardless of the size of organization involved.

The bottom line is that scale does matter in enterprise software delivery. This book has explicitly focused on the implications of this scale on effective enterprise software delivery. The industrialization offered by supply chain approaches helps address the challenges this scale can bring. Many of the ideas have particular relevance in large-scale situations, and the illustrations I've used throughout the book have highlighted several examples.

However, I also view the balance of agility and industrialization as critical to all scales of enterprise software delivery. SMEs can find value from this thinking by gaining a deeper understanding of the role they play in the software supply chain, improving their approach to collaborative delivery across their teams, and interacting with partners in their own supply chains in a more effective way.

10.3.2 The Impact of Process Maturity

The move toward industrialization of enterprise software delivery depends on a maturity of approach to software delivery that is essential to enact the changes necessary for success. It can be argued that any approach that requires the management and control of a software supply chain presupposes that the organization has in place a set of management practices that enable that vision to be executed in practice.[2] A number of important observations can be made with regard to the relationship between organizational maturity and supply chain thinking.

I'll begin by noting that there is an existing wealth of research and practice in understanding organizational maturity and its impact in general on enterprise software delivery. The importance of a mature set of software delivery practices is at the heart of several important areas of work, perhaps best exemplified by the maturity levels defined in the Software Engineering Institute (SEI) capability maturity models (CMM) and the integration of those models (CMMI) [35].

The CMMI describes a framework for examining the process maturity of an enterprise software delivery organization. As illustrated in Figure 10.1, the lower levels of the CMMI scale (levels 1 and 2) characterize organizations with minimal ability to understand the processes they employ in enterprise software delivery and with little visibility into the results they obtain to support disciplined improvements. According to this view, it's only with improved levels of maturity (levels 3, 4, and 5) that the measures necessary for sustained optimization activities are available.

Unfortunately, the studies carried out at the SEI and elsewhere over the last decade indicate that as many as 70 percent of all enterprise software delivery organizations fall into the lowest two maturity categories. Such low maturity organizations are unlikely to make effective changes toward greater industrialized software delivery approaches because they lack necessary standardization, do not follow predictable processes, and have no baseline of measures on which to steer those improvements toward a satisfactory result.

---

2. According to Thomas Edison, "A vision without execution is hallucination."

CMMI Maturity Levels

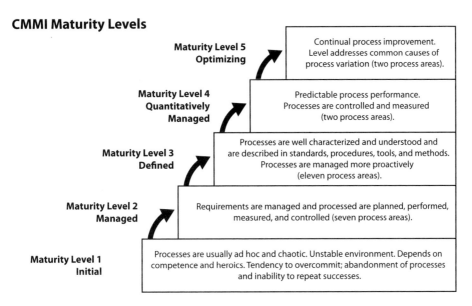

Figure 10.1 *A simplified view of the five levels of maturity in the SEI capability maturity model for software*

This observation cannot be taken lightly. However, it does not obviate the need for most organizations to begin the journey that is necessary for making important changes to their enterprise software delivery approaches. Indeed, it provides us guidance and benchmarks that can aid that transition. For example, specifically in regard to software outsourcing, a key element of the supply chain vision, there are two main ways in which process maturity as indicated by the CMMI has been used.

First, in recent years outsourcers have been using the CMM and CMMI to demonstrate the rigor, repeatability, and efficiency of their delivery capability to potential clients. Most often, these outsource delivery organizations gain certification at the highest levels of the maturity scale for the software factories that they use to deliver software and services to clients. In that way, they can demonstrate to clients that they employ repeatable, optimized processes in their enterprise software delivery, and they can validate for their own management that they use standardized techniques that efficiently produce optimal results. The higher levels of CMM maturity support the kinds of statistically controlled optimization essential for efficient delivery.

Second, outsourcee groups have been using CMM as an assessment approach to evaluate potential outsourcers.[3] This is an approach encouraged by the SEI

---

3. www.keane.com/resources%2Fpdf%2FWhitePapers%2FOutsourcingCMM.pdf.

in its adaptation of the CMM to acquisition activities (the so-called software acquisition CMM [77]). In this approach, the key process areas in CMM levels 2 and 3 become the basis of a scorecard for evaluating the practices in use by the outsourcer and provide a mechanism for understanding and managing software outsourcing risks.

One of the most interesting observations to be made with regard to process maturity and supply chains is that significant challenges are faced when there is a mismatch in maturity between the different groups that must collaborate across that supply chain. For example, there is an increased chance of failure when a company that is operating at CMM level 2 maturity decides to outsource to a CMM level 5 company located in a different part of the world. While initially the immature outsourcing company may see outsourcing cost savings through lower labor rates and increased flexibility of its staffing, the savings are likely to be wasted due to the instability of management processes, inexperience in measurement, and lack of visibility into critical project-planning activities.[4] In such situations, benchmarks and improvement frameworks such as the CMM can act as an essential tool for identifying areas of maturity mismatch where agreement across the supply chain are essential, and these frameworks can offer a roadmap for improving supply chain performance with a phased approach.

In short, I believe that maturity of an enterprise software delivery organization can be a strong indicator of the challenges it will face in industrializing enterprise software delivery. Increasing an organization's level of success with software factory models, particularly outsourcing, can be obtained by using frameworks for improvement (such as the Software Acquisition CMM) across the software supply chain.

However, I must note that the CMM and similar improvement frameworks are primarily optimized for large enterprise adoption (as can be expected given their heritage in large government software programs). Hence the maturity of an organization with respect to the CMM does not necessarily mean it is well adapted to all classes of supply chains—particularly those that involve many organizations of different sizes, cultures, and specialties.[5] As always, maturity is a relative measure and is highly dependent on the context of enterprise software delivery. This is true in general, including in industrialized approaches to software delivery.

---

4. http://ezinearticles.com/?The-Biggest-Challenge-to-Outsourcing-Success—Differences-in-Processes-and-CMM&id=1262120.

5. http://advice.cio.com/remi/cmm_might_be_mature_but_is_it_adapted.

10.3.3 Software Is Not Manufactured; It Is Crafted and Evolved

The idea of "industrializing" software delivery, and in particular the use of the term *software factory*, is a clear attempt to draw an analogy with manufacturing disciplines to provide a useful way of thinking about industrialization of enterprise software delivery that builds on the lessons from that domain. From this perspective, it invokes an image with many positive characteristics of governance, efficiency, control, and predictability.

But the term *software factory* can also be viewed as a provocation. Many negative connotations imply mundane, repeated tasks that promote uniformity and rote activities, suppressing creativity and innovation. For many people it is the "softness" of software (its malleability and infinite variety) that is the source of its value. The industrialization of enterprise software delivery must not be construed as the death of innovation in software.

This dichotomy between the need for control and the need for creativity is perhaps best illustrated in the writings of Walker Royce [78]. To examine innovation in software, Royce draws an analogy between enterprise software delivery and movie making. He explains that both activities struggle with this blend of rigor and creativity, and that early stages of the process involve significant "scrap and rework" as part of the creative process. In these early stages, it's usually a mistake to minimize rework, as it stifles needed creativity and flexibility. However, later in the process there must be a great deal of focus on reducing rework to eliminate inefficiencies.

The result of this tension is an important blend of artistic creativity supported by extensive engineering and management for production, postproduction, and distribution of the completed work. Furthermore, Royce states that what is needed is a "steering leadership style rather than the detailed plan-and-track leadership style encouraged by conventional wisdom." The coordination and planning is generally less detailed and rigorous at the beginning of a project and increases over time when more is known on which to base detailed plans and drive consistency.

It is important to align Royce's observations with the supply chain approaches and software factories discussed in this book. In particular, it's a mistake to view the industrialization of enterprise software delivery as aimed purely at a mechanical style of software delivery maniacally focused on reducing cost. Rather, I'll highlight several ways in which Royce's observations on innovation can provide important lessons for the industrialization of enterprise software delivery:

- Even in highly innovative situations, specializations and supply chain approaches are employed to control costs and manage risks. In movie making this is via companies that specialize in aspects of design, digital technology, and postproduction editing. A movie studio brings together a wide variety of skills in a complex network of relationships to ensure the creativity necessary in some areas can be marshaled effectively into a satisfying and profitable result. The same pressures, approaches, and challenges face enterprise software delivery in producing systems that match stakeholders' needs and provide value to the organization.

- Different software delivery styles are appropriate for different kinds of projects. For example, there are aspects of software delivery that may be well matched to waterfall styles of delivery where initial planning can be signed-off before software construction takes place. This is perhaps more akin to production studios that create many movies in the same style or based on common themes. While in other situations with greater amounts of innovation and uncertainty, more iterative and agile techniques are necessary. For some highly innovative movies, film companies spend a great deal of their resources in creating new technologies and techniques for capturing the vision and intent of the movie. It is essential that such process variation is understood, supported, and managed.

- Project management and planning is not a single event, but rather a relationship that evolves through discovery, negotiation, and redirection. Account must be taken of where this flexibility is necessary, particularly in relationships across organizational boundaries where contractual arrangements may be necessary. For movies, we see great emphasis on managing large productions to cost and deadline. However, we also see many changes necessary throughout production to meet emerging market needs, to adapt to new social and political conditions, or to overcome technical challenges. This flexibility is essential to success.

- Adaptation of the delivery process throughout its execution may require changes in the measurement, governance, and control of enterprise software delivery. While difficult to manage, such variation must be expected and accounted for. For movies, the ultimate measure is the box office revenue—how many people pay to watch the movie in a theater or purchase the subsequent DVD. However, other important measures can have great impact, including ease of adaptation to television or computer games, merchandising, and so on. As with software, many of these secondary measures can become dominant over the lifetime of a system or solution. They must be considered as part of the overall project planning.

Finally, we can also note that Royce's ten management principles for agile software delivery have direct relevance to industrialized approaches to enterprise software delivery. With some amount of reinterpretation and rewording, they offer excellent guidance for how to approach supply chains and software outsourcing to maximize collaboration and reinforce innovative delivery:

- Reduce uncertainties by first agreeing with all parties on an architectural framework and a clear set of architectural principles.

- Establish a set of variation points and a governance process that allows an adaptive life-cycle process that accelerates variance reduction and provides clear points of innovation.

- Reduce the amount of custom development through shared asset reuse, a common asset repository, and standardized middleware components.

- Enhance visibility and transparency with emphasis on measuring the cost of change, quality trends, and progress trends.

- Communicate honest progressions and digressions with all stakeholders. Problems should be surfaced as early as possible, and their resolution should be the focus of all partners.

- Build into the process formal and informal ways to collaborate regularly with stakeholders within and across organizations to renegotiate priorities, scope, resources, and plans.

- Continuously integrate releases and test usage scenarios with evolving breadth and depth, using these activities as a primary means of coordination for all parties.

- Establish a collaboration platform that enhances teamwork among potentially distributed teams, making sure it is particularly suited to work across different geographic and organizational boundaries.

- Maintain control, but do not be slaves to the initial plan. Enhance the freedom to change plans, scope, and code releases through automation.

- Establish a governance model that guarantees creative freedoms where it provides most value to organizations, teams, and practitioners within the broader governance framework.

10.3.4 Supply Chain Weaknesses

The move toward a software supply chain brings a number of risks that are common across every set of partnerships. Frankly speaking, reliance on other organizations brings with it a potential lack of insight and control. Several possible pitfalls must be addressed:

- *Failure to deliver on time, with quality, or to agreed specifications.* Any partnership relies on trust, respect, and open dialogue. However, in enterprise software delivery these must be supported by clear approaches to ensure that agreements are being met. A variety of inspection approaches can be employed to help reinforce those agreements, and many supply chains include review and analysis activities to ensure that artifacts being created are as complete, consistent, and effective as possible.

- *Suppliers going out of business.* The reliance on partners always opens the possibility that those partners become so essential to an organization's enterprise software delivery that it would be catastrophic if they ceased to be in business. Many contingencies are possible, with most organizations opting to multisource key components to ensure competition or to escrow key source code to ensure access to it.

- *Partners optimizing for different needs or becoming competitors.* With the dynamics of the market economy, suppliers are often under pressure from many clients for enhancements and new features. It's not always clear that your organization's needs will have highest priority or will be in the best interest of the supplier. Also, the supplier may move to offer competitive capabilities or may be acquired by a competing organization. Again, dependence on a single partner can aggravate this risk, and measures are needed to mitigate it. In addition, some organizations look to invest in joint partnerships to place business constraints on the partners in a supply chain where the alignment of priorities across the partners is much more explicit.

- *Malware, trapdoors, and intellectual property theft.* Attention to issues of security and protection of intellectual property are necessities in today's environment. Effective techniques are necessary to ensure that clear agreements are in place and are being followed. It's common, for example, to scan all delivered code from outsourced suppliers for various known security problems, to set up external security teams to monitor all aspects of software development and delivery, and to run periodic compliance audits to ensure that all parties are following the agreements.

- *Different motivations, costs, roles, and cultures.* In the end, it must be accepted that different organizations in a supply chain will be operating in different contexts. This diversity is the source of much strength but also requires careful understanding and management. Misunderstandings and miscommunication can arise from these differences, and sensitivity is essential. For example, many organizations are beginning to address cultural differences between geographically distributed teams with awareness activities that help participants understand the working contexts and social climates of the dispersed teams.

10.3.5 Summary

Despite our best efforts, the move toward more diverse, distributed organizations based on software supply chains introduces challenges that must be recognized and addressed. The risks I've raised here are indicative of the hurdles that must be overcome to create effective approaches to industrialized enterprise software delivery. While many of these issues are common supply chain issues, they are exacerbated by two important factors:

- *The world is not flat.* High-speed networks and technology advances have enhanced communication, but distances between teams still play a major role in causing misunderstandings, misinterpretation, and mistrust.[6]

- *Motivation and culture matter.* In matters of enterprise software delivery, we all carry around a large amount of context and history at the personal, team, and organizational levels. Efforts to standardize across these differences will have limited impact. Rather, finding ways to embrace and support that diversity promises more success.

Far from trying to dominate and erase these issues, industrialized approaches to enterprise software delivery must recognize the challenges for what they are and introduce techniques that address them within the context of high-performance supply chains.

10.4 Lessons from Other Domains

Industrialization and supply chain approaches to solution delivery are not new. Indeed, there is a rich history of experiences in how to improve the consistency, predictability, and efficiency of solution delivery in several domains, including software-intensive systems. Here I'll look at three areas of particular relevance: evolutionary acquisition and through-life capability management (TLCM), supply chain management, and lean manufacturing.

---

6. With all due respect to the views expressed by Friedman [17].

10.4.1 Evolutionary Acquisition and TLCM

For many years, the defense industry has been focusing attention on the need to provide ways to maximize the capability it delivers while increasing flexibility and managing costs. A great deal can be learned from the kinds of approaches and practices it has adopted with respect to industrializing enterprise software delivery. Here I describe two major directions of particular relevance: evolutionary acquisition and TLCM.

Over the past decade, evolutionary acquisition approaches have become the preferred strategy for the rapid acquisition of defense technologies in the United Kingdom and United States. Traditionally, major defense systems have had notoriously long acquisition and deployment phases; in some instances, by the time the technology is delivered, it is already redundant, outdated, or obsolete. In reaction to this, an evolutionary approach delivers capability in increments, recognizing the need for future capability improvements up front. Each increment provides useful and supportable operational capabilities that can be developed, produced, deployed, and sustained. Major enhancements and preplanned product improvements are managed as separate increments.

Several studies have examined the ways in which evolutionary acquisition is being realized in major defense programs [79,80]. While they identify challenges with managing large defense programs using an evolutionary approach, they also indicate that several important success patterns have emerged:

- Evolutionary acquisition promotes flexibility, but a level of agreement and consistency across the supply chain has been essential to avoid potential confusion.

- Evolutionary acquisition requires greater collaboration and involvement of all project roles (including business, technical, and program management) throughout the program.

- Incremental and spiral-based models for evolutionary acquisition enhance the ongoing negotiation and replanning of major elements of the programs.

The result of these studies reveals that an evolutionary approach to acquisition creates, in effect, a supply chain approach that considers a defense system to be an evolving system of capabilities that must be readily upgraded and enhanced to address evolving needs. It is well matched to the kinds of approaches and thinking that have been explored in our discussion on the industrialization of enterprise software delivery.

TLCM addresses the need in defense systems to deliver maximum availability of platforms, systems, and assets through their operational life. TLCM translates the requirements of defense policy into an approved set of practices that deliver the required capabilities throughout a system's life and across all contributors to the delivery supply chain (including the different defense lines-of-business). The intent is for TLCM to offer a comprehensive way of looking across the whole life cycle to ensure that an appropriate balance is maintained between short-term innovation and longer-term support needs.

Essential to TLCM is the ability to coordinate and visualize the many different activities and artifacts that are produced throughout a large defense program. The ability to capture, visualize, and understand the multiple inter-dependencies of the required systems-of-systems is a hugely complex task. It requires the coordination, agreement, and collaboration of all contributors and stakeholders across the program. In the defense community's experience, this broad view of system delivery is an essential approach for managing ongoing costs and prioritizing change.

To summarize, defense systems acquisition and delivery requires greater flexibility and efficiency. It is driving new ways of working that bring important lessons for the industrialization of enterprise software delivery. The importance of these approaches cannot be overemphasized. This point is underscored by the UK Ministry of Defence's explicit beliefs that these approaches toward assembling systems from a robust commercial supply chain are critical to its success. The UK defense strategy is based on the fact that "a greater proportion of [the UK Ministry of Defence's] overall business is available to industry than in any other major defence nation, and growing expertise in the combination of systems engineering skills, agility and supply chain management required to deliver through-life capability management gives the UK defence industry a comparative advantage."[7]

10.4.2 Supply Chain Management

It has long been recognized that success in many business activities requires careful focus on the relationships between all suppliers involved in the delivery of goods and services to customers. This view has been highlighted throughout the twentieth century with moves toward greater automation in the creation and assembly of many goods and most recently in the diversification and globalization of supply of parts used in assembly. The result has been explicit attention to understanding the supply chain: the facilities, functions, and activities

---

7. From page 6 of [81].

associated with the flow and transformation of goods and services from raw materials to customer solutions [82].

The primary goal for many companies has been to overcome inefficiencies that result from the siloed behavior across various departments and groups (e.g., between marketing, finance, research, and product development). To ensure that the supply chain is operating as efficiently as possible and generating the highest level of customer satisfaction at the lowest cost, companies have invested in supply chain management processes and associated technology.

However, with the growing complexity of many companies' networks of suppliers, managing the supply chain has become increasingly important and challenging. For example, connecting suppliers requires managing the flow of information throughout the supply chain to attain the level of synchronization that will make it more responsive to customer needs while lowering costs. Consequently, much of the attention has been focused on issues associated with supply chain integration:

- Information sharing among supply chain partners to provide early detection of problems, improve response time, increase trust between suppliers, and reduce the instability that can occur due to delivery anomalies (the so-called bullwhip effect)

- Collaborative planning, forecasting, replenishment, and design to lower costs and improve customer satisfaction

- Coordinated procurement, workflow, production, and operations to reduce production inefficiencies and increase responsiveness to new customer demands

- Adoption of new business models and technologies to allow innovation in product creation and delivery, increase efficiency, and support entry into new markets

There are many close parallels between this broad view of supply chain management and the experiences I've explored with respect to the industrialization of enterprise software delivery throughout this book. The experiences, detailed analysis, and investigation of the past decade have particularly clear applicability. Here we can look at three specific areas of alignment that illustrate this affinity.

First, current literature on supply chain management offers insight into the focus areas and market directions that are driving research and practice in this area. These insights provide direct support for the major themes of this book:

- Collaborative planning with design partners, distributors, and suppliers to increase transparency and visibility across the supply chain

- Real-time commitments for design, production, inventory, and capacity planning to offer just-in-time delivery of goods and on-demand services

- Flexible logistics options to ensure timely fulfillment and increase agility in providing value to the customer

- Increased visibility and reporting across multiple vendors and carriers to enhance decision making and ensure delivery of goods

- Personalized content and services for increased interaction and alignment to customer needs

Second, analyses of the success criteria and delivery patterns from numerous case studies have begun to uncover the high-priority areas for organizations looking to obtain differentiation from their supply chain. In particular, organizations who are successfully managing their supply chains in today's dynamic, global marketplace demonstrate the following practices:

- View the supply chain as a strategic asset and a differentiator (e.g., Dell's innovative direct-to-consumer sales and Volkswagen's build-to-order manufacturing approach)

- Create unique supply chain configurations that align with the company's strategic objectives, particularly as they relate to outsourcing, multichannel delivery, and customer service

- Reduce supply chain uncertainty by investing in technologies that enhance forecasting, encourage collaboration across suppliers, and improve integration between suppliers and customers

Finally, industry efforts around supply chain management have resulted in standardization on frameworks that encourage consistent approaches to the management and measurement of supply chain solutions. Most notably, the Supply Chain Council,[8] a multi-industry, nonprofit organization with more than eight hundred members, has created a supply chain operations reference model (SCOR) that integrates well-known concepts of business process reengineering, benchmarking, and process measurement into a cross-functional framework for improvement. The SCOR model is a very interesting example of how focus on the supply chain can lead to important improvements in the

---

8. http://supply-chain.org.

consistency and efficiency of solutions that require the interactions of many teams and organizations. A number of organizations have used SCOR to implement a phased approach to supply chain improvement and report notable successes.[9] The direct application of SCOR to the industrialization of enterprise software delivery would seem an obvious and valuable research direction to pursue.

10.4.3 Lean Manufacturing

Traditional supply chain manufacturing emphasized cost control. However, there are many other important factors to consider in delivering high-quality, innovative products to the marketplace. In particular, throughout the 1950s and 1960s, ideas about efficiency linked to customer value became increasingly important in manufacturing domains. Based on key examples such as Toyota, the ideas have led to the concept of the lean enterprise. In this context, *lean* is a philosophy that seeks to eliminate waste in all aspects of a company's production activities: human relations, vendor relations, technology, and the management of materials and inventory.

The concept has evolved into an industry-independent management philosophy where *lean thinking* is about eliminating waste by focusing on delivering more customer value while at the same time improving growth and profitability. Many different interpretations of this thinking are possible, and a wide variety of materials, techniques, and practices have resulted. However, for our purposes, the basic ideas of lean thinking are well articulated in these five core lean principles:

- *Value.* Understand what adds value for the customer.

- *Value stream.* Understand how the organization generates customer value.

- *Flow.* Maximize speed and minimize cost by achieving continuous flow.

- *Pull.* Deliver value on a just-in-time basis based on actual customer demand.

- *Perfection.* Continuously improve the performance of your value streams.

As illustrated in Figure 10.2, the target of these lean principles is to help eliminate waste that can be found in seven areas.[10] While the areas of waste in

---

9. www.casestudyinc.com/supply-chain-case-study.

10. These originated with Toyota's Chief Engineer Taiichi Ohno and are widely discussed in literature on lean manufacturing.

Figure 10.2 are clearly geared toward manufacturing, it's interesting to examine them from the perspective of industrializing enterprise software delivery:

- *Bad quality.* Originally focused on parts not being delivered to their specification, attention to reducing errors and improving the consistency of all manufactured parts and assemblies proves necessary. As in enterprise software delivery, reducing scrap and rework is a primary target for eliminating waste.

- *Overproduction.* The main source of overproduction is manufacturing an item before it is required or without clear visibility into market demands. In enterprise software delivery, closer relationships and continuous collaboration with the business owners must be developed to increase agility in delivery as the market need evolves.

- *Excess inventory.* Excess inventory is normally associated with poor process alignment across different work centers in a production process. As in enterprise software delivery, a clearer view of the end-to-end delivery process allows optimization across all stages of development and delivery.

- *Transport.* In manufacturing, there is a lot of time spent moving different parts and assemblies from one location to another within the production process. Often the transportation time can be reduced by redesign of the production process to reduce the steps and to localize hand offs. Similar optimizations in enterprise software delivery can be made by improving agreements between teams in the supply chain and by avoiding converting artifacts between different formats as they are moved through the development and delivery process.

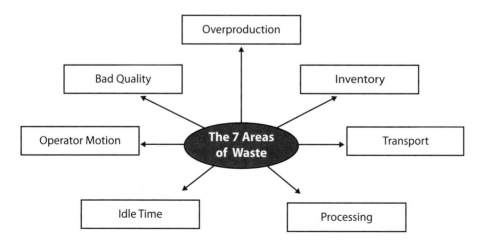

Figure 10.2 *The focus on the seven areas of waste in lean manufacturing*

- *Processing.* In manufacturing organizations, there are many cases where use of expensive, high-precision equipment could be replaced by simpler processing that proves to be as effective and reduces overall costs. Often in enterprise software delivery there are similar situations where complex processes and software tools are put in place for development and delivery without any understanding of the value they bring to the overall solution.

- *Idle time.* Much of the waste in production time is due to long lead times and bottlenecks in the production process where goods are left waiting for processing. In enterprise software delivery we also see a great deal of time diverted from core delivery tasks as a result of poor communication, misunderstandings, failed automation, and so on.

- *Operator motion.* The manufacturing process can put stresses on individuals that cause inefficiency in their tasks and can lead to longer-term health and safety problems. In enterprise software delivery, performance can also be severely affected by hours spent doing mundane tasks that are better automated, attending meaningless meetings to address issues that should be easily resolved using available data, and creating documents that will not be read.

In recent years, the application of lean thinking to software development has been proposed [13]. This has been the basis for a large number of enabling practices, tools, and techniques that help enterprises maximize customer value and avoid waste.

What we learn from applying lean thinking to enterprise software delivery is that a broader view of the organization with emphasis on feedback and organizational learning can direct efforts toward the primary goal of generating customer value. That is an essential lesson for the industrialization of enterprise software delivery. Furthermore, many of the sources of waste in manufacturing processes are a result of poorly aligned processes, inefficient communication, and lack of focus on value in decision making. Such issues are clear targets for the three key areas of enterprise software delivery: collaboration, automation, and visibility.

10.5 Examples and Illustrations

In examining any new approach, it's as important to discuss examples of failure as it is to highlight successes. Unfortunately, our failures are typically not well documented and rarely publicized. This makes a detailed review of failure patterns not possible. However, in general we have good understanding of why software fails [60]. Sometimes it's due to single critical technical errors. But far more often it's a combination of reasons that are buried in the complexity of enterprise software delivery.

In the following sections, I describe three vignettes[11] of software failure that highlight particular challenges in enterprise software delivery where outsourcing, supply chains, and software factory approaches have contributed to the failure. Drawing from available public information, I summarize the examples, and in each case, I make a number of observations.

10.5.1 US State Government Outsourcing

Over the past few years a major trend in US state governments has been toward outsourcing large parts of the state's IT services. Using this approach, many states have been able to reduce costs while improving capability for their citizens. However, there have also been notable problems.

A recent review analyzed several large outsourced IT services projects in US state governments that had suffered major issues.[12] In states such as Texas, Indiana, and Virginia, public discussions have been held about the poor performance and lack of results from their outsourced contracts. In particular, the state governments have complained that their expectations concerning delivery from the outsourced providers have not been met.

The results of these analyses have highlighted three key areas of concern related to such approaches:

- The cost-saving aspects of the relationship were overemphasized without the development of a clear collaborative relationship between the supplier and the consumer of services.

- There was little flexibility in the definition and evolution of the contract between suppliers and consumer. In particular, the only recourse for addressing disputes appeared to be public debate and eventually lawsuits.

- Success in these outsourcing contracts was enhanced through long-term commitment, open dialogue, and constant feedback across all parties.

Of course, many reports and analyses have pointed out that there are many more challenges to be overcome in outsourcing software delivery. From these US state government experiences we can see in concrete terms that the dialogue

---

11. These are small-scale illustrations highlighting a few key points, rather than detailed case studies.

12. www.cio.com/article/602072/Don_t_Mess_with_Texas_7_Lessons_From_State_IT_Outsourcing _Disasters?source=CIONLE_nlt_insider_2010-08-05.

between outsourcer and outsourcee is a critical one. It must be a relationship built on trust and it requires continued discussion to be effective.

10.5.2 Nokia Product Development and Delivery

Throughout the 1990s, Nokia maintained a dominant position in the delivery of mobile phones and other handheld devices. It had a reputation for producing market-leading solutions in advance of all other competitors. By the year 2000 Nokia had over 50 percent market share and a stock market valuation in excess of $300 billion. This situation changed quickly in the early years of the twenty-first century. By 2010, Nokia had lost significant market share, and its stock market valuation had dropped to one tenth of its peak in 2000.

It's not so much that Nokia is not continuing to hold very good market share; at least 40 percent of all phones come from Nokia. Rather, there appear to be two major issues:

- Nokia has stumbled badly when faced with increasing competition from new market players, fast-paced technology changes, and a revolution in customer demands. It is no longer seen as a market leader. Several recently released products were very poorly received and simple user tasks were found to be too complex.

- Nokia sells a wide variety of phone models and supports three different operating systems. This diversity is difficult to justify to the market and complex to maintain in practice. Incompatibilities and diversity mean that the core software platform, Symbian, is not available to all models, and hence Symbian-based applications do not run on all models.[13]

A compelling article looks at Nokia's challenges in bringing new products to market and in particular examines how new players such as Apple have been able to leapfrog Nokia's previously dominant market position.[14] The article makes important observations regarding the culture, organization, and technical approach of the company. And, most interestingly, it focuses attention on three important areas of relevance to the themes of this book:

- *The negative impact of factory thinking on innovation in products.* The company turned much of its focus to commoditization and scaleability of delivery of its devices with immense pressure on driving down costs. This

---

13. www.forbes.com/2008/08/18/nokia-iphone-symbian-tech-wire-cx_bc_0818nokia.html.
14. www.hs.fi/english/article/Knock+Knock+Nokias+Heavy+Fall/1135260596609.

had the unfortunate effect of reducing focus on providing innovation in products and supporting novel ideas into production.

- *Lack of visibility into design and delivery activities necessary to make key decisions that crossed organization and responsibility boundaries.* The move toward fixed lines of business and focus competencies increased problems when designing and integrating all the components of the system. Local optimizations were often at the expense of the overall solution.

- *Poor connection between product managers and customers and across the rest of the delivery organization.* Coordination and communication paths across the organization were not sufficient enough to be flexible and timely in decision making. Many weeks were wasted waiting for decisions that would have allowed good ideas to be moved forward, developed, and delivered.

The need to maintain balance between standardization and innovation is a major lesson from the Nokia experiences for industrialized enterprise software delivery.

10.5.3 FAA Large Project Management

Each day, the Federal Aviation Administration (FAA) is responsible for managing more than 30,000 commercial flights that move 2,000,000 passengers around the United States. There are more than 500 air traffic control towers, 180 terminal radar control centers, and 20 en route centers. A significant element of the FAA's task is controlled and delivered by a series of software-intensive systems.

Since the 1980s, the FAA has been undertaking a major modernization of its systems for air traffic control (ATC).[15] This is a large, extensive, and complex undertaking affecting every aspect of the software that is used by the FAA in supporting ATC. The long and difficult history of this effort has received a great deal of scrutiny, and many different reviews and analyses have taken place, many of them available in the public domain (e.g., many reviews undertaken by the US Government Accounting Office, the Software Engineering Institute, and many other agencies supporting government programs).

To comprehend the challenges being faced by the FAA, consider the en route air traffic control systems that manage air traffic flying across major regions in the United States. The software systems responsible for this rely heavily on

---

15. For example, there are reports that the FAA estimated about $20 billion to replace and modernize software-intensive ATC systems between 1982 and 2003 and that, due to overruns, the amount spent will be as much as $51 billion by the end of 2010. See www.gao.gov/new.items/d04227t.pdf.

a large set of software systems amounting to millions of lines of source code written almost forty years ago in languages such as Jovial, FORTRAN, and several flavors of Ada. To improve those systems, the FAA has embarked on many ambitious software renovation programs. The latest, the en route automation modernization (ERAM) program, began to replace that systems used at the twenty en route centers in 2008.[16]

The work at the FAA to modernize their software is an extreme example of large-scale software delivery in a very complex environment with high government oversight. The modernization has been executed through use of many different contractors and subcontractors organized across several programs, initiatives, and projects. Hence, to some degree, it can serve as an important case study on the challenges of a supply chain approach to enterprise software delivery. While there are many possible lines of discussion,[17] in this context I provide a limited review of the series of actions that were identified as particularly influential in making improvements in these projects:

- Introduction of incremental development and delivery styles and away from very lengthy delivery periods where little practical progress could be demonstrated

- Explicit definition of a system architecture blueprint to provide a common basis for managing the integration of artifacts delivered by subcontractors across the many projects

- Improved processes for integrated software and system acquisition to help with selecting and managing their investments

- Focus on collaboration among technical experts and system users to create integrated teams that worked together to identify needs, assess their viability, and define their priorities

- Greater feedback from the projects that had been completed or were in flight to assist with future acquisition, management, and planning

These improvement areas provide useful reminders to those embarking on an industrialized approach to enterprise software delivery, with respect to using actual performance data to guide and readjust plans during any long, complex delivery cycle.

---

16. www.faa.gov/air_traffic/technology/eram.

17. Many thousands of pages of analysis by the GAO cannot be reduced to just a few bullets. Rather, I simply try to give a flavor of the kinds of improvement areas that were adopted.

10.6 Conclusions

As we drive enterprise software delivery organizations toward greater efficiency, many interesting approaches to industrialization of software delivery can be introduced. Each brings with it a series of important opportunities for improvement but can also raise challenges, introduce risks, and create instabilities in an existing organization.

In this chapter I discuss important areas of variability and risk associated with introducing supply chain and software factory approaches. I'll summarize this discussion by highlighting six main lessons:

- *Lesson 1*. Use the characteristics of the enterprise to guide where and how industrialized approaches to enterprise software delivery can be more readily applied.

- *Lesson 2*. Assess the process maturity of the enterprise and pay attention to differences in how it relates to the maturity of other organizations in the software supply chain.

- *Lesson 3*. Don't overly focus on standardization and cost cutting to the extent that it stifles innovation and creativity.

- *Lesson 4*. Know your supply chain weaknesses and have explicit approaches in place to address them.

- *Lesson 5*. Seek to gain insights from experiences in other domains with a history of supply chain management and industrialized delivery of solutions.

- *Lesson 6*. Learn from other people's failures and document your failures so that you (and others) can learn from them.

By understanding and applying these lessons, greater confidence can be gained and improved success is possible when industrializing enterprise software delivery.

Chapter 11

The Future of Global Enterprise Software Delivery

Chapter Summary

I discuss several interesting and important directions for the future of global enterprise software delivery. With rapid evolution and adoption of new enterprise software technologies, the pressures on enterprise software delivery organizations are growing. I note the following:

- Cloud-based technologies not only provide new infrastructure choices for solution delivery to clients; they also represent opportunities for the global enterprise software delivery organization to optimize, become more efficient, and coordinate more effectively.

- Global delivery models will continue to evolve, allowing new forms of supply chains and requiring different organizational relationships.

- The wide availability of intelligent devices has caused a rapid change in demand and expectations from end users resulting in high pressure on global enterprise software delivery organizations to deliver more capability more often to more kinds of devices than ever before.

- The combination of these and several other advances places enormous pressure on global enterprise software delivery organizations to rethink the balance between efficiency of delivery and innovation in new capability. Achieving the right balance between these is a key challenge such organizations will face for the foreseeable future.

11.1 Introduction

There are many important and interesting advances taking place that will have an impact on the future of enterprise software delivery. Industry analyst reports, software journals, and company web pages all list many critical factors for the future. Several noteworthy recent events have especially provoked consideration of the deeper implications on global enterprise software delivery.

The first observation concerns the availability of computing resources. It's been suggested that perhaps 20 percent of all the servers bought in recent years are being acquired by a small group of companies (such as Microsoft, Amazon, Google, and Yahoo).[1] This massive consolidation of computing power is being housed in vast warehouses where tens of thousands of servers deliver computing resources to consumers around the world. The investment in infrastructure is driving down the cost of obtaining computing power and storage. Nicholas Carr refers to this as "the big switch" from locally owned computer resources to IT as a commodity utility provided by a handful of public infrastructure providers, where users can choose the services they want driven by low-cost suppliers [16].

The second observation pertains to the way consumers are accessing services. By 2015 it is estimated that there will be in excess of 1 trillion interconnected devices around the world.[2] Each of these systems contains software that allows data to be collected and analyzed, items to be positioned and tracked, and information to be communicated in a bewildering number of forms. Society now relies on an array of systems combining sensors, communications, data management, and information analytics.

Furthermore, these devices are the platform for delivering many kinds of services. For example, in January 2010, Apple announced that more than 3 billion apps had been downloaded from its app store for use on its iPhone device.[3] In general, industry analyst company IDC predicts that the number of mobile application downloads worldwide will grow from 10.9 billion in 2010 to 76.9 billion in 2014.[4] A large percentage of these apps today are games or offer trivial functionality. However, a growing percentage are business applications or apps that interact with business applications running back-office services.

---

1. http://blogs.ft.com/techblog/2009/03/how-many-computers-does-the-world-need.

2. For example, see www.readwriteweb.com/enterprise/2010/06/ibm-a-world-with-1-trillion-co.php.

3. www.apple.com/pr/library/2010/01/05appstore.html.

4. www.idc.com/about/viewpressrelease.jsp?containerId=prUS22617910&sectionId=null&elementId
=null&pageType=SYNOPSIS.

The third observation concerns the use of communities and new ways of interaction. In 2006, the online movie-rental company Netflix offered a prize of $1 million to whoever came up with the best way to improve on the company's movie recommendation algorithms. There were more than 40,000 groups who responded with solutions. The prize was subsequently awarded to a team of seven people who provided Netflix with a much more accurate approach to movie recommendation. This was adopted by Netflix to improve its services to customers.[5] We have seen many other interesting examples of open-source and open-community activities in recent years. This is the latest example of *crowdsourcing*, one of several new ways that businesses are connecting with the broader community to offer more transparency and interactivity within their markets. The willingness to disrupt traditional business practices to introduce these new ways to innovate more effectively indicates how serious businesses are about rapidly improving their products.

These new advances result in many known and countless unknown implications for enterprise software delivery, management, and evolution. In this chapter, I examine some of these areas and offer comments and projections about how these trends will further accelerate scaleable agile practices and the move toward supply chains in enterprise software delivery.

11.2 The Beginning of the End, or the End of the Beginning?

The history of enterprise software delivery reflects a constant reinvention of the way software-intensive systems deliver capabilities to their consumers. We've witnessed the move from mainframe computers to PCs, from PCs to supercomputers, and from computing grids to Internetworked cloud computing. With each of these evolutions, enterprise software delivery has experienced growth periods followed by realignment as new computer platforms and new software paradigms emerge to gradually replace the incumbent approaches.

According to what we see referred to as Bell's law, a new platform emerges about every ten years to offer improved functionality in new areas, accompanied by lower prices for existing capabilities compared to those of the incumbent platform.[6] These platforms (or "computer classes") have included

5. The Netflix approach is discussed here: www.nydailynews.com/tech_guide/2009/09/21/2009-09-21_netflix_prize.html.

6. www.ieee.org/portal/site/sscs/menuitem.f07ee9e3b2a01d06bb9305765bac26c8/index.jsp?&pName=sscs_level1_article&path=sscs/08Fall&file=Bell.xml&xsl=article.xsl;jsessionid=QnYzNLpckg5Js4Tf22LYSRPYgNTkyy8N1VzZ1fPh5gX0mFKQpC1x!-1706892250!NONE.

mainframes (1960s), minicomputers (1970s), networked workstations and personal computers (1980s), web-servers and n-tier architectures (1990s), web services (2000s), and mobile devices connected to networked computers (2003). The next platform evolution appears to be upon us: service-based delivery on a cloud platform.

There is a great deal of excitement (and associated hype) around this new platform. Cloud computing, software as a service (SaaS), and easy access to computing power through Internet-based connections have changed many aspects of how computer-based services are accessed. There are many important implications for enterprise software delivery.

This reworking of enterprise software delivery is recognized by some groups as the start of the *enterprise 3.0* era, a combination of the emerging cloud-based platform supporting an enterprise software delivery organization constructed from a software supply chain.[7] This idea of the extended enterprise recognizes that modern enterprises are not monolithic organizations. Rather, all kinds of entities extend and expand the boundaries of the enterprise and make collaboration and supply chain management critical to their success.

What's more, billions of connections among systems and users accessing continuously updated data from multiple devices anywhere in the world require a redefinition of what we mean by an *enterprise system*. SaaS and cloud computing have not just provided a new platform for existing applications; they have opened up completely new ways to think about the services and solutions supported by the enterprise software delivery organization. For example, the traditional idea of "an application" may not even be relevant anymore. Consequently, delivery of client-facing capabilities may soon be considered the result of providing a highly customized solution for some market segment by bringing together only the resources needed for that solution and doing so on a model where almost all the infrastructure and development are outsourced in one form or another. The software may have been developed by an outsourced team from a system integrator, storage might be purchased on demand from a cloud infrastructure vendor, quality of the delivered solution may be the responsibility of a specialist testing company, and the solution may be deployed to a public SaaS platform to provide more open access to its users. And this whole cycle may be accomplished in a matter of hours, rather than weeks.

In summary, enterprise software delivery remains as critical to the enterprise as ever. The emerging SaaS and cloud platform introduces new opportunities for efficient delivery of capabilities. This view of enterprise 3.0 is the basis for accelerating industrialization of enterprise software delivery across the software supply chain.

---

7. www.sramanamitra.com/2007/02/26/enterprise-30-saas-ee.

11.3 Into the Clouds

The arrival of cloud computing is by far the most conspicuous trend in recent times, and it's likely to have the most wide-scale impact on enterprise software delivery in the coming years. Whether viewed as a natural extension of Internet-based computing or a completely new phenomenon, high-bandwidth global interconnectivity and cheap processors and storage have fueled moves to create large computing centers that can act as massive computing hubs to serve organizations that may be distributed around the globe. These centralized computing centers can be created by a single organization, shared between organizations, or be provided by third parties as a resource that can be acquired as necessary. All these give rise to the possibility that enterprise software delivery can be coordinated more effectively via shared service centers and can be supported more efficiently using a flexible set of hardware and software services that can expand and contract as the organization's needs evolve.

This move toward a centralized approach for greater flexibility and efficiency in enterprise software delivery is not new. As illustrated in Figure 11.1, enterprise software delivery organizations have been on a multiyear journey toward greater efficiency and effectiveness. From the earliest days of computing, there have been moves to centralize computer resources, share access to costly

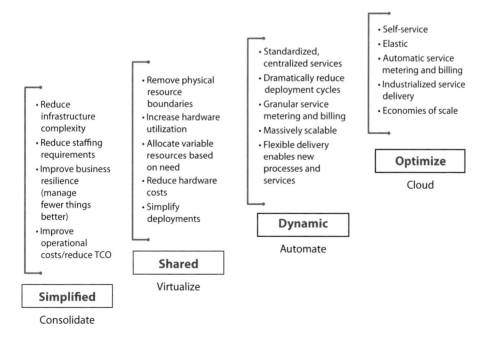

Figure 11.1 *The evolving efficiency focus of enterprise software delivery organizations*

infrastructure, increase flexibility of access to common services, and improve responsiveness to peak demands for capabilities. In recent years, this journey has taken the enterprise software delivery organization from a focus on simplification toward greater sharing and virtualization of its delivery infrastructure. What is new in the recent trend around cloud computing is the technology infrastructure that now makes the next step possible, driven by a business environment that is forcing efficiencies across enterprise software delivery, by the expanding global nature of our organizations and their supply chains, and by a broader business reevaluation of the role of IT services in support of the organization's value to its stakeholders.

There are many primers on cloud computing (e.g., [48,83]), and there have been several insightful analyses published on cloud computing and its impact (e.g., [84,85]). Rather than replay those themes here, I'll provide a short contextual review of cloud computing and then focus on the most important implications of this trend for enterprise software delivery.

11.3.1 Understanding the Cloud

The broad notion of cloud computing is composed of many different elements, and several different perspectives are possible. I'll describe three dimensions of cloud computing that help us understand the breadth and impact of this approach on enterprise software delivery.

11.3.1.1 Characteristics of a Cloud Approach

In general, the main characteristics of a cloud computing approach is to deliver "convenient, on-demand network access to a shared pool of configurable computing resources (e.g., networks, servers, storage, applications, and services) that can be rapidly provisioned and released with minimal management effort or service provider interaction."[8] The value of this approach is that it offers a great deal of flexibility to consumers of those resources. In particular, capabilities can be rapidly and elastically provisioned to scale up when demands for those capabilities increase, and similarly, they can be rapidly released to scale down when demand reduces.

Supporting this elasticity of capabilities are two key enablers that are essential to make the approach practical. The first is to allow the consumers of the resources to be able to self-provision the capabilities they need and to obtain (near) immediate access via a set of provision automation services. The second is a monitoring and measurement approach that allows pay-per-use accounting for those resources being consumed. The richness of these two enablers helps to

---

8. The US National Institute of Standards and Technology (NIST) definition of cloud computing: http://csrc.nist.gov/groups/SNS/cloud-computing/cloud-def-v15.doc.

distinguish cloud computing from previous attempts to offer pooled virtualized services that typically were restricted to a very limited set of options and required expensive and time-consuming interventions from a service provisioning team for the majority of changes to the configuration.

In enterprise software delivery, the flexibility that is possible with cloud computing approaches is critical. Not only does this flexibility encourage the kinds of dynamic relationships that characterize supply chain approaches; it also provides much more explicit ways to look at infrastructure costs and assign those costs to the role of each organization and team, and it encourages global delivery approaches more suited to today's highly diverse enterprises.

11.3.1.2 Cloud Deployment Models

Cloud computing services are made available to users in a variety of ways. Two significant variations have emerged that polarize two ends of a delivery spectrum: *private* and *public* clouds.

For organizations with many teams requiring access to common capabilities, it can be effective to create a private cloud computing solution that serves those teams and is managed by the enterprise software delivery organization. The technologies and processes necessary for creating a cloud solution are acquired and dedicated to that organization's needs. The main advantages of a private cloud computing approach are clear: teams are quickly given access to the cloud services, teams have elasticity of use of those services, and metering provides accurate accounting (and even allows cross-charging) of those services to their consumers. Private cloud computing services can be created by organizations when they require the flexibility offered by shared, virtualized capabilities but are not able (or are unwilling) to accept the implications of sharing those capabilities with other organizations.

In contrast, one of the most compelling directions for cloud computing is the emergence of public cloud capabilities. Several organizations provide cloud-based capabilities that are readily accessible over a public infrastructure such as the Internet. Multiple organizations share the use of that infrastructure (so-called multitenancy) and thereby reduce costs for both the cloud users and cloud supplier. The use of a third-party provider of resources over a public infrastructure can offer great cost savings to the consumer, increases the flexibility and availability of the services, and eliminates wasted investment in infrastructure acquisition, setup, and service administration.

However, public cloud solutions also have significant disadvantages for many organizations that require the security, privacy, and reassurance of a privately owned cloud-base solution. As a result, various hybrid models of cloud computing are also possible. For example, some organizations use private cloud capabilities for key aspects of their business, and they make use of public cloud services where there are less concerns about performance and data privacy. Similarly, many public cloud-computing providers are able to offer dedicated infrastructure capabilities to clients to ensure their availability and increase confidence about security and privacy of data.

11.3.1.3 *Service Models for the Cloud*

With respect to the capabilities being made available through cloud computing, there is a huge array of offerings and a wide variety of ways of packaging, delivering, and charging for those capabilities. I'll highlight three clear categories of capabilities being offered through cloud computing models.

The first involves infrastructure as a service (IaaS). A starting point for offering cloud-based services is to provide the organization with dependable, scalable, and expandable hardware (CPU, storage, networking). These capabilities may be offered directly as the service that the end users consume or be used as the foundation for building virtualization layers and higher-level services. For example, if a team requires an additional terabyte of disk space to manage the temporary data needed for a series of system tests, a cloud-based solution would be able to accommodate that request (whether implicitly or explicitly made) rather than having the team to look for an available machine or go through any complex acquisition approval process.

A number of services must support the IaaS, including supplying the abilities to pool highly available CPUs and storage (perhaps differentiated by particular kinds of hardware characteristics), meter the capacity and utilization of resources, bill and chargeback for consumed services, audit and analyze for compliance to specific norms and standards, and so on. The IaaS services must guarantee particular functional and nonfunctional requirements will be met in areas such as performance, response time, availability, and so on. One example of this approach is IaaS applied to large-scale development and test teams across the IBM Tivoli organization. In IBM Tivoli, there are more than six thousand software practitioners in thirty-eight labs around the world responsible for a wide variety of software delivery tasks. A recent analysis revealed that they were using more than 30,000 servers, with typical utilization between 5–9 percent per server. By introducing a cloud-based IaaS solutions, IBM Tivoli has been able to deliver to all practitioners a set of common desktop images housed in a central set of managed systems running IBM's own cloud software. Within two years of this switch, IBM was able to demonstrate vastly reduced services, provisioning times for new projects, and capital expense reductions of more than $10 million, and it accumulated operation expense savings of more than $11.5 million.

The second category, platform as a service (PaaS) delivers a more complete computing platform for developing and delivering applications. In particular, a

PaaS offering will include operating-system and other middleware capabilities typically with the latest versions of the software, updates, and patches applied. For example, often when an organization wants to test a new application, it needs to acquire and configure each computer platform on which the application must be tested. This may mean several different platform variations with combinations of operating system, database, web server, and so on. In a PaaS approach, specific platform combinations are requested and provisioned using a cloud computing model. Typically, a limited set of PaaS solutions is available for use by default. In addition, users may be able to define specialized stacks of software that combine the available platform elements to provision a specific PaaS solution that meets their needs.

An important variation on the PaaS approach is that the platform may itself be a development and delivery platform for new cloud-based services. For example, the Amazon web services platform (AWS) is a PaaS offering that delivers a fully functional development and delivery capability for organizations wanting to deliver solutions that run on the Amazon IaaS offering called the Amazon elastic compute cloud (EC2) and that integrate with a set of solution components they have created to execute on that infrastructure. Similarly, Salesforce.com provides Force.com as the PaaS offering for creating new solutions that integrate with its Salesforce.com solution elements.

The PaaS approach is very appealing to two kinds of organizations. First, smaller organizations can take advantage of PaaS to access a wide set of platform variations without the capital investment necessary for each of them. Second, for larger organizations, the PaaS approach offers standardization to ensure that teams use the same technology base with appropriate versions of each component of the platform installed there.

An interesting illustration of the application of this approach is within a large financial institution that has almost five thousand people in its enterprise software delivery organization spread across local sites and three different systems integrators (SIs). These included substantial offshore teams located in India. The organization was struggling with the challenges of maintaining an effective software development and delivery workbench across the organization. Failings due to inconsistencies across development and test tools had been identified as major factors in several high-profile software delivery delays. As a result, the organization created a standard corporate-wide development and delivery workbench as a PaaS offering that it mandated across the global enterprise software delivery organization. Due to its cloud-based foundation, this provided a consistent solution with easy management and configuration essential for the business to match its diverse organizational structure.

The third category is SaaS. Most organizations interested in the cloud computing model are not software development companies. Rather, they use the enterprise software as a means to support and differentiate their businesses. They are looking to have business or domain-specific capabilities offered as a service whereby they simply make use of that service when and as they need it and in the quantity they need at the time. This has resulted in a very large set of offerings now available in a SaaS model.

Again, both public and private cloud approaches are possible. In the public cloud category there are now some very well-established examples of SaaS. One example is Gmail, Google's e-mail service that provides a SaaS e-mail capability that is widely used by individuals and increasingly deployed in businesses. Another well-known example is the cloud-based sales management service from Salesforce.com. Both of these examples exhibit the key characteristics of today's SaaS offerings: Internet-based access to a core organizational capability that is provided on a pay-per-use model with a great deal of elasticity in the underlying technology. This kind of simplification of service provisioning is very appealing to organizations that see no value in the investment and administration required to maintain close control of that capability in house.

Many examples of SaaS offerings for software development and deployment are already commercially available. For example, one software vendor[9] offers several cloud-based software delivery workbenches aimed at different sizes of teams and different blends of software delivery roles. These offerings are available in a variety of pay-per-use schemes according to different operational needs.

11.3.2 Impact on Enterprise Software Delivery Organizations

There has been a great deal written about the impact of cloud computing approaches in the world of software delivery. Undoubtedly the impact is being felt broadly across the industry with the restructuring of many software vendors to deliver Internet-based services, the creation of new markets for computing capabilities, and the emergence of powerful new technology infrastructure providers that have redrawn the traditional boundaries between software, hardware, and service delivery. While there are many interesting lines of discussion, I concentrate here on the impact that cloud computing is having on the enterprise software delivery organization. In particular, I look at three key areas: the changing role of enterprise IT, the economics of enterprise software delivery, and the redesign of the enterprise data center.

11.3.2.1 The Role of Enterprise Software Delivery

In most commercial companies, the delivery and support of enterprise software capabilities is the responsibility of a core enterprise software delivery group. It

---

9. See www.oncloudone.net.

has traditionally been responsible for acquisition, installation, management, and support of all computing infrastructure elements. It has had the responsibility and authority for governing all enterprise software services and for offering the capabilities required as efficiently as possible at the service levels demanded by the users of those services.

For a number of years, there has been pressure on the company's central enterprise software delivery group. Not only have different organizational groups and departments begun to wrestle some control from the central team, but more recently, the moves to outsource key capabilities to reduce delivery costs has led companies to rethink the scope and role of enterprise software delivery. For many, this has resulted in a "utility" view of those services—they can be seen as a metered resource akin to electricity and water. They are necessary for the business to function but offer little differentiation and therefore require little special attention or investment.[10]

The introduction of cloud computing approaches further enhances this utility view of software delivery. It can be seen as accelerating the disintegration of the enterprise software delivery organization by giving users much greater flexibility to obtain services directly without the need for specialized, expensive service support for acquisition and administration. Furthermore, it is possible to go as far as renaming *users*, who consume centrally provisioned enterprise software services, as *choosers* of suppliers of those services with the characteristics considered appropriate to their needs [86].

But this trend certainly does not mean the death of the enterprise software delivery organization. Rather, it points to a redefinition of the organization's role. With cloud computing, enterprise software delivery organizations are essential to success. They are needed to define standards, manage the workflow for service authorizations, manage change life cycles and chargebacks to suppliers, ensure service levels are being met, mediate during disagreements across the supply chain, and so on. All these activities are stretching current skills and support systems to the limit, with many enterprise software delivery teams struggling to evolve to meet these needs and understand the role they now play in delivering enterprise software to the business.

11.3.2.2 Financial Transparency

The introduction of cloud computing in enterprise software delivery organizations creates challenging changes in the financial aspects of their tasks. Two particular areas are worth highlighting.

First, the availability of IaaS, PaaS, and SaaS based on cloud computing technologies has introduced a level of price transparency and competitiveness that

---

10. The most explicit version of this perspective is represented in the writing of Nicholas Carr, with his open question "Does IT matter?" [15].

has raised the stakes for enterprise software delivery organizations. Potential users of computing services can go to public cloud computing providers to see clear, explicit rates for how much specific services will cost. Whether it is the price for a terabyte of data storage or the cost for performing load testing on a new application, any potential consumer of those services has transparency into a pricing structure that can be used for financial calculations, return on investment (ROI) analyses, and competitive bids. Consequently, every enterprise software delivery organization is being forced to become more transparent in its financial structure. It must understand, manage, and reveal its costs to potential consumers inside the enterprise.

For many such organizations, this is a painful exercise. Business leaders in those companies can now openly challenge the enterprise software delivery organization on the value it delivers to the business and form opinions about how the efficiency of the delivery of those services can be improved. If the answers are not clear and defensible, the threat of using an external service supplier looms.

To increase the financial pressure further, the budgets in most enterprise software delivery organizations are largely viewed as capital expenses, with high initial investment in technology that depreciates over time. On the other hand, cloud-based services are usually viewed as operational expenses because they are "leased" for the time they are needed. Hence they are expensed as they are used and can be allocated to their specific users in a more straightforward charge-back mechanism. For many companies, the switch from capital to operational expense can be very attractive from an accounting perspective, and many arguments are made that it is far more easily managed as part of the company's budgeting activities.[11]

In summary, due to financial pressures such as these, the enterprise software delivery organization must become much more expert in understanding its cost structures, in justifying where and how those costs are assigned, and in understanding the value those services deliver directly and indirectly to the business. Unfortunately, for many organizations, cost accounting and value analysis are not currently areas of strength.

11.3.2.3 Data Center of the Future

Many organizations invest significantly in setting up and running the enterprise data centers that house their primary computing resources. In many cases, this investment includes specialized power-management systems, heating and cooling systems, energy management infrastructure, and much more. The complexity

---

11. In practice, the discussion about capex versus opex is much more complex than this, as summarized here: www.cio.com/article/484429/Capex_vs._Opex_Most_People_Miss_the_Point_About _Cloud_Economics.

of this task can be overwhelming for all but the most advanced organizations. As a result, in the past few years consolidation and data center outsourcing have been the trends. Specialist organizations can set up, run, and manage those data centers using their experience and skills to ensure efficiency, quality, and value.

Cloud computing represents a natural extension of the consolidation and outsourcing of the enterprise data center. The basic ideas of cloud computing are also the foundations of data center design: modular components, elasticity of resources, virtualized capabilities, metering of usage, and self-administration for provisioning.[12]

An interesting example of this thinking was expressed by John Suffolk, UK government chief information officer (CIO), who described his plans for a UK-wide government cloud computing infrastructure, the *G-cloud*. Specifically, he identified several objectives for the G-cloud: "Focus on getting desktop designs standardized; rationalize the morass of telecommunications infrastructures into a 'network of network' under the Public Sector Network Programme; rationalize the data centers; drive through the open source, open standards and reuse strategy; surround each of those individual elements with the Green IT strategy and our Information Assurance strategy."[13]

This thinking has also led to a further trend: use of public cloud computing infrastructures to house enterprise data centers. The major providers of the public cloud computing infrastructure, such as Amazon, Google, and Microsoft, now also support the hosting of enterprise data centers within their infrastructure. Leveraging the massive investments they have made in their cloud computing infrastructure, these vendors provide all the capabilities necessary to manage the data center for an enterprise software delivery organization.

Massive server farms are being constructed to deliver incredible amounts of computing capability to users.[14] In 2008, it was estimated that Google had more than 1 million servers and that Microsoft, in its bid to catch up, was deploying at least 20,000 new servers per month.[15]

This scale of investment in infrastructure allows those companies to offer very high performance, elasticity of supply, and built-in support for high availability, redundancy, failover, disaster recovery, and so on. Recent improvements

---

12. www.forbes.com/2009/12/12/datacenter-amazon-computers-technology-cio-network-sperling.html.

13. As reported at http://cloudcomputing.sys-con.com/node/1007821.

14. For example, the Microsoft data center that opened in Chicago in June 2009 is 700,000 square feet and constructed from a number of preconfigured containers, each one housing between 1,800 and 2,500 servers. See http://blogs.technet.com/b/msdatacenters/archive/2009/09/28/microsoft-celebrates -chicago-data-center-grand-opening.aspx.

15. *The Economist*, "Down on the Server Farm," May 24, 2008.

in security and guarantees of availability and response time have changed the thinking that public cloud infrastructure can be used only for "less critical data." This is a direction that will continue to put pressure on traditional enterprise data center approaches.

11.3.3 Summary

A high level of excitement surrounds cloud computing and the promises that it brings to enterprises to reduce cost and increase flexibility of service delivery. Many organizations are already involved in pilots or are actively using cloud technologies and cloud-based services. Over the coming years, the massive excitement will be tempered with the reality that in some respects cloud is "just another deployment platform." Hence the use of this platform will require a wealth of supporting capabilities to both create enterprise solutions *for* the cloud and to take advantage of solutions and services *on* the cloud.

Initially, we've seen traditional enterprise software solutions ported to the cloud platform and included in platform images that can be uploaded to a cloud infrastructure. This is an important starting point for enterprise system use on the cloud. However, it's very limited in terms of many of the important usage scenarios for cloud technology. There is less understanding of which new enterprise software capabilities, services, and approaches will be needed in much more complex scenarios. For example, we're already seeing interesting scenarios that are raising new challenges for enterprise software delivery organizations:

- Several teams are deploying business applications onto a public cloud infrastructure for access by clients around the world. How do those teams collaborate to share information to ensure that they don't place sensitive data on the public infrastructure? What coordination is employed by the teams to ensure the management of shared images is handled effectively?

- Multiple system integrators and specialist vendors must deliver different parts of key enterprise solutions as part of a software supply chain that must be integrated to be delivered into production. How can the cloud be used as the delivery platform to coordinate and govern delivery and integration of these components?

These, and many more such scenarios, are stretching conventional processes, skills, and technologies for enterprise software delivery. Software delivery organizations are actively working on new deployment approaches that provide the additional governance, visibility, and control that is demanded in such situations.

11.4 Sourcing Options

Vendor management has always played an important role in the enterprise software delivery organization. Specialist processes and teams are in place in many organizations to examine potential suppliers, issue requests for proposals, evaluate and choose among proposals, issue contracts, manage vendor performance, and so on. In some domains, this role is very well established (e.g., telecommunications, aerospace, and government systems). For others, the necessary skills and experience are in very short supply.

The last few years, however, has seen accelerated use of vendors to deliver services, particularly with respect to outsourcing key aspects of enterprise software delivery tasks. We've now accumulated a multiyear history of using outsourced suppliers for enterprise software delivery, globalization of enterprise software delivery organizations, and widespread offshoring of development and delivery capabilities. During this time, the approaches in use have significantly matured. Many variations exist, but as illustrated in Figure 11.2, we can highlight three distinct categories of sourcing approaches.

In *single sourcing*, an organization selects an outsourced provider to deliver specific capabilities. Typically, the provider is managed based on utilization for the effort delivered as part of the contract, with this effort being the basis for a fixed price or rate-based fee. The provider is responsible for how it delivers that service and offers little insight to the acquiring organization on its progress during delivery, outside of the agreed contract.

Single Sourcing	Multisourcing	Cosourcing
• Country-Based Delivery	• Onshore/Offshore	• Networked Global Centers
• Utilization Based	• Deliverables Based	• Outcome Based
• Limited Collaboration	• Core Team Collaboration by Project	• Community Collaboration Across Process and Technology
• No Workflow Management	• Limited Workflow Management	• Component-Based Workflow Management
• No Reuse	• Ad Hoc Reuse	• Systematic Reuse
• Limited Visibility	• Visibility of Standard Project Metrics	• Pervasive Transparency of All Project Artifacts
• Provider Processes	• Ad Hoc Improvement Processes	• Continuous Improvement with Lean
Technology Platform		
• Stand-Alone Development and Project Management Tools	• Limited Tool Integration and Collaboration Capability	• Integrated Technology Platform Enabling Real-Time Collaboration and AD/M Automation

Figure 11.2 *Evolution of sourcing options and their main characteristics*

Often an organization will make use of *multisourcing* to use specialists in different business areas or to reduce risks from dependence on a single supplier [72]. Normally the providers are organizationally and geographically distributed, requiring the acquiring organization to spend more effort coordinating across the suppliers, measuring and managing the delivered artifacts, ensuring consistency and quality, project managing the different tasks to align results, and so on.

Consequently, in *cosourcing*, a more explicit partnership is created between the consumers and suppliers of services.[16] Here, there is shared responsibility and ownership of results between all parties, with well-defined communication and coordination channels preestablished. This may include shared investment in setting up and delivering service centers, and the creation of a common set of processes and tools for coordinated delivery of services.

Further complicating the range of sourcing options is the emerging use of broader community involvement. Open-source and crowdsourcing approaches create communities that can be used to provide broad input for organizations. At one extreme, this can be through reuse of precreated open-source components, and at the other extreme, projects may gain input (including ideas, comments, code, etc.) from the use of communities of people who have interest in those projects. In some cases, broad requests for services can be made to receive the best response from as large a community as possible. While benefits from this approach are obtained, there are also many challenges to the enterprise software delivery organization in managing this model.

Each of these options (and their many variations) brings with it a series of advantages and disadvantages that make it more or less suitable in different enterprise software delivery situations. As a result, most organizations employ a hybrid set of sourcing approaches that is complicated to define, organize, and manage. Hence, while many organizations have vendor-management experience, they are realizing that too often that experience is of limited value in a world becoming dominated by the following trends:

- *Extensive diversity in sourcing options.* Many organizations are able to be effective with each sourcing option individually but are overwhelmed by the complexity that arises with the combination of these approaches. The most important role of the enterprise software delivery organization in this scenario is to manage key cross-cutting concerns, such as architectural coherence, security, performance, and business continuity. This is

---

16. www.mbaknol.com/international-business/the-concept-of-co-sourcing

extraordinarily difficult in a hybrid sourcing situation—across multiple process, organizational, political, and geographical boundaries.

- *Rapid acquisition-deployment-release cycles.* For many organizations, there are long lead times involved with any vendor acquisition (typically measured in months from initial request for service to deployment). New technologies and business demands require this cycle to be substantially faster (taking days or hours). Currently, processes are not typically in place to encourage or support this acceleration.

- *Specialization of service delivery direct to consumers.* One of the consequences of cloud computing and SaaS solutions has been increasing "disintermediation" between service consumers and service providers.[17] It is now much more straightforward for business units to bypass corporate technology providers to acquire services directly from the vendors with zero deployment and administration costs. Such actions are placing greater pressure on enterprise software delivery organizations to support and manage business units involved in those activities to understand their actions and to maintain overall corporate governance.

- *Increased financial management and cost transparency.* The broader use of sourcing partners is raising questions about cost management and financial analysis across delivered services to the business. On the one hand, the use of cloud-based offerings can make costs much more transparent to the business. Yet cost-reduction pressures are also forcing short-term tactical decisions that make strategic management of enterprise software delivery extremely difficult. For example, some companies have simply cancelled all projects that will take more than nine months to implement on the basis that such projects cannot demonstrate ROI within a year.

As a result of these trends, many enterprise software delivery managers now view their role as much more focused on activities related to project management and cost management and away from the technology aspects that are often their interests and heritage. As illustrated by companies such as Nokia, misunderstanding this changing role of software delivery can have profound consequences and lead to frustrations that can be major

---

17. According to Wikipedia, *disintermediation* is "the free market removal of intermediaries in a supply chain": http://en.wikipedia.org/wiki/Disintermediation.

contributing factors to lack of innovation and failure to bring quality products to market.[18]

11.5 The Third Wave

Three major technology waves have dominated enterprise solution delivery during the last decade: The first wave was a result of the rapid adoption of Internet-based technology around the world. Situations unthinkable only a few years ago are now commonplace, with fast broadband access available from most homes. For example, the United States has seen broadband adoption increase nearly sevenfold from 2001 to 2009, from 9 percent to 63.5 percent.[19] As a result, most businesses and governments have spent a great deal of effort from the late 1990s preparing their solutions for Internet access, launching new Internet-based businesses, and seeking to develop strategies that leverage the global reach of the Internet.

Just as enterprises began to come to terms with the first wave, a second wave began. In the early 2000s we began to see the first signs of social networks becoming more important in enterprise software delivery. Initially viewed as no more than extended newsgroups, initiatives such as Myspace, Twitter, and Facebook exemplify the major impact social networking has had on not just how people interact but also how they acquire goods and services, inform each other of new events, form opinions and preferences, and drive awareness. By 2005, every major enterprise organization had taken steps to use social networks to interact with its markets, understand and anticipate new trends, connect its global work force, and so on.

Now the third wave has arrived. The availability of high-function, Internet-connected mobile devices has brought with it the possibility for enterprise solutions to be accessible anywhere at any time. A large number of people carry around in their pocket a device capable of connecting to enterprise systems anywhere in the world to analyze information from many sources and to share news, information, and opinions with large numbers of people almost instantaneously. Mobile devices have become essential to many people's way of life—as indispensable to them as their credit card or wallet.

This third wave has fueled the explosive growth of applications especially created for use on those mobile devices. A bewildering assortment of applications is available for use, supporting entertainment, information, business, and many other needs. Again, this has had a significant impact on the

18. www.hs.fi/english/article/Knock+Knock+Nokias+Heavy+Fall/1135260596609.
19. www.websiteoptimization.com.

enterprise software delivery organization. In particular, this third wave has required enterprise software delivery organizations to make the following advances:

- *Deploy existing services to mobile devices as an important new delivery platform.* With the variety of devices available, this has often greatly increased the development, testing, and delivery cycle and has required additional investment in infrastructure and skills.

- *Look for new ways to leverage mobile devices as an alternative channel for delivering services to clients.* New opportunities to deliver services are possible by designing services that extend existing capabilities.

- Increase the responsiveness and flexibility of enterprise solution delivery to make existing solutions accessible to mobile devices and to create new apps that not only function on those devices but also take advantage of the device's unique capabilities.

This final point, concerning the flexibility to create new mobile device apps, is particularly intriguing. Not only is there a very wide variety of apps available for mobile devices, but the usage patterns for those apps is placing interesting new demands on the enterprise software delivery organization. The dominant pattern is that mobile device owners download and use a large number of apps, with the majority of applications having very short lifetimes.[20] End users expect new capabilities to be available frequently, to find new services on demand, and to readily consume combinations of services from many different providers. This forces a responsiveness and rapidity of change that is stretching existing enterprise software delivery approaches to their breaking point.

What's more, many enterprises are only now waking up to the business implications involved with this huge market for mobile content and applications.[21] As enterprises seek to take advantage of this emerging market for ubiquitous content, information, and communications, they are beginning to see limitations in traditional business models. Many of the new services involve partners in their delivery, and a competency of working in supply chains is essential. The inexperience of many companies in this regard is becoming a major limitation. Demonstrating the competency to deliver a positive customer

---

20. According to MUBIQUO (www.mubiquo.com), the owners of Android and iPhone devices download an average of nine apps a month. Often they are only used for a short time, perhaps even only for one day.

21. www.globaltelecomsbusiness.com/Article/2316072/The-third-wave-of-transformation.html.

experience across services created by multiple parties at an acceptable price and at acceptable profit margins is clearly critical. It can be argued that the emerging significant players in the delivery of mobile device apps (such as Apple) clearly demonstrate their understanding of managing the supply chain for software and services. Creating strong commercial partnerships with supply chain partners is an essential cultural and operational change that many companies are currently undergoing.

11.6 Conclusions

For more than fifty years enterprise software delivery organizations have been required to adjust and adapt to continual changes in technology, operating environments, and consumer needs. Whether from mainframe to PC or from thick client access to web browsers, these changes have resulted in challenges addressed through new practices and approaches and supported with tools and skills necessary for success.

Currently, the evolving world economy is driving globalization activities at every level of business. Among the several ways in which this globalization will affect the way teams deliver enterprise software, the most important is that software delivery will be viewed from the perspective of a global supply chain in which multiple delivery partners will collaborate within and across organizational boundaries to deliver effective solutions at lowest cost.

Here I've highlighted several important directions that are bringing their share of challenges to enterprise software delivery:

- Cloud computing is stripping away control from the enterprise software delivery organization, bringing cost pressures that are forcing transparency in pricing and diversifying the software supply chain.

- Increased sourcing options for services are adding complexity to the supply chain and increasing the need for more sophisticated approaches to vendor management in enterprise software delivery.

- Rapid growth in the use of mobile devices is accelerating the pace of change in enterprise software applications and requiring additional investments to deploy solutions to many more platforms.

Current approaches to enterprise software delivery are only the first steps to understanding and supporting the kinds of collaborative interactions that must be supported in the coming years. In three areas in particular there will be significant activity:

- *Software factories.* The primary model of enterprise software delivery has shifted toward specialized "centers of excellence" where skilled resources are shared across projects or lines of business. This approach has improved cost efficiency but has often been at the cost of flexibility and time to market due to resource shortages. The move to software factories is aimed at accelerating skills centralization by applying product-line engineering and supply chain experiences from manufacturing domains to the area of enterprise software delivery. We are beginning to see initial approaches to software factories used in SIs such as Accenture, Cognizant, Wipro, and TCS. The approach is viewed as a general model that can be applied much more broadly in enterprise software delivery. However, significant work is still required to develop these approaches to software factory governance, reporting, and control.

- *Outsourcing.* All organizations, to some degree, have taken advantage of global resources to manage cost. Initially, rather simple models of global outsourcing were applied to offload standardized tasks such as maintenance and test activities. However, more recently, more complex and innovative uses of offshore and outsourced resources have emerged. Continued cost pressure will drive further use of outsourcing in enterprise software delivery. Currently, the staff augmentation model most widely used will likely be superseded by more value-added models using outcome-based service delivery techniques. Coordination, management, and control of outsourcing and offshore relationships will be a major challenge to large enterprises. Enterprise software delivery will be enhanced in these areas to deliver greater support for emerging usage patterns with real-time collaboration and rich interaction across global teams.

- *Multisourcing and crowdsourcing.* The challenges that we see in new delivery models often result from the increased risks of moving to supply chains of partners delivering key services and artifacts. Many kinds of risks must be actively managed: suboptimal performance of suppliers, partners being acquired or going out of business, failure to deliver against contract, security and intellectual property exposure, and so on. Some of these risks can be addressed by moving toward multisourcing (using several providers of similar or aligned capabilities) and crowdsourcing (placing services out to wider markets for supply from a greater community). However, these approaches also introduce additional risks. A big focus for future enterprise software delivery will be on how to support, manage, and adapt to these different relationship models while helping to understand and mitigate risks.

The industrialization of enterprise software delivery is already on the path to adapt to these needs. We see a great deal of activity taking place to recognize and meet these challenges and look forward to many future advances in this area.

Appendix A

Enterprise Software Delivery Revisited

Chapter Summary

I discuss the main characteristics of enterprise software delivery organizations and the tasks that they typically perform. In particular, I emphasize the breadth and depth of the challenges they must address and the ways in which they organize and focus efforts to overcome them. I highlight the following:

- The pressures and expectations on enterprise software delivery organizations is growing at the same time that budgets are shrinking.

- The organization of activities and resources focuses around the main areas of work, separating *run* and *change* activities and emphasizing governance and control across those areas.

- A critical aspect of an enterprise software delivery organization concerns balancing the portfolio of applications and system maintenance activities with new investment.

- Complexity is an inherent issue in their activities and is seen in many aspects of what is carried out, particularly with regard to understanding and managing changes in software and systems.

A.1 Introduction

The chief information officer (CIO) of a large bank recently explained his strategy for the coming year very simply by expressing his enterprise software delivery focus in the form of three primary questions:

- How do I get a better understanding of how I am currently spending money, and how do I optimize my resources as effectively as possible to deliver on my enterprise software commitments?

- What decisions are we making that have significant impact on our deployed enterprise software, and how do I improve decision making to invest more in the areas that are of high value to my business?

- What key enterprise delivery practices are most successful, and how do I support their wider adoption and use in my organization?

On face value, these are rather obvious and straightforward questions and may even be seen as rather narrow or naïve. However, they capture the essence of the challenge facing enterprise software delivery today. The magnitude of the task being faced is a consequence of a number of factors—most notably, the complexity involved in managing a large portfolio of solutions across diverse business domains with a highly distributed work force of varied skills and increasingly demanding consumers. Intense pressures on delivering enterprise software in many business domains are the result of several convergent factors, including the following:

- *End-user expectations.* The amount of personnel that access and use software-intensive solutions in their day-to-day activities has increased, and their expectations for those systems has also increased.

- *Cost to create solutions.* Changes occur in regard to who is developing and evolving those solutions and what it costs to specify, implement, and maintain them.

- *Speed of change.* The fast pace of business change demands that enterprise software can be reconfigured quickly as those needs change.

- *Technology churn.* A range of new technologies have emerged that require renovation of the enterprise computing platform and delivery of capabilities to new devices.

- *Auditing and compliance.* There is increased accountability for how software is developed to ensure it meets the business needs.

As a result, enterprise software delivery organizations are in the midst of significant changes in how their role is perceived within the broader business context, how they should be organized for greatest efficiency and impact, what kinds of solution architectures support the increased flexibility demanded, and how they balance investments for greatest effect across a large, diverse portfolio of solutions.

In the remainder of this appendix, I review the structure and role of the enterprise software delivery organization, examine the nature and impact of the pressures that are forcing change, and illustrate through a series of real-world examples the extent and impact of the challenges facing such organizations. I start by looking at how a typical enterprise software delivery organization is organized and the day-to-day challenges it faces. Then I briefly review the structure of a typical enterprise system before concluding with some illustrations and observations that serve as motivation for the major themes addressed in this book.

A.2 The Enterprise Software Delivery Organization

It's not easy to put your arms around what is really meant by *enterprise software* or the *enterprise software delivery organization* that is responsible for the software's development, delivery, and ongoing maintenance. Fundamentally, enterprise software is any software-intensive solution or product that provides core services to an organization in its daily business. Consequently, the enterprise software delivery organization is a support organization with responsibility for the creation, evolution, or ongoing operation of an enterprise's computer systems. However, that description seems to ignore a number of the key characteristics that motivate the work and value that the group provides. For many organizations, enterprise software delivery is primary to the organization's success. It provides the infrastructure that the organization relies on for smooth operation of its key business processes, provides key information-focused services that differentiate the organization's business offerings, and supports a wide variety of stakeholders who communicate through a common set of information managed by the group.[1]

For this reason, I begin this analysis with an overview of the primary roles and functions supported in a typical enterprise software delivery organization. While I use examples and illustrations from several business domains, for this

---

1. For example, to customers of an online financial services company, the enterprise software "is" the organization. In contrast, many companies view their enterprise software very much as a supporting function necessary to help deliver other kinds of goods and services to clients.

analysis I place particular emphasis on traditional IT delivery organizations as one primary class of enterprise.

A.2.1 Organizational Approaches

Enterprise software delivery is typically organized around two main axes. These are *core business processes (core)* and *line of business processes (LOB)*. While reporting relationships may differ, LOB is typically partitioned based on the market being served and products delivered to that market, with funding for projects related to the value the LOB derives from that investment. Core processes revolve around functions that are more naturally centralized and provide value more generally to the organization or across a range of LOBs. Examples of processes that are typically centralized include many of the support activities such as human resources (HR), marketing, and research. However, depending on the organization, the core activities may also include many other activities, such as data-center management, tools standardization, and infrastructure procurement.

This distinction between LOB and core may seem artificial and arbitrary. But in practice it is particularly important and shapes many of the decisions made in enterprise software delivery. The different characteristics of core and LOB include the following:

- Core activities typically include day-to-day operations in the data centers. As such, they have responsibility for the ongoing operation of key IT services and command a lot of authority. Roles such as database administrator (DBA) and system administrator (sysadmin) have responsibility for many aspects of the main computing resources on operational systems. For example, typically no hardware is added to the corporate network and no software or data are placed onto corporate systems without sign off from these roles.

- The incentives and metrics for success of core and LOB activities are different. Core practices place primary value on stability, efficiency, and persistence. They are measured via service level agreements (SLAs) that use explicit definitions of machine downtime, response time, and backlog of support requests. For LOB practices, the pressure is on speed of innovation, fast turnaround of new solutions to meet project needs, introduction of new capabilities to match competitor offerings, and customization for different end-user stakeholder requests. They are measured by direct impact on business revenue, responsiveness to new requests, and usability of delivered solutions.

Indeed, this basic separation of core versus LOB is the basis for a series of important decisions about the overall function and organization of enterprise software delivery. As illustrated in Figure A.1, a number of organizational options are possible, each with its own strengths and weaknesses:[2]

- *Dedicated LOBs* can be defined for each key business domain; for example, in a banking company these may be for retail banking, personal banking, Internet banking, trading and options, and so on. Each LOB is responsible for its own software development and delivery with projects that are largely locally controlled. This makes IT teams directly responsible for the business they serve through specialization of the practices and tools, and it creates deep local knowledge of business practices. However, this also limits sharing across the LOBs and encourages duplication of resources and platforms across the organization.

- *Common services* focus on centralizing major capabilities across the organization to create services specializations that may be called on by projects initiated by the LOBs. Typically, this simplifies the services provided, reduces overlaps, and provides more governed IT expenses. However, projects now are much more complex to execute and may require a series of agreements among services teams to align resources and priorities. Visibility and governance of delivery requires particular attention.

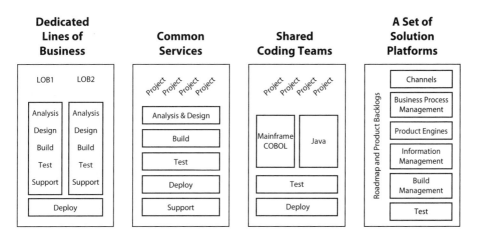

Figure A.1 *Examples of enterprise software delivery approaches*

---

2. Of course, in addition to these four common patterns, several variations and hybrid approaches are also possible.

- *Shared coding teams* create "solution delivery centers" that specialize in the technology platforms of interest. The goal is to create a highly efficient technology base, optimizing resources and reducing support costs. Each of the LOBs will assume more business design responsibility and treat the solution delivery centers as technology partners in delivery. While this can be efficient to operate, the result can be a highly technical IT organization with little direct business knowledge. A sharp distinction between business and technical communities may limit business flexibility and agility.

- *A set of solution platforms* can be created as a common infrastructure for all enterprise software delivery. The projects are driven by an enterprise-wide road map and strategy that governs priorities and guides resource decisions. This focuses attention on reusable infrastructure and services and toward product-line thinking. Success requires a very strong cross-enterprise strategy that is driven across all LOBs and the IT organization, with clear change management practices. Without that strong leadership, these platforms can become an impediment to change rather than an extensive framework to be leveraged.

In practice, therefore, the organizational structure of the enterprise shapes many aspects of the dynamics, politics, and decision making in large corporations, and its influence cannot be overstated. At a lower level within the main organizational units, understanding the specific roles and responsibilities offers great insight into the way many of today's enterprise software delivery organizations function.

In summary, the enterprise software delivery organization has responsibility for the delivery of enterprise software in support of the business. Consequently, the primary challenge is to map those business needs into priorities and actions that optimize the organization's performance. The structure of the organization reflects the pressures being faced to maintain deployed systems while driving innovation to support new and emerging business needs.

A.3 Managing an Enterprise Software Portfolio

For most organizations, their enterprise software delivery challenges are dominated by the need to manage a large, complex portfolio of solutions that have been developed, acquired, inherited, and upgraded over a significant period of time—often several decades [87]. Hence the need to support new business activities is severely limited by the need to continue operation of existing systems. The consequence is that the vast majority of related spending is used to maintain ongoing operations. Many such organizations view their highest priority to be activities aimed at business continuity, and they carefully monitor the ratio of their investments between *running* the enterprise and *changing* the enterprise.

The extent to which concerns about ongoing system maintenance dominate will vary across organizations depending on their business domain, previous investments, and delivery history. However, it's not unusual to hear examples of companies where up to 80 percent of the budget is directed toward ongoing system maintenance. This leaves only a small fraction of the budget for introducing new and innovative enterprise solutions to build for the future. What's more, any budget cuts typically aggressively target this ability to innovate because it's frequently much harder to shut down ongoing operations than delay the delivery of some future capability.

The extent of this budget challenge is effectively illustrated in many recent surveys,[3] Based on such surveys, we see that an average of over 60 percent of IT investment is directed toward ongoing operation costs, with that figure rising significantly in recent years. The situation is a little better for IT capital budget allocation, where such surveys show that an average of over 50 percent of the budget is used to maintain current IT capabilities.

While many factors contribute to this extensive investment in ongoing systems, one of the most dominant factors is the extent of overlap and duplication in the set of applications that are used across the business. Most organizations have many years of enterprise software delivery history, have refocused business lines and markets as a result of strategic adjustments, and have complex combinations of systems delivery infrastructures as a result of acquisitions, mergers, and reorganizations. The extent of this challenge is illustrated in Figure A.2. Here we see the result of a high-level application portfolio analysis for a large bank.

To examine the breadth of enterprise software it supports, the organization created a framework for analysis based on its key business processes. From this analysis, it was able to identify significant enterprise software overlap in many of those business process areas. For example, more than one hundred different enterprise systems directly address some aspect of *clearing* and *settlement* business processes, and almost one hundred address the processes of managing balances and positions. Through such an analysis, the enterprise software delivery organization can target strategic efforts to rationalize the portfolio as a basis for simplification and cost reduction.

Of course, managing and governing this extensive portfolio of solutions is a major activity for any enterprise software delivery organization. Much effort is required to create and manage an up-to-date inventory of existing solutions and to understand the range of projects that are being executed to manage, update, evolve, and extend that set of solutions. Such a project portfolio view

---

3. For example, see "The State of Enterprise IT Budgets" reports at www.forrester.com.

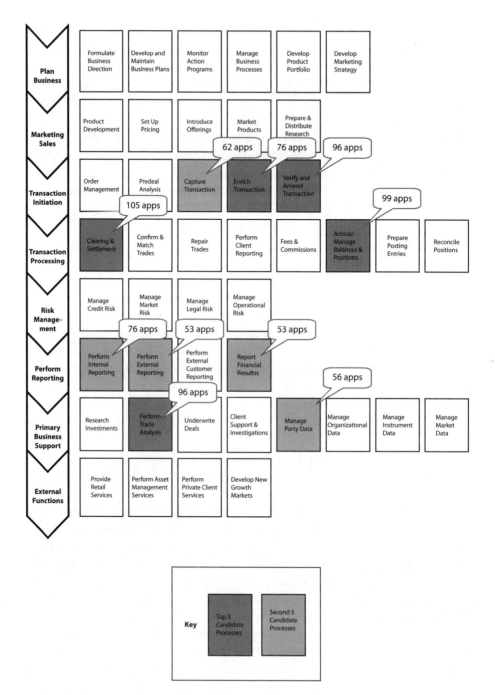

Figure A.2 *An analysis of the application portfolio for a large banking organization*

may provide details about individual projects and the systems they impact (data about their ownership, size, investment, business function, etc.), relationships among those projects (data about their technical, business, and resource interdependencies and interactions), and their current and planned investments (data about their resource requirements, resource expenditure, projected cost, and timelines).

Many different analysis techniques and supporting application portfolio management tools are used to catalogue the broad set of enterprise software activities taking place in a enterprise organizations. In a typical large bank, for example, there may be hundreds of ongoing projects in-flight at any time, each of them affecting one or more existing enterprise software solutions. Project costs and delivery times are carefully managed to ensure resources are being used to the best effect in moving these enterprise solutions forward.

A.4 Examining the Mix of Portfolio Solutions

The business solutions delivered by enterprise software delivery organizations differ significantly depending on a variety of factors. However, some common patterns can be used to describe the basic mix of solutions that form the typical enterprise software portfolio. Here I expand upon the split between core and LOB activities to describe that collection of systems for which the enterprise software delivery organization is responsible, and I use a simple classification of the function of those solutions and the technologies from which they are constructed.

A.4.1 The Role of Packaged Applications

So far in this appendix, I've looked at the pressures facing enterprise solutions delivery from the perspective of the organizational structure and the complexity of the enterprise software portfolio. Central to this discussion has been the need to ensure that there is an appropriate balance across the enterprise software portfolio to maintain current operations while investing in future needs. This requires significant attention to ensure that the applications are prioritized correctly to provide high value to the business. The primary function of the enterprise solutions delivery organization involves supporting the business by delivering and operating mission-critical applications to support the key business processes. Over the past few years, organizations have recognized that for many of these key business processes, there is a great deal of commonality. A large number of business processes are critical functions within the organization but do not necessarily offer any particular competitive value in the specific business role being accomplished. This includes activities such as sales management, customer relationship management, and human resource management. Consequently, the last decade has signified a reliance on "packaged" enterprise solutions from third-party vendors such as SAP Siebel and Oracle.

Many papers and books explore the role and importance of these packaged applications [88,89] and describe specific solutions in great detail [90,91]. I won't repeat that work here, but I will make the following points:

- Acquiring and installing packaged applications is seen as a low-cost route to common functionality, allowing businesses to focus development resources on value-added LOB solutions. Packaged applications increase standardization of core business processes both within and across organizations and can help the organization to work more effectively with partners and suppliers.

- Adjusting and configuring these packaged applications forms a considerable development effort. Often, these systems cover a wide range of business processes that must be significantly aligned with the way the organization currently does business. Hence the effort to customize the packaged application can be a substantial multiyear investment.

- Ongoing enhancements and upgrades to the packaged applications must be carefully aligned with all other enterprise software delivery activities. The packaged application vendors will work to their own specific schedule that must be considered in the planning and execution of the broader enterprise software delivery portfolio. Such dependencies inherently increase risk and reduce flexibility.

A.4.2 Business Integration

As organizations continue to exploit Internet-based technologies for competitive advantage, one of the most important directions has been to vastly expand both business-to-consumer and business-to-business delivery channels. Business integration is seen as key to the agility needed to gain and maintain competitive advantage. Consequently, one of the most fundamental pushes in the last few years for the enterprise software delivery organization has been to optimize the business supply chain and provide more explicit support for understanding and implementing rapid business process change through the reconfiguration of the enterprise software that supports it [92].

This has led to two important changes in the way enterprise software are delivered. First, portals and rich customer applications are seen as the common user interface to expose aggregate functionality and act as enterprise knowledge repositories. These portals offer a common way to aggregate information from many different sources to deliver integration "on the glass" in front of the user. Hence the user is able to make more informed business decisions through the combination of information available regardless of the variety of data sources, complex back-office systems, or disparate enterprise solutions that underlie it. Also, as business needs change, there is a great deal of flexibility because the displayed information accessible through the portal can be reconfigured and reorganized; this helps avoid complex reengineering of the underlying enterprise software itself.

Second, where more fundamental integration among enterprise software is required, there is increasingly common use of service-oriented architecture (SOA) approaches as the architectural underpinning to provide integration across the enterprise and with partners. The basic idea of an SOA approach is to construct the enterprise software as a well-defined collection of capabilities (i.e., services) offered to other potential consumers of those capabilities via explicit service interfaces and to consume the capabilities of other enterprise software through their external service interfaces. Service-based systems are possible because of commercial service management technologies that support service catalogues, service connection, and service-based transaction behavior (such as service execution logging, and restarting services on failure). By designing and executing enterprise software in this way, the focus of design is on the business process interactions and the services required to support them, with service interactions seen as much more explicit parts of the overall system model.

A.4.3 Balancing Enterprise Software Delivery Needs

One of the most challenging aspects for many enterprise software organizations is to balance the enterprise software delivery activities in a way that optimizes their capabilities in support of the businesses needs. The tendency in many enterprise delivery organizations is for a series of specializations to be built up across the organization. This is a result of a number of forces:

- Disparate enterprise systems have typically been managed by disparate business teams. Many of these enterprise systems are very large and complex, and they may have been in operation for many years. As a result, significant personal experience and expertise is built up over that time by the team responsible for each system.

- In operating as a supply chain, it's clear that enterprise solutions frequently interact with partner systems as part of an extensive value chain. These partner systems are typically managed separately, with an external team governed by priorities and goals that differ from the core enterprise software delivery organization.

- For a series of organizational and auditing reasons, operational control functions are usually implemented separately from the business teams defining the requirements for new systems and the delivery teams responsible for ongoing delivery of services. While this independence aids compliance and supports overall management of external regulations, it also complicates systems delivery by dividing authority across different independent groups.

- Longer-term strategic decision on platform and delivery standards must be considered from an organizational perspective, independent of any one enterprise software concern. Also, for most organizations, there is a bewildering set of technology, business, and market-driven standards to track, understand, and prioritize. The standards that do exist are complex and frequently poorly governed, and they may require customization per line of business.

- New technology is acquired and delivered to add new operational capability or to refresh existing capabilities. Too frequently this technology is added without sufficient thought to the existing infrastructure and information assets, with the result that it may duplicate what exists and hence add to the complexity rather than easing it.

- Outsourcing has brought saving in labor costs but highlighted the poor practices in communication, process definition, governance, and business/IT alignment across the different domains, enterprise software, departments, and management chains.

Overall, the enterprise solutions delivery organization must address a complex collection of systems of varying architectural characteristics, acquired from different sources. We can view these systems in a series of categories and examine the specific stakeholder concerns inherent in each one.

As illustrated in Figure A.3, there are several categories of systems, each with their own characteristics, challenges, and concerns. While many aspects of these systems are of interest, it's important to highlight the specific issues that must be faced when supporting each category of systems.

A.4.3.1 Core Business Application Concerns

The following is a list of core business application concerns:

- Core business applications require significant investment to maintain and evolve. The health of the core business applications is usually the highest priority concern. As discussed earlier, a majority of an enterprise delivery organization's budget is devoted to this effort.

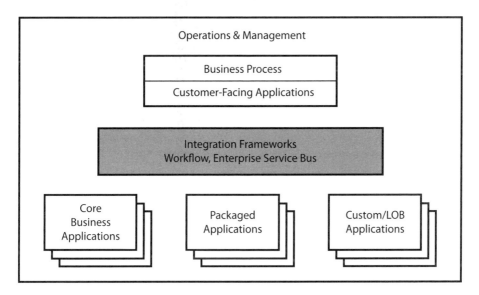

Figure A.3 *The main categories of solutions in a typical large enterprise software portfolio*

- As new business processes emerge, an important concern is how to appropriately leverage functionality from existing systems "outside the silo" of its existing operation. Integrating with these core capabilities is both a necessity and a major risk to ongoing operations.

- Knowledge about the architecture and operation of existing systems varies enormously. There is a constant need to catalogue the current inventory as a basis for decision making on cost reduction and to keep that information accurate with respect to the many changes that take place over time.

- More frequently we see different access channels required to existing systems, notably Internet-based access to core business capabilities. This requires secure, efficient access to those capabilities, even if they were developed more than a decade ago.

A.4.3.2 *Packaged Application Concerns*
The following is a list of packaged application concerns:

- A packaged application delivers a complex collection of capabilities based on supporting a standardized set of business processes. As expected, these must be customized to align with the organization's specific business processes. In many cases, the pack is updated to reflect more accurately how business is conducted in that organization. Additionally, the organization's business processes may be adjusted to align more closely with those supported by the packaged application.

- The size and business impact of a packaged application deployment can be significant. As a result, such systems are typically deployed incrementally and supported by a careful set of practices around training, installation, rollout, and change management. For example, to manage deployment, the packaged application may be deployed one business unit at a time, one business function at a time, one geographic area at a time, or in some combination based on the organization's needs.

- Adaptation and configuration of the packaged application is an ongoing process that continues throughout the lifetime of the solution's use. Implementation and deployment of the packaged application must be considered a work in progress that must be constantly adjusted to the changing business requirements and reassessed with each new packaged application release.

- Very few organizations can be entirely supported by a single set of packaged applications. As a result, a major effort is required to integrate the packaged application services with those of the other operational systems. In this sense, the packaged application is one component of a larger enterprise solution that must be understood and managed collectively. This complex set of interactions may be particularly brittle in the light of system changes, and it often requires specialist consulting attention and dedicated tooling to maintain.

A.4.3.3 Custom Application Concerns

The following is a list of custom application concerns:

- Specialized, custom applications will still be required to meet business needs and differentiate the organization from competitive offerings in the market. Such applications may be of any size and criticality and will need to be supported from inception through to deployment. The enterprise software delivery organization is responsible for all aspects of this, and it must use contemporary techniques and technologies to deliver the solutions to meet the business needs as optimally as possible.

- Furthermore, in most business domains there are periodic changes that may require reworking major parts of the enterprise software portfolio in order to align with those changes. Examples of such changes include new governance and auditing regulations (e.g., SOX and Basel II compliance in financial services industries), additional security and reporting rules (e.g., passenger flight documentation in light of perceived terrorist threats), and government mandates (e.g., tax law amendments and monetary policy changes). Broad changes such as these require a lot of planning, assessment, and potential upgrades across many systems.

- Reacting quickly to day-to-day market conditions can enable an organization to take advantage of market shifts before competitors have time to react (the so-called first-move advantage). These kinds of changes have particularly profound effects in consumer industries such as the automotive industry, telecommunications, and entertainment services industries. Succeeding in such a market requires fast replanning and turnaround of system changes and focuses on the ability to quickly assess the potential impact of these market changes on existing systems and in-flight projects and to implement them with a high degree of predictability.

A.4.3.4 Integration Concerns

The following is a list of integration concerns:

- This drive for flexible assembly and reassembly of system capabilities has led many enterprise software delivery organizations to focus attention on a system integration infrastructure as a critical component of their solution portfolio. This integration hub, or "enterprise service bus," raises the profile of integration activities from a one-time effort toward a plug-and-play model for enterprise software delivery. This infrastructure forms the heart of an integrated suite of enterprise software services that together deliver business value to the organization.

- The capacity for integrating systems and services from outside the organization must be included in any integration strategy. In addition to the traditional challenges of system integration, connection to systems outside the organization introduces additional concerns around security, privacy, intellectual property, and so on. This can add significantly to system complexity and increases the ongoing maintenance challenges. For example, specific gateways for the systems may need to be configured for partner use, isolated from normal system access mechanisms, and multiple levels of security analysis may need to be implemented to reduce risk from outside access to internal data.

- Latest trends in enterprise software delivery include the need to support a wide variety of technologies both for user interaction and for back-office connectivity. In addition to access from PCs and other computer devices, it's now much more likely that enterprise software will need access from handheld devices, portable devices, mobile phones, and a host of new interconnected systems. Many different operating systems and communications applications of varying kinds will run on these devices. Continual technology churn requires a great deal of investment in new ways to surface business processes and data to new devices in ever more meaningful ways.

A.4.3.5 Business Concerns

The following is a list of business concerns:

- The business requirements provide the context for defining the enterprise software delivery organization's role, impact, and success. A strong relationship with the business analysts and business leaders is a determining factor in how well the enterprise delivery organization performs its tasks and strongly influences how it is perceived. Unfortunately, all too frequently this relationship is strained, and at times it is broken. The main causes of this are the divergent operating worlds for both communities and a failure to find common ground on which to cooperate on, plan for, and execute the business goals.

- Fundamental to success is the need to articulate the business processes as clearly as possible as the basis for understanding the effectiveness of current enterprise software. Business process modeling and analysis are core activities of the business analyst. They form the major input to the enterprise software delivery organization. A key focus for the communication between business people and the enterprise software delivery organization is the alignment of these business process models to the services of the implemented enterprise software. Such process models are particularly important in business improvement efforts, where the starting point is typically a business process reengineering effort.

- Perhaps the most frequent cause of conflict across the boundaries between business and enterprise software delivery is a lack of coordinated change management. Operational systems are affected by changes in business function as well as changes in system implementation. Each will likely have impact on the other, often in unintentional and destructive ways. Managing these changes in a coordinated way is vital.

- New projects to add system capabilities or improve existing capabilities must, in the end, be justified in terms of their value to the business. The return on investment (ROI) for some kinds of changes (such as improvements to system security or support for new auditing regulations) can be easily defined. However, in general, it proves difficult to justify many enterprise software projects in ways that allow the business leaders and enterprise software teams to agree on delivery priorities. Too often, business cases to support investment in new projects are poorly defined and supported by weak improvement metrics and unsubstantiated ROI projections.

A.4.3.6 Operations Concerns

The following is a list of operations concerns:

- There are many difficult challenges in operating a large, complex enterprise software portfolio at the service levels required by the business (minimum downtime and maximum access at all times) wherever the organization operates across the world and for every hour of every day of every year. The ramifications of this, of course, are enormous, and it would be foolish to try to summarize them here in a few words. I'll simply note that operating and managing the enterprise software portfolio for a large organization is one of the most complex tasks in any business. It is the source of most of the systems capability provided to the business and the destination for most of the enterprise software budget required to make it possible.

- Particularly challenging in this context is to understand the impact of any enterprise software change on not only the business functions being delivered but also on the ongoing operational aspects of the systems in place. Updates cannot be introduced if there is any risk that they compromise operational factors such as system performance, data access, information security, and so on. Consequently, significant analysis is performed before any change is allowed to be introduced into operation.

- As the ongoing operational and support aspects consume a lot of the costs in computing budget for most organizations, they're also the target for a great deal of pressure to reduce those costs and to be as effective as possible in the use of resources. This has led in recent years to a number of important trends, including the globalization of enterprise software delivery. Two dimensions of this that are of interest here are the movement of operations functions to offshore locations and the outsourcing of operations to third-party organizations. While both of these can improve the cost management aspects of operations, they also can increase the distance (physically and conceptually) between the enterprise software delivery organization and the operation of those systems when deployed. Without careful attention, this gap increases the chances for misalignments between the teams, which can have catastrophic and expensive impacts.

- Most businesses are looking to broaden access to their services to clients in new ways, tie together formally distinct capabilities, and interact using new business models. All these require a move to greater external access to enterprise software from parties outside of the organization. They clearly introduce additional stress on the operational aspects of enterprise software. For example, one impact of this is that much greater attention is placed on concerns about fraudulent and malicious access to information, scams and attacks, vandalism, and espionage. In light of this, every enterprise system must be assessed and monitored continually.

A.5 Enterprise Integration Issues

For many organizations, the challenge of developing enterprise software in isolation is dwarfed by the complexity of how to understand that system's interactions with others to deliver the services it provides. There are two specific aspects of this challenge that can be distinguished.

The first aspect, which we will call *delivery integration*, is the deployment and management of enterprise software into operation [93]. There are many aspects of this problem that arise from the key operational concerns associated with the deployment of any large system: controlling external access, continuous operation in the face of failure, redundancy and backup of data, power management, and so on. These concerns are important individually for each enterprise software system, but the main challenge arises in collectively managing an extensive portfolio of enterprise software such that these operational concerns can be adequately addressed. So for example, it may be relatively straightforward to perform a security assessment on a single system to ensure that Internet-based access to data is restricted. However, with a portfolio of several hundred systems interacting in multiple ways, the potential access paths and security implications across those systems are much more difficult to understand, assess, and manage.

The second aspect, which we will call *design integration*, is the planned interaction that occurs between enterprise software in order to perform their business function effectively [94]. The business as a whole does not plan and design every enterprise software solution as an independent "island" of business function and data. In fact, it's quite the opposite. It is essential that each enterprise software solution plays a role in the broader needs of the organization and augments the existing capability in well-understood ways. This planned integration across enterprise software is an essential part of the enterprise software delivery role. Unfortunately, it's also one of the most challenging to realize in practice.

In the following sections, I explore more of this design integration challenge. I use three illustrations that highlight different complexities that must be addressed: the complexity of business process integration, the complexity of service interfaces, and the complexity of the supply chain.

A.5.1 Business Process Complexity

The main starting point for the complexity challenges faced by enterprise software delivery organizations is at the business process level. To a large degree, most businesses have a very hard time clearly describing the business domain in which they operate, the business functions they perform, and the primary business processes that capture how they carry out those functions. If you discuss the detailed business processes supported by a typical large organization, you are very soon overwhelmed by the complexity of how the organization views its business—the roles, activities, tasks, resources, business rules, priorities, alternatives and exceptions, and so on.

In practice, as illustrated in Figure A.4, the business process view presented by many organizations consists of a complex set of processes and interactions that are almost impossible to understand without significant experience and domain knowledge. As seen in this diagram, the business process elements are shown tightly interconnected with the data they manipulate, the enterprise software that implements those processes, and the technology that underpins them.

To address this complexity, enterprise software delivery organizations have been working with business process analysts to clarify the key business processes and obtain a clearer shared view of the structure of those business processes and their realization in specific enterprise software. By introducing a more disciplined approach to business process analysis [95], the business processes can be defined in a standard business process modeling notation (BPMN) [96]. Such business process models can then be more easily shared, analyzed, and transformed into other artifacts, such as service descriptions.

Figure A.5 illustrates the way in which a more systematic approach to business process analysis is possible. In the upper part of Figure A.5, we see the different processes that form the *arrangement management* business areas from the *propose* to *close* steps in the life cycle. Each of these business processes is described in detail (the lower part of Figure A.5) in the business process model shown. This business process model can be used as the basis of analysis, and

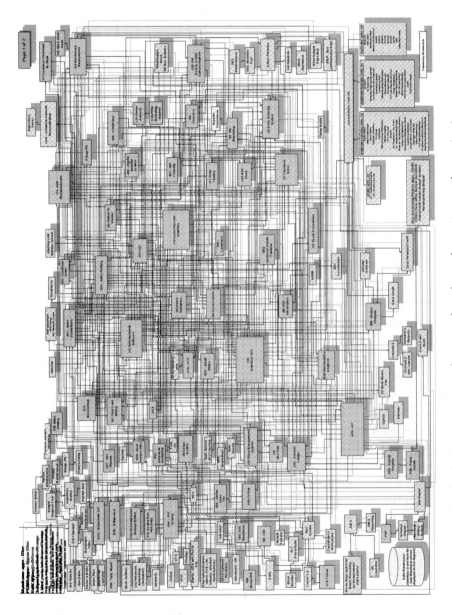

Figure A.4 *A complex business process architecture for a large electronics retail organization*

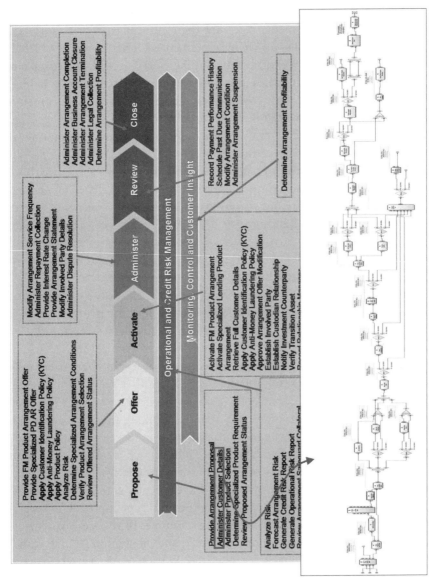

Figure A.5 *An example business process analysis for banking processes around Arrangement Management*

it can be linked directly into the specific enterprise systems that implement the business process.

A.5.2 Service Interface Complexity

Many organizations have recognized that their current enterprise software have a great deal of overlap in their implemented functionality, which is realized in a very varied collection of technologies. To provide a clearer picture of what the organization has and how this intersects, it can be helpful to abstract the technical details to consider the wide collection of capabilities those systems deliver to the business as a portfolio of services accessed through their interfaces and realized through one or more components that offer an implementation of that service with particular delivery characteristics. This combination of a service-oriented interface model realized through a component-based implementation provides a clean conceptual approach that helps the organization reason about its current capabilities and forms the basis for planning new development projects as part of an integrated solution.

This kind of service-oriented thinking, and the consequent SOA, is particularly helpful in understanding the interactions among systems. Service models explicitly record how each service interface exposes its capabilities to others, and the way that one service performs its task is often through access to a number of other services via their available service interfaces. To complete this approach, a more dynamic way of connecting services is possible by recording which services are available at any point in time, and allowing a service to query for, and connect to, another service's interfaces at runtime.

To some extent, this form of service-oriented thinking (perhaps under different terminology) has been part of enterprise software development for many years. However, the recent availability of specialist service-focused technologies encourages and supports this way of designing systems and system interactions. For example, service description standards have recently emerged and can be used as part of a service catalogue, query, and connection approach in several different vendor-supported technologies. For example, IBM bases many of its solutions on the universal description, discovery, and integration (UDDI) standard for service discovery; the reusable asset specification (RAS) for service cataloging; and the service-oriented method and architecture (SOMA) approach for service design and delivery.

That said, the simplicity of a service view is severely challenged when we look at the scalability of applying it within a large organization. For example, the component model for a single division of a global financial services organization can often consist of hundreds of items to describe the organization's enterprise software as a collection of components and their interactions through their service interfaces. While the component model imposes some structure, the complexity of such a view can be overwhelming. While it may aid conceptual planning, it is far from clear how in practice such a complex component model can be used effectively to identify overlaps, inefficiencies, and optimization opportunities across a set of enterprise software. The enterprise software delivery organization must find ways to deal with this level of complexity in service level design using a variety of service-based design techniques and best practices.

A.5.3 Supply Chain Complexity

For organizations deploying packaged applications as a core element of the enterprise software approach, there is greater standardization on the business processes and service architecture. In effect, the packaged application implements a specific set of business processes, realized as a set of services and delivered as deployable components. To a large degree, this standardization is the main reason many organizations adopt a packaged application solution rather than implement the functionality from scratch themselves.

However, introducing a packaged application solution also requires a significant integration effort. In many cases, this effort is primarily directed at how the packaged application implementation can be inserted into the existing technology infrastructure in some reasonable way and how the existing systems surrounding it much be adjusted to ensure that the packaged application functions effectively in this context. For example, in many integrations with SAP, care is needed to design how the SAP components connect to the messaging bus to consume and deliver messages to the rest of the system. Data sources must also be connected to SAP to manage the enterprise data across the organization. Other packaged applications also need to be integrated into this system; for example, packages such as Siebel may be used to handle associated business processes such as sales management and demand management processes.

In effect, the result of any such integration effort is a supply chain of different solutions integrated across a number of message backbones for communication and coordination. Such architecture is typical of complex enterprise software integration, particularly where external trading partners are consuming services in a broader business value chain. The supply chain architecture naturally fits the loosely coupled integration approach necessary to support the flexibility required for such solutions.

A.6 Managing Change

An interesting exercise for understanding any complex system (computer-based or otherwise) is to ask the question, What happens when something changes? Much can be learned by examining the implications of any particular change in the system and by tracking the individual steps involved in its execution. This is also true with enterprise software delivery. In this case, it is instructive to look at changes at two different levels. First, at the tactical level, I consider a change in a capability delivered by a single enterprise solution. Second, at the strategic level, I consider how changes across the enterprise solutions are planned and delivered.

A.6.1 Tactical-Level Change Management

There are frequent changes in individual components across an enterprise software portfolio as a result of fixes and upgrades, rearchitecture, and replacement. Of course, there are many technical aspects to understanding and delivering many of these changes. However, just as important to all changes is the process by which those changes are prioritized, agreed, implemented, delivered, and deployed. For some situations, some informality in this process is possible. But for many organizations, there are strict, highly governed practices that must be followed to avoid errors, misunderstandings, and malicious intent.

As illustrated in Figure A.6, a change to a system can be part of a complex set of activities that validate and govern the change throughout its life cycle. In this process extract, we see that the different artifacts and supporting tasks interact across the primary process phases (in the middle of the diagram). Enacting the changes requires a number of change authorizations, validation, and coordination tasks.

Furthermore, in many industries such changes need to be auditable. That is, each step must not only be done; it must also be seen to have been done via a clear record of what took place, when, and who was responsible for the action (perhaps with formal sign off at each stage). It's often found that in those situations more time is spent deciding what to change and documenting the change than actually implementing the change itself.

A.6.2 Strategic-Level Change Management

While many changes arise on an ad hoc basis due to the discovery of defects and other stakeholder input, many changes are also necessary to maintain the overall architecture of the enterprise software (e.g., to introduce a new user

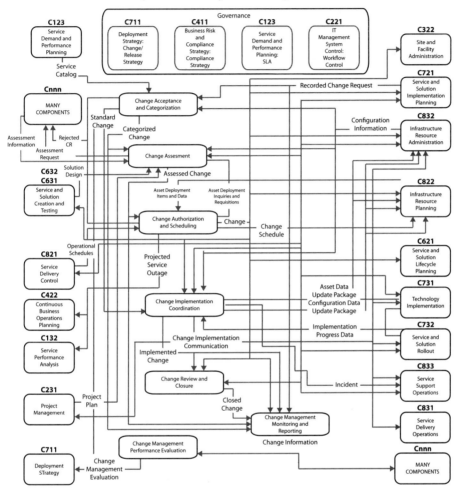

CBM4IT C722 Change Deployment Control
Physical Information System View—Target Situation

Figure A.6 *An extract from a process description for change deployment in a large IT organization*

interface layer to ease multichannel access to core services), to make fundamental upgrades to the technology infrastructure (e.g., moving to a new version of an operating system platform), or to realize a program-wide enhancement (e.g., to introduce a new security logging mechanism). These kinds of strategic changes frequently affect many systems and must often be introduced in a number of phases over some significant period of time.

In Figure A.7, I illuminate the kinds of strategic changes that are typical by showing the phased plan that was defined by a large retail organization

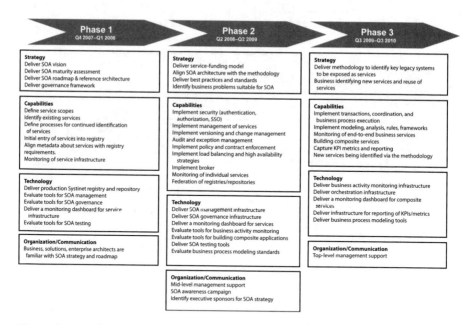

Figure A.7 *A phased strategic change plan for a large retail organization*

as it planned its future directions. Here we see that over a three-year period there were a large number of strategic change projects being executed, categorized into four areas: *strategy*, *capabilities*, *technology*, and *organization/communication*. Each of the items in each category could have a major impact on many of the deployed enterprise software and indirectly impact all in-flight projects. Strategic changes such as these require their own approval and governance process, often at least as complex as the tactical change process described earlier.

A.7 Conclusions

As enterprise software delivery organizations seek to improve their efficiency and provide greater value to the businesses they serve, they face many challenges. Underlying these challenges is the basic concept of managing complexity. This shows in the organizational structure of the company, the systems being managed, and the variety of systems that form the enterprise software portfolio. In this appendix, I examine the following elements:

- To explain how enterprise software delivery organizations relate and govern, I describe their typical structure.

- To analyze the basic operation of enterprise software delivery organizations, I examine the basic elements of the enterprise systems for which they are responsible.

- To discuss the balance of different skills and activities that is necessary, I describe the composition of an enterprise software portfolio typically managed by an enterprise software delivery organization.

References

[1] F. Brooks, *The Mythical Man-Month: Anniversary Edition*, Addison-Wesley, 1995.

[2] C. Jones, *Applied Software Measurement: Global Analysis of Productivity and Quality, Third Edition*, McGraw-Hill, 2008.

[3] C. Jones, *Software Engineering Best Practices: Lessons from Successful Projects in Top Companies*, McGraw-Hill, 2009.

[4] T. DeMarco and B. Boehm, *Controlling Software Projects*, Yourden Press, 1983.

[5] T. DeMarco and T. Lister, *Peopleware: Productive Projects and Teams*, Dorset House, 1999.

[6] I. Sommerville, *Software Engineering, Ninth Edition*, Addison-Wesley, 2010.

[7] G. Booch, J. Rumbaugh, and I. Jacobson, *Unified Modeling Language User Guide*, Addison-Wesley, 2005.

[8] G. Booch, J. Rumbaugh, and I. Jacobson, *Object-Oriented Analysis and Design with Applications, Third Edition*, Addison-Wesley, 2007.

[9] J. Rumbaugh, I. Jacobsen, and G. Booch, *Unified Modelling Language Reference Model*, Addison-Wesley, 2007.

[10] E. Gamma, R. Helm, R. Johnson, and J. Vlassides, *Design Patterns: Elements of Reusable Object-Oriented Software*, Addison-Wesley, 1993.

[11] M. Cohn, *Succeeding with Agile: Software Development with Scrum*, Addison-Wesley, 2009.

[12] R. C. Martin, *Agile Software Development: Principles, Patterns, and Practices*, Prentice Hall, 2002.

[13] M. Poppendieck and T. Poppendieck, *Lean Software Development: An Agile Toolkit*, Addison-Wesley, 2003.

[14] P. Kruchten, *Rational Unified Process*, Addison-Wesley, 2002.

[15] N. Carr, *Does IT Matter?*, Harvard Business Press, 2004.

[16] N. Carr, *The Big Switch: Rewiring the World from Edison to Google*, Harvard Business Press, 2009.

[17] R. Friedman, *The World Is Flat: A Brief History of the 21st Century*, Farrar, Straus, and Giroux, 2005.

[18] R. Kalakota, M. Robinson, and S. Sharma, *Global Outsourcing: Executing an Onshore, Nearshore, and Offshore Strategy*, Mivar Press, 2005.

[19] D. Brown, *The Black Book of Outsourcing: How to Manage the Changes, Challenges, and Opportunities*, John Wiley, 2005.

[20] B. Boehm, *Software Engineering Economics*, Prentice Hall, 1991.

[21] W. Royce, *Software Project Management: A Unified Framework*, Addison-Wesley, 2010.

[22] D. Leffingwell, *Scaling Software Agility: Best Practices for Large Enterprises*, Addison-Wesley, 2007.

[23] R. Pressman, *Software Engineering: A Practitioners Approach*, McGraw-Hill, 2009.

[24] F. Buschmann et al., *Pattern-Oriented Software Architecture, Volume 1: A System of Patterns*, John Wiley Press, 1996.

[25] R. Hopkins and K. Jenkins, *Eating the IT Elephant: Moving from Greenfield Development to Brownfield*, IBM Press, 2008.

[26] TOGAF version 9.1, www.opengroup.org/togaf.

[27] COBIT Framework for IT Governance and Control, www.isaca.org/knowledge-center/COBIT.

[28] "CAST Worldwide Application Software Quality Study" (2010), available at http://research.castsoftware.com.

[29] C. Alberts et al., *Continuous Risk Management Guidebook*, Software Engineering Institute (SEI) series, Addison-Wesley, 1996.

[30] P. Naur and B. Randell, eds., "Software Engineering: Report of a Conference Sponsored by the NATO Science Committee, Garmisch, Germany, 7–11 Oct. 1968," http://homepages.cs.ncl.ac.uk/brian.randell/NATO.

[31] B. Randell and J. N. Buxton, eds., "Software Engineering Techniques: Report of a Conference Sponsored by the NATO Science Committee, Rome, Italy, 27–31 Oct. 1969," http://homepages.cs.ncl.ac.uk/brian.randell/NATO.

[32] R. Hunter and R. Thayer, eds., *Software Process Improvement*, Wiley-IEEE Computer Society Press, 2001.

[33] W. Humphrey, "Software Process Improvement at Hughes Aircraft," *IEEE Software* 8(4): 11–23, July 1991.

[34] B. Boehm, "A Spiral Model of Software Development and Enhancement," *ACM Computer*, May 1988.

[35] Software Engineering Institute (SEI), "CMMI for Development, Version 1.3, CMU/SEI-2010-TR-033," SEI report, November 2010, www.sei.cmu.edu.

[36] P. Clements and L. Northrop, *Software Product Lines: Patterns and Practices, Third Edition*, Addison-Wesley, 2001.

[37] A. W. Brown, *Large-Scale Component-Based Development*, Prentice Hall, 2000.

[38] J. Greenfield, K. Short, S. Cook, and S. Kent, *Software Factories: Assembling Applications with Patterns, Models, Frameworks, and Tools*, Wiley Press, 2004.

[39] P. Harmon, *Business Process Change, Second Edition*, Morgan Kaufman, 2007.

[40] L. Fredendall and E. Hill, *Basics of Supply Chain Management*, CRC Press, 2000.

[41] J. Geunes and P. Pardalos, *Supply Chain Optimization*, Springer Verlag, 2010.

[42] N. Bieberstein, S. Bose, M. Fiammante, and K. Jones, *Service-Oriented Architecture (SOA) Compass: Business Value, Planning, and Enterprise Roadmap*, IBM Press, 2005.

[43] M. Hotle and S. Landry, "Application Delivery and Support Organizational Archetypes: The Software Factory," Gartner Research Report G00167531, May 2009.

[44] IBM, "Give Your Software Factory a Health Check: Best Practices for Executing with Reduced Risk and Cost for Real Results," IBM white paper, September 2009.

[45] IBM, "Application Assembly Optimization: A New Approach to Global Delivery," IBM white paper, August 2009.

[46] M. Goethe et al., *Collaborative Application Lifecycle Management with IBM Rational Products*, IBM Redbooks, 2008.

[47] D. S. Frankel, J. Parodi, and R. Soley, eds., *The MDA Journal: Model Driven Architecture Straight from the Masters*, Meghan Kiffer Press, 2004.

[48] G. Reese, *Cloud Application Architectures: Building Applications and Infrastructures in the Cloud*, O'Reilly Press, 2009.

[49] R. Sood, *IT, Software, and Services: Outsourcing and Offshoring*, AiAiYo Books, 2005.

[50] I. Oshri and J. Kotlarsky, *Global Sourcing: Doing Better through Outsourcing and Offshoring*, Springer, 2010.

[51] S. Sahay, S. Krishna, and B. Nicholson, *Global IT Outsourcing: Software Development across Borders*, Cambridge University Press, 2007.

[52] R. Sangwan et al., *Global Software Development Handbook*, Auerbach Publications, 2006.

[53] A. W. Brown and G. Booch, "Collaborative Development Environments," in *Advances in Computers*, vol. 59, 2–27, Academic Press, 2003.

[54] J. Strubing, "Designing the Working Process: What Programmers Do Besides Programming," in *User-Centered Requirements for Software Engineering Environments*, Springer, 1994.

[55] E. Yourdon, *Death March*, Prentice Hall, 1997.

[56] A. Leon, *Software Configuration Management Handbook, Second Edition*, Artech, 2004.

[57] C. Schwaber, "The Changing Face of Application Lifecycle Management," Forrester Report, August 18, 2006.

[58] A. Cockburn, *Agile Software Development*, Addison-Wesley, 2001.

[59] M. Cohn, *Succeeding with Agile*, Addison-Wesley, 2006.

[60] R. Charette, *Why Software Fails*, IEEE Spectrum, 2005.

[61] M. L. Hutcheson, *Software Testing Fundamentals: Methods and Metrics*, John Wiley Press, 2003.

[62] Software Engineering Institute, "Software Risk Management," Technical Report CMU/SEI-96-TR-012, June 1996.

[63] P. Clements, R. Kazman, and M. Klein, *Evaluating Software Architectures: Methods and Case Studies*, Addison-Wesley, 2002.

[64] P. Kroll and M. Cantor, *Software and System Development with the IBM Measured Capability Improvement Framework*, IBM white paper, May 2009.

[65] N. Ayewah, et al., "Using Static Analysis to Find Bugs," *IEEE Software* 25(5): 22–29, September/October 2008.

[66] B. Chess and J. West, *Secure Programming with Static Analysis*, Addison-Wesley, 2007.

[67] J. Allen, S. Barnum, R.J. Ellison, G. McGraw, *Software Security Engineering: A Guide for Project Managers*, Addison-Wesley, 2008.

[68] R. J. Ellison, et al., "Evaluating and Mitigating Software Supply Chain Security Risks," SEI Report CMU/SEI-2010-TN-016, May 2010.

[69] W. Royce, K. Bittner, and M. Perrow, *The Economics of Iterative Software Development*, Addison-Wesley, 2009.

[70] W. Royce, "Measuring Agility and Architectural Integrity," *International Journal of Software Informatics*, 5(3): 414–33, 2011.

[71] K. E. Wiegers, "Automating Requirements Management," *Software Development* 7(7): 1–5, 1999.

[72] L. Cohen and A. Young, *Multisourcing: Moving Beyond Outsourcing to Achieve Growth and Agility*, Harvard Business Press, 2005.

[73] A. W. Brown, "A Case Study in Agility-at-Scale Delivery," *Proceedings of The 12th International Conference on Agile Software Development, XP2011*, Springer Verlag, 2011.

[74] "An Introduction to OpenUP: The Open Unified Process," http://www.eclipse.org/epf/general/OpenUP.pdf.

[75] K. Beck, *Extreme Programming Explained, Second Edition*, Addison-Wesley, 2004.

[76] M. Lacity, L. Willcocks, and J. W. Rottman, "Global Outsourcing of Back Office Services: Lessons, Trends, and Enduring Challenges," *Strategic Outsourcing: An International Journal* 1(1): 13–34, 2008.

[77] M. Phillips, "The CMMI for Acquisition, Version 1.3," Technical report CMU/SEI-2011-TR-010, March 2011.

[78] W. Royce, "Successful Software Management Style: Steering and Balance," *IEEE Software* 22(5): 40–47, September/October 2005.

[79] B. Grey, "Review of Acquisition for the Secretary of State for Defence," UK Ministry of Defence, October 2009.

[80] M. Lorell, J. Lowell, and O. Younnosi, *Evolutionary Acquisition: Implementation Challenges for Defense Space Programs*, Rand Corp., 2006.

[81] "Defence Industry Strategy: Defence Whitepaper," UK Ministry of Defence, Cm 6697, December 2005.

[82] M. Christopher, *Logistics and Supply Chain Mangement, Third Edition*, Prentice Hall, 2005.

[83] J. Rhoton, *Cloud Computing Explained: Implementation Handbook for Enterprises*, Recursive Press, 2009.

[84] T. Mather, S. Kumaraswamy, and S. Latif, *Cloud Security and Privacy: An Enterprise Perspective on Risks and Compliance (Theory in Practice)*, O'Reilly, 2009.

[85] M. Bennioff, *Behind the Cloud: The Untold Story of How Salesforce.com Went from Idea to Billion-Dollar Company and Revolutionized an Industry*, Jossey-Bass, 2009.

[86] R. Yanosky, "From Users to Choosers: The Cloud and the Changing Shape of Enterprise Authority," in *The Tower and the Cloud*, Educause, 2008, http://www.educause.edu/thetowerandthecloud.

[88] D. Linthicum, *Enterprise Application Integration*, Addison-Wesley, 1999.

[87] B. Maizlish and R. Handler, *IT Portfolio Management: Unlocking the Business Value of Technology*, Wiley Press, 2005.

[89] J. Dean and A. Gravel, eds. *COTS-Based Software Systems: Proceedings of the First International Conference ICCBSS, 2002*, Springer Verlag, 2002.

[90] N. Muir, *Discover SAP*, SAP Press, 2009.

[91] A. Passi, *Oracle E-Business Suite Development and Extensibility Handbook*, Osbourne Oracle Press, 2009.

[92] J. Schmidt and D. Lyle, *Lean Integration: An Integration Factory Approach to Business Agility*, Addison-Wesley, 2010.

[93] J. Humble and D. Farley, *Continuous Delivery: Reliable Software Releases through Build, Test, and Deployment Automation*, Addison-Wesley, 2010.

[94] C. Finkelstein, *Enterprise Architecture for Integration: Rapid Delivery Methods and Technologies*, Artech House, 2006.

[95] J. Jeston and J. Nelis, *Business Process Management, Second Edition: Practical Guidelines to Successful Implementations*, Butterworth-Heinemann, 2008.

[96] S. White and D. Miers, *BPMN Modeling and Reference Guide*, Future Strategies, 2008.

Index

Note: Page numbers followed by *f* indicate figures; those followed by *n* indicate notes.

FREE
Online Edition

Your purchase of *Enterprise Software Delivery* includes access to a free online edition for 45 days through the **Safari Books Online** subscription service. Nearly every Addison-Wesley Professional book is available online through **Safari Books Online**, along with thousands of books and videos from publishers such as Cisco Press, Exam Cram, IBM Press, O'Reilly Media, Prentice Hall, Que, Sams, and VMware Press.

Safari Books Online is a digital library providing searchable, on-demand access to thousands of technology, digital media, and professional development books and videos from leading publishers. With one monthly or yearly subscription price, you get unlimited access to learning tools and information on topics including mobile app and software development, tips and tricks on using your favorite gadgets, networking, project management, graphic design, and much more.

Activate your FREE Online Edition at
informit.com/safarifree

STEP 1: Enter the coupon code: LSJUHFH.

STEP 2: New Safari users, complete the brief registration form.
Safari subscribers, just log in.

If you have difficulty registering on Safari or accessing the online edition,
please e-mail customer-service@safaribooksonline.com